Pocket

BUSINESS

FRENCH

DICTIONARY

third edition

English-French/French-English

Anglais-Français/Français-Anglais

General Editor
PH Collin

French Editor
Françoise Collin

A&C Black

Originally published by Peter Collin Publishing

Third edition published 2003
Second edition published 2001
First edition published 1998

A&C Black Publishers Ltd
38 Soho Square
London WID 3HB

British Library Cataloguing in Publications Data

A Catalogue record for this book is
available from the British Library

ISBN 0 7136 7735 X

Text computer typeset by A&C Black

Preface

This pocket dictionary is for any business person, business student or traveller who needs to deal with the language of business. It contains over 5,000 essential business terms in French and English with clear and accurate translations.

Abbreviations

adj	adjective
adv	adverb
f	feminine
fpl	feminine plural
m	masculine
mf	masculine or feminine
mpl	masculine plural
n	noun
v	verb

Préface

Ce dictionnaire vous offre 5 000 mots et expressions indispensables lors de vos voyages d'affaires à l'étranger. Le format étudié, la liste de mots choisis avec soin et les traductions au point en font un outil tout à fait convivial.

Abréviations

adj	adjectif
adv	adverbe
f	féminin
fpl	féminin pluriel
m	masculin
mf	masculin ou féminin
mpl	masculin pluriel
n	nom
v	verbe

Contents

Table des matières

English-French
Anglais-Français

Aa

A1 *[condition]*
excellent(e) *ou*
parfait(e)
abandon (v)
abandonner *ou*
renoncer à
abandon an action
[legal] renoncer
aux poursuites *ou* à
un procès
abatement (n)
réduction (f)
abroad à l'étranger
absence absence (f)
absence: in the
absence of en
l'absence de
absent (adj)
absent(e)
absolute monopoly
monopole (m)
absolu
accelerated depre-
ciation amortisse-
ment (m) accéléré
accept (v) *[agree]*
accepter

accept (v) *[take*
something]
accepter
accept a bill
accepter une traite
accept delivery
of a shipment
réceptionner des
marchandises *ou*
prendre livraison
d'un envoi
accept liability
for something
accepter la
responsabilité de
quelque chose
acceptable (adj)
acceptable
acceptance (n)
acceptation (f)
acceptance of an
offer
acceptation (f)
d'une offre
acceptance
sampling test (m)
sur échantillon
accommodation
address adresse (f)
postale *ou* boîte (f)
à lettre

accommodation bill
billet (m) de
complaisance *ou*
effet (m) de
complaisance
according to
selon *ou* suivant *ou*
conformément (à)
account (n)
compte (m)
account: on
account en
acompte
account executive
responsable (mf) de
clientèle *ou*
responsable de la
gestion du budget
d'un client
account for (v)
rendre compte de *ou*
justifier
account in credit
compte (m)
créditeur
account on stop
compte (m) bloqué
accountant (n)
comptable (mf)
accounting (n)
comptabilité (f)

accounting
procedures
méthodes (fpl)
comptables
accounts department
service (m) de la
comptabilité
accounts payable
comptes (mpl)
fournisseurs *ou*
dettes (fpl)
accounts receivable
comptes (mpl)
clients (mpl) *ou*
créances (fpl)
accrual (n)
accumulation (f) *ou*
capitalisation (f)
accrual of interest
capitalisation (f)
des intérêts
accruals (n)
compte (m) de
régularisation
accrue (v) courir
ou s'accumuler
accrued interest
intérêt (m) couru
accumulate (v)
accumuler *ou*
s'accumuler

accurate (adj)
exact(e) *ou*
précis(e) *ou*
correct(e)
acknowledge (v)
receipt of a letter
accuser réception
d'une lettre
acknowledgement
(n) accusé (m) de
réception
acquire (v) a
company faire
l'acquisition d'une
société *ou* acheter
une société
acquisition
acquisition (f)
across-the-board
(adj) général(e) *ou*
généralisé(e)
act (n) loi (f)
act (v) agir
act of God
catastrophe (f)
naturelle
acting (adj)
intérimaire
acting manager
directeur (-trice)
intérimaire

action *[thing done]*
action (f)
action *[lawsuit]*
procès (m) *ou*
poursuite (f) *ou*
action (f)
action for damages
poursuite (f) en
dommages-intérêts
actual (adj)
réel (-elle) *ou*
véritable
actuals (n) chiffres
(mpl) réels
actuarial tables
tables (fpl) de
mortalité
actuary (n)
actuaire (mf)
ad *or* **advert (n)**
annonce (n)
(publicitaire)
add (v) ajouter *ou*
augmenter
add on (v) 10% for
service ajouter 10%
pour le service
add up (v) a
column of figures
additionner une
colonne de chiffres

addition (f) [calcu-lation] addition (f) *ou* somme (f)
addition [thing added] addition (f)
additional (adj) supplémentaire
additional charges frais (mpl) supplémentaires *ou* supplément (m)
additional premium prime (f) additionnelle
address (n) adresse (f)
address (v) adresser
address a letter *or* a parcel adresser une lettre *ou* un colis
address a meeting prendre la parole à une réunion
address label étiquette (f) (avec *ou* pour) adresse
address list répertoire (m) *ou* fichier (m) d'adresses

addressee (n) destinataire (mf)
adequate (adj) adéquat(e) *ou* suffisant(e)
adjourn (v) ajourner *ou* remettre
adjourn a meeting lever la séance; ajourner une réunion
adjudicate (v) in a dispute se prononcer sur un litige *ou* sur un conflit
adjudication (n) jugement (m) *ou* décision (f) *ou* arrêt (m)
adjudication tribunal conseil (m) d'arbitrage
adjudicator (n) arbitre (m) *ou* juge (m)
adjust (v) ajuster *ou* modifier
adjustment (n) ajustement (m) *ou* modification (f)

admin (n)
[informal:adminis-
tration] (d')
administration;
administratif (-ive)
admin costs frais
(mpl) adminsitratifs
ou de gestion
administration (n)
administration (f)
ou gestion (f)
administrative
(adj)
administratif (-ive)
administrative
expenses frais
administratifs *ou*
frais de gestion
admission (n)
admission (f) *ou*
entrée (f)
admission charge
entrée (f)
admit (v) *[confess]*
avouer *ou*
reconnaître
admit (v) *[let in]*
admettre
(quelqu'un) *ou*
laisser entrer
(quelqu'un)

ad valorem ad
valorem *ou* propor-
tionnel(-elle) (à la
valeur)
ad valorem tax
taxe proportionnelle
advance (adj)
anticipé(e)
advance (n)
[increase]
hausse (f) *ou*
augmentation (f)
advance (n) *[loan]*
avance (f)
advance (v)
[increase]
augmenter
advance (v) *[lend]*
avancer (de
l'argent) *ou* prêter
(de l'argent)
advance booking
réservation (f) à
l'avance
advance on account
avance (f) *ou*
acompte (m) *ou*
provision (f)
advance
payment paiement
anticipé

advertise (v)
mettre *ou* insérer
une annonce; faire
de la publicité
**advertise a new
product** faire de la
publicité pour un
produit nouveau
advertise a vacancy
annoncer un poste
(dans un journal)
advertisement (n)
annonce (f);
publicité (f)
advertiser (n)
annonceur (m)
advertising (n)
publicité (f) *ou*
réclame (f)
advertising agency
agence (f) de
publicité
advertising budget
budget (m) de
publicité
**advertising
campaign**
campagne (f)
publicitaire *ou*
campagne de
publicité

advertising manager
responsable (mf) de
la publicité
advertising rates
tarifs (mpl)
publicitaires
advertising space
espace (m)
publicitaire
advice note avis
(m) d'expédition
advise (v) *[tell what
happened]* informer
ou aviser (de)
advise (v) *[what
should be done]*
conseiller
**adviser *or* advisor
(n)** conseiller
(-ère)
affidavit (n)
déclaration (f) sous
serment
affiliated (adj)
affilié(e)
affirmative (adj)
affirmatif (-ive)
afford (v) pouvoir
se payer *ou*
s'acheter *ou* s'offrir
quelque chose

after-sales service
service (m)
après-vente (SAV)
after-tax profit
bénéfice (m) après
impôts
agency (n)
agence (f)
agenda (n) ordre
du jour (m)
agent (n)
[representative]
représentant(e)
agent (n) *[working
in an agency]*
agent (m)
**AGM (annual
general meeting)**
assemblée (f)
générale annuelle
agree (v) *[accept]*
accepter *ou*
convenir de
agree (v) *[approve]*
accepter *ou* approuver
agree (v) *[be same
as]* concorder
(avec)
**agree to do
something** accepter
de faire quelque chose

agree with *[be
same as]* concorder
(avec) *ou*
correspondre (à)
agree with *[of same
opinion]* être
d'accord avec
quelqu'un
agreed (adj)
accepté(e) *ou*
convenu(e)
agreed price prix
convenu
agreement (n)
contrat (m) *ou*
accord (m) *ou*
convention (f)
agricultural (adj)
agricole
aim (n) objectif
(m) *ou* but (m)
aim (v) viser (à) *ou*
avoir pour but (de)
air (n) air (m)
air freight transport
(m) par avion *ou*
fret (m) aérien
**air freight charges
or rates** tarifs
(mpl) de transport
par avion

air letter
aérogramme (m)
air terminal
aérogare (f)
airfreight (v)
expédier par avion
airline (n)
compagnie (f) (de
navigation) aérienne
airmail (n) poste
(f) aérienne
airmail (v) envoyer
par avion
airmail sticker
étiquette (f)
'par avion'
airport (n)
aéroport (m)
airport bus
autobus (m) de
l'aéroport
airport tax taxe (f)
d'aéroport
airport terminal
terminal (m)
(d'aéroport)
airtight packaging
emballage (m)
hermétique
all expenses paid
tous frais payés

all-in tout compris;
toutes taxes
comprises (TTC)
all-in price prix
(m) net *ou* tarif (m)
tout compris
all-out strike grève
(f) totale *ou*
générale
all-risks policy
assurance (f) tous
risques
allocate (v)
affecter *ou* attribuer
ou distribuer
allow *[permit]*
permettre
allow a discount
accorder *ou* consentir
une remise
**allow 10% for
carriage** ajouter
10% pour le
transport
allowance (n)
allocation (f) *ou*
indemnité (f)
**allowance (n) for
depreciation**
provisions (fpl)
pour dépréciation

alphabetical order ordre (m) alphabétique
alter (v) changer *ou* modifier
alteration (n) changement (m) *ou* modification (f)
alternative (adj) autre *ou* de remplacement
alternative (n) alternative (f); solution (f)
amend (v) rectifier *ou* modifier *ou* corriger
amendment amendement (m) *ou* modification (f) *ou* correction (f)
American (adj) américain (-aine)
American (n) Américain (-aine)
American dollar dollar (m) (américain)
amortization (n) amortissement (m)
amortize (v) amortir *ou* rembourser (un prêt *ou* une dette)

amount [of money] montant (m) *ou* somme (f)
amount owing somme (f) due
amount paid montant (m) versé *ou* versement (m)
amount to (v) s'élever à *ou* se monter à
analyse *or* analyze (v) analyser
analyse the market potential étudier le potentiel du marché
analysis (n) analyse (f)
announce (v) annoncer
announcement (n) déclaration (f) *ou* annonce (f)
annual (adj) annuel (-elle)
annual accounts comptes (mpl) annuels *ou* comptes de l'exercice

annual general meeting (AGM) assemblée (f) générale annuelle

annual report rapport (m) annuel

annual return rendement (m) annuel

annualize (v) annualiser

annualized percentage rate (APR) taux (m) effectif global (TEG)

annually (adv) annuellement *ou* chaque année

annuity (n) rente (f)

annul (v) *[contract]* annuler *ou* résilier (un contrat)

answer (n) réponse (f)

answer (v) répondre

answer a letter répondre à une lettre

answer the telephone répondre au téléphone *ou* prendre un appel

answering machine *or* **answerphone (n)** répondeur (m) téléphonique

answering service permanence (f) téléphonique

antedate (v) antidater

anti-inflationary measures mesures (fpl) anti-inflationnistes

apologize (v) s'excuser

apology (n) excuse (f)

appeal (n) *[against a decision]* appel (m) (d'un jugement)

appeal (n) *[attraction]* attrait (m)

appeal (v) *[against a decision]* faire appel (d'un jugement)

appeal to (v) *[attract]* attirer *ou* séduire

appear (v) *[seem]* paraître *ou* sembler

appendix (n) annexe (f)

applicant for a job
candidat(e) à un
emploi
application (n)
demande (f)
application for a job
candidature (f) à un
poste *ou* demande
(f) d'emploi
application form
formulaire (m)
de candidature
ou de demande
(d'emploi)
apply for (v) *[ask
for]* demander *ou*
solliciter
apply for a job solliciter un emploi *ou*
poser sa candidature
à un poste
apply in writing
faire une demande
par écrit
apply to (v) *[affect]*
concerner
appoint (v) nommer
appointee (n)
personne nommée à
un poste; candidat(e)
retenu(e)

appointment (n)
[job] poste (m) *ou*
emploi (m)
**appointment
[meeting]**
rendez-vous (m)
**appointment [to a
job]** nomination (f)
**appointments
book** carnet (m) de
rendez-vous
appointments vacant
offres (f) d'emploi
appreciate (v) *[how
good something is]*
apprécier
**appreciate [increase
in value]** augmenter
en valeur *ou*
s'apprécier
appreciation (n)
*[how good something
is]* appréciation (f)
**appreciation [in
value]** augmentation
(f) en valeur *ou*
appréciation (f)
appropriate (v)
[funds] affecter *ou*
destiner *[une
somme à un projet]*

approval (n)
approbation (f)
approval: on
approval *or* on
appro à l'essai *ou* à
condition
approve (v) the
terms of a contract
approuver les termes
d'un contrat
approximate (adj)
approximatif (-ive)
approximately
(adv) environ *ou*
approximativement
APR (annualized
percentage rate)
TEG (taux effectif
global)
arbitrate (v) in a
dispute arbitrer un
conflit
arbitration (n)
arbitrage (m) *ou*
médiation (f)
arbitration board *or*
arbitration tribunal
comité (m) de
conciliation
arbitrator (n)
arbitre (mf)

area (n) *[of town]*
secteur (m) *ou*
quartier (m)
area *[region]* région
(f) *ou* zone (f)
area *[subject]*
secteur (m) *ou*
domaine (m)
area *[surface]*
surface (f)
area code
[telephone]
indicatif (m) de zone
area manager
directeur (-trice)
régional(e)
argument (n)
discussion (f) *ou*
dispute (f)
arrange (v) *[meet-*
ing] arranger *ou*
organiser
arrange *[set out]*
arranger *ou* disposer
arrangement (n)
[compromise]
accord (m) *ou*
compromis (m)
arrangement
[system]
organisation (f)

arrears (n)
arriéré (m)
arrival (n) arrivée (f)
**arrivals [at airport,
etc.]** arrivées (fpl)
arrive (v) arriver
article (n) [clause]
article (m) ou
clause (f)
article [item]
article (m)
**articles of
association** statuts
(mpl) d'une société
**articulated lorry or
articulated vehicle**
semi-remorque (m ou
f);poids lourd (m)
as per advice
suivant avis
as per invoice selon
facture
as per sample
selon échantillon ou
conformément à
l'échantillon
**asap (as soon as
possible)** aussitôt
que possible ou dès
que possible
ask (v) demander

**ask someone to
do something**
demander à
quelqu'un de faire
quelque chose
**ask for (v) [ask a
price]** demander
(un prix)
ask for [something]
demander ou réclamer
quelque chose
ask for a refund
demander un
remboursement
**ask for further
details or particulars**
demander des
renseignements
supplémentaires
**assembly (n)
[meeting]**
assemblée (f)
**assembly
[putting together]**
assemblage (m) ou
montage (m)
assembly line
chaîne (f) de
montage
assess (v) évaluer
ou estimer

assess damages
évaluer les
dommages
assessment (n) of
damages évaluation
(f) des dommages
asset (n) actif (m)
asset stripping
dépeçage (m) d'une
entreprise (après
son rachat)
asset value valeur
(f) de l'actif
assets and liabilities
l'actif et le passif *ou*
doit (m) et avoir (m)
assign a right to
someone attribuer
un droit à quelqu'un
assignee (n)
cessionnaire (mf)
assignment (n)
[cession] cession
(f) *ou* transfert (m)
assignment [work]
tâche (f)
assignor (n)
cédant(e)
assist (v) aider
assistance (n) aide
(f) *ou* assistance (f)

assistant (n)
assistant(e)
assistant manager
directeur (-trice)
adjoint(e)
associate (adj)
associé(e)
associate (n) asso-
cié(e); collègue (mf)
associate company
société (f) affiliée
ou filiale (f)
association (n)
association (f)
assurance (n)
assurance (f)
assurance company
compagnie (f)
d'assurance-vie
assurance policy
police (f)
d'assurance-vie
assure (v) some-
one's life assurer
quelqu'un sur la vie
attach (v) attacher
ou joindre
attachment (n)
[email] pièce (f)
jointe
attack (v) attaquer

attend (v) *[meeting]* assister à *[une réunion]*

attend to (v) s'occuper de (quelque chose)

attention (n) attention (f)

attorney (n) fondé (m) de pouvoir

attract (v) attirer

attractive salary salaire attrayant *ou* intéressant

auction (n) enchère (f) *ou* vente (f) aux enchères

auction (v) vendre aux enchères

auction rooms salle (f) des ventes *ou* hôtel (m) des ventes *[enchères]*

audit (n) audit (m)

audit (v) vérifier *ou* réviser

audit (v) the accounts vérifier les comptes

auditing (n) vérification (f) *ou* révision (f) comptable

auditor (n) audit (m) *ou* auditeur (m); commissaire (m) aux comptes

authenticate (v) authentifier *ou* homologuer

authority (n) autorité (f)

authorization (n) autorisation (f)

authorize (v) *[give permission]* autoriser

authorize payment autoriser le paiement

authorized (adj) autorisé(e)

availability (n) disponibilité (f)

available (adj) disponible

available capital capital disponible

average (adj) moyen (-enne)

average (n) moyenne (f)

average: on average en moyenne

average (n) *[insurance]* avaries (f)
average (v) établir une moyenne; atteindre une moyenne
average price prix moyen
avoid (v) éviter
await (v) instructions attendre les instructions
award (n) *[decision]* décision (f) *ou* sentence (f)
award (v) attribuer
award a contract to someone donner *ou* adjuger un contrat à quelqu'un

Bb

back (n) dos (m)
back orders commandes (f) en attente

back pay rappel (m) *ou* arriéré (m) (de salaire)
back up (v) *[computer file]* sauvegarder
back up (v) *[financially]* appuyer *ou* étayer
backdate antidater
backer (n) sponsor (m); bailleur (m) de fonds
backhander (n) pot-de-vin (m)
backing (n) *[financial]* appui (m) (financier)
backlog (n) travail (m) en retard *ou* en attente
back office (n) back office (m)
backup (adj) *[computer]* de sauvegarde
backup copy disquette (f) de sauvergarde
backwardation déport (m)

bad buy mauvais achat (m)

bad debt créance (f) douteuse

bag sac (m)

bail (v) someone out cautionner quelqu'un

balance (n) solde (m) *[d'un compte]*

balance (v) équilibrer *ou* solder *ou* arrêter *[compte]*

balance (v) (a budget) équilibrer (un budget)

balance brought down *or* brought forward solde (m) à nouveau; ancien solde; solde reporté

balance carried down *or* carrried forward solde (m) à ce jour; solde à reporter

balance due to us solde (m) à recevoir

balance of payments balance (f) des paiements

balance of trade balance (f) commerciale

balance sheet bilan (m)

ban (n) interdiction (f); embargo (m)

ban (v) interdire

bank (n) banque (f)

bank (v) *[cheque]* mettre *ou* déposer à la banque

bank with (v) avoir un compte en banque (à *ou* au)

bank account compte (m) bancaire

bank balance *[bank account]* solde (m) *ou* position (f) (d'un compte)

bank base rate taux (m) de base bancaire

bank bill *[GB]* effet (m) bancaire *ou* traite (f) bancaire

bank bill *[US]* billet (m) de banque

bank book livret (m) *ou* carnet (m) de banque

bank borrowings
emprunts (m)
bancaires
bank charges frais
(mpl) bancaires *ou*
agios (mpl)
bank credit crédit
(m) bancaire
bank deposits
dépôts (mpl)
bancaires
bank draft traite (f)
bancaire
bank holiday jour (m)
férié
bank loan prêt (m)
bancaire
bank manager
directeur (-trice)
d'agence
bank mandate
mandat (m) de
paiement
bank statement
relevé (m) de
compte (bancaire)
bank reserves
réserves (fpl)
bancaires
bank transfer vire-
ment (m) bancaire

bankable paper effet
(m) escomptable *ou*
bancable
banker banquier (m)
banker's draft
traite (f) bancaire
banker's order ordre
(m) de virement
bancaire
banking (n)
banque (f) *[activité
bancaire]*
banking hours
heures (fpl) d'ouver-
ture des banques
banknote billet (m)
de banque
bankrupt (adj)
failli(e) (adj)
bankrupt (n)
failli(e) (n)
bankrupt (v) causer
ou entraîner une
faillite
bankruptcy (n)
faillite (f)
bar chart diagramme
(m) en bâtons;
histogramme (m)
bar code code (m)
(à) barres

bargain (n) *[cheaper than usual]* affaire (f) *ou* occasion (f)
bargain (n) *[deal]* marché (m) *ou* affaire (f)
bargain (n) *[Stock Exchange]* vente (f) d'un lot d'actions
bargain (v) discuter *ou* marchander
bargain offer offre (f) exceptionnelle
bargain price prix (m) sacrifié *ou* prix exceptionnel
bargaining (n) marchandage (m) *ou* négociation (f)
bargaining position prise (f) de position dans les négociations
bargaining power position (f) de force dans les négociations
barrier barrière (f) *ou* obstacle (m)
barter (n) troc (m)
barter (v) troquer
bartering échange (m) *ou* troc (m)

base (n) *[initial position]* base (f)
base (n) *[place]* siège (m)
base (v) *[in a place]* avoir son siège
base (v) *[start to calculate from]* (se) baser sur *ou* calculer à partir de
base year année (f) de référence
basic (adj) *[most important]* de base *ou* essentiel (-elle)
basic (adj) *[simple]* de base
basic discount remise (f) de base *ou* remise habituelle
basic tax taux (m) d'impôt moyen
basis base (f)
batch (n) *[of orders]* paquet (m) *ou* liasse (f)
batch (n) *[of products]* lot (m)
batch (v) grouper
batch number numéro (m) de lot

batch processing
traitement (m)
par lots
bear (n) *[Stock
Exchange]* baissier
(m) *ou* spéculateur
(m) à la baisse
bear (v) *[carry]* porter
bear (v) *[interest]*
porter intérêt
bear (v) *[pay for]*
supporter *[frais]*
bear market marché
(m) à la baisse *ou*
marché baissier
bearer (n) porteur (m)
bearer bond titre
(m) *ou* obligation
(f) au porteur
begin (v)
commencer
beginning début (m)
behalf: on behalf of
au nom de
belong to (v)
appartenir à
below-the-line
expenditure
dépense (f)
exceptionnelle
(hors bilan)

benchmark (n)
(point de) référence
(f) *ou* repère (m)
beneficiary (n)
bénéficiaire (mf) *ou*
ayant droit (m)
benefit (n) allocation
(f) *ou* prestation (f)
ou indemnité (f)
benefit from (v)
profiter de *ou*
bénéficier de
berth (n) poste
(m) d'amarrage
berth (v) accoster
ou mouiller *ou*
arriver à quai
best (adj)
le meilleur,
la meilleure
best (n) le mieux
best-selling car
voiture la plus en
demande
bid (n) *[at an
auction]* offre (f)
ou enchère (f)
bid (n) *[offer to buy]*
offre (f) *ou* mise (f)
bid (n) *[offer to do
work]* devis (m)

bid (n) *[tender]*
soumission (f)
bid (v) faire une
soumission *ou* une
offre
**bidder (n) *[at an
auction]***
enchérisseur (m)
bidder *[for tender]*
soumissionnaire (m)
**bidding (n) *[at an
auction]*** enchère (f)
bilateral (adj)
bilatéral(e)
bill (v) facturer *ou*
présenter la facture
bill (n) *[US]* billet
(m) de banque
**bill (n) *[in a restau-
rant]*** addition (f)
**bill (n) *[in
Parliament]*** projet
(m) de loi
**bill (n) *[list of
charges]*** facture (f)
ou note (f)
**bill (n) *[written
promise to pay]***
traite (f)
bill of exchange
lettre (f) de change

bill of lading
connaissement (m)
bill of sale contrat
(m) de vente *ou*
acte (m) de vente
billing (n)
facturation (f)
billion milliard (m)
bills for collection
effets (mpl) à recevoir
bills payable effets
(mpl) à payer
bills receivable
effets (mpl) à
recevoir
binding (adj) qui
lie *[par contrat]*
black economy
économie (f)
parallèle; travail (m)
au noir
black list (n) liste
(f) noire
black market
marché (m) noir
blacklist (v) mettre
sur la liste noire
blame (n)
reproche (m);
responsabilité (f)
blame (v) reprocher

blank (adj)
blanc (blanche)
blank (n) *[empty square]* blanc (m)
blank cheque chèque (m) en blanc
blister pack
blister (m)
block (n)
[building] bloc (m)
d'immeubles
block (n) of shares
paquet (m) *ou* bloc (m) d'actions
block (v) bloquer
block booking
réservation (f)
en bloc
blocked currency
devises (fpl) non
convertibles
blue chip titre (m)
de premier ordre *ou*
valeur (f) sûre
**blue-chip invest-
ments** placements
(mpl) de père de
famille
board (n) *[group of
people]* conseil (m)
ou comité (m)

board (v) monter à
bord de
board meeting *[of
directors]* réunion
(f) du conseil
d'administration
board of directors
conseil (m)
d'administration;
directoire (m)
board: on board
à bord
boarding card *or*
boarding pass carte
(f) d'embarquement
ou d'accès à bord
boardroom (n)
salle (f) de réunion
(du conseil
d'administration)
bona fide
de bonne foi
bond *[borrowing by
government]* bon
(m) (du Trésor) *ou*
obligation (f)
bonded warehouse
entrepôt (m) de la
douane
bonus (n) bonus
(n) *ou* prime (f)

bonus issue
émission (f)
d'actions gratuites
book (n)
livre (m)
book (v) réserver
book sales ventes
(fpl) enregistrées
book value valeur
(f) comptable
booking (n)
réservation (f)
booking clerk
préposé(e) à la
vente des billets
booking office
bureau (m) de
location *ou* des
réservations
bookkeeper
employé(e) (n) aux
écritures
bookkeeping
comptabilité (f)
ou tenue (f)
de livres
boom (n) période
(f) d'expansion *ou*
boom (m)
boom (v) devenir
prospère

boom industry
industrie (f) en
pleine croissance *ou*
en pleine expansion
booming (adj)
prospère (adj) *ou*
florissant(e) (adj)
boost (n)
poussée (f)
boost (v) pousser
ou relancer *ou*
réactiver
border (n)
frontière (f)
borrow (v) emprunter
borrower (n)
emprunteur (-euse)
borrowing (n)
emprunt (m)
borrowing power
capacité (f)
d'emprunt
boss (n) *[informal]*
patron (-onne)
bottleneck (n)
goulot (m) *ou* goulet
(m) d'étranglement
bottom (n) fond (m)
bottom line
résultat (m) net *ou*
bénéfice (m) net

bought ledger
grand livre (m)
des achats
bought ledger clerk
employé(e) aux
écritures (du grand
livre des achats)
bounce (v)
[cheque] (chèque)
sans provision
box number
numéro (m) de
boîte postale
boxed set (présenta-
tion sous) coffret (m)
boycott (n)
boycott (m) *ou*
boycottage (m)
boycott (v)
boycotter
bracket (n) *[tax]*
tranche (f)
bracket (v) together
grouper *ou* réunir *[les*
éléments d'une liste]
branch (n) succur-
sale (f); agence (f)
[d'une banque]
branch manager
[company] directeur
(-trice) de succursale

branch manager
[bank] directeur
(-trice) d'agence
branch office suc-
cursale (f); agence
(f) *[d'une banque]*
brand (n) marque
(f) *ou* nom (m)
brand image image
(f) de marque *ou*
réputation (f)
brand loyalty fidélité
(f) à la marque
brand name marque
de fabrique *ou* nom
de marque
brand new tout
neuf (toute neuve)
breach of contract
non respect (m) *ou*
rupture (f) de
contrat
breach of warranty
non respect (m)
ou rupture (f) de
garantie
break (n) pause (f)
ou arrêt (m)
break (v) *[contract]*
rompre (un accord
ou un contrat)

break down (v)
[itemize] ventiler
les frais
break down (v)
[machine] être en
panne *ou* avoir une
panne
break down (v)
[talks] échouer;
prendre fin
break even (v)
rentrer dans ses frais
break off (v)
negotiations
arrêter *ou* rompre
les négociations
break (v) the law
enfreindre la loi
breakages (n)
casse (f)
breakdown (n)
[items] détail (m)
ou ventilation (f)
breakdown (n)
[machine]
panne (f) *ou*
défaillance (f)
breakdown (n)
[talks] rupture (f)
breakeven point
seuil (m) de
rentabilité

bribe (n)
pot-de-vin (m)
bribe (v) acheter *ou*
corrompre quelqu'un
brief (v) informer
ou donner des
explications
briefcase (n)
serviette (f) *ou*
porte-documents (m)
bring (v) apporter
ou amener
bring a civil action
intenter un procès à
quelqu'un
bring in *[yield]*
rapporter
bring out *[launch]*
produire *ou* lancer
British (adj)
britannique *ou*
anglais (-aise)
brochure brochure (f)
broke *[informal]*
fauché(e) *ou* sans
le sou
broker (n)
courtier (m)
brokerage *or* bro-
ker's commission
courtage (m) *ou* com-
mission (f) (d'agent)

brown paper papier (m) kraft

bubble pack blister (m)

budget (n) *[government]* budget (m)

budget (n) *[personal, company]* budget (m)

budget (v) budgéter *ou* budgétiser

budget account *[in bank]* compte (m) crédit

budget deficit déficit (m) budgétaire

budgetary (adj) budgétaire (adj)

budgetary control contrôle (m) budgétaire

budgetary policy politique (f) budgétaire

budgeting préparation (f) de budget; budgétisation (f)

build in (v) incorporer *ou* intégrer

building society société (f) de crédit immobilier

built-in incorporé(e) *ou* intégré(e)

bulk (n) grande quantité

bulk buying achat (m) en gros

bulk shipment expédition (f) en vrac

bulk: in bulk en gros; en vrac

bulky volumineux (-euse)

bull (n) *[Stock Exchange]* spéculateur (m) à la hausse *ou* haussier (m)

bull market marché (m) haussier *ou* à la hausse

bulletin (n) bulletin (m)

bullion (n) lingots (mpl) (d'or ou d'argent)

bureau (n) de change bureau (m) de change

bus (n) bus (m) *ou* autobus (m)

business (n) *[commerce]* affaires (fpl) *ou* entreprise (f)

business [company]
entreprise (f)
business [discus-sion] question (f)
ou point (m)
business: on business
pour affaires
business address
adresse (f) du
bureau *ou* du lieu de
travail
business call visite (f)
d'affaires
business card carte
(f) professionnelle
business centre cen-
tre (m) *ou* quartier
(m) des affaires
business class
[travel] classe (f)
affaires
business equipment
équipements (mpl)
de bureau
business gift
cadeau (m) d'affaires
business hours
heures (fpl) d'ouver-
ture *ou* de bureau
business letter
lettre (f) d'affaires

business lunch
déjeuner (m) d'affaires
business premises
local (m) à usage de
bureaux; locaux
(mpl) commerciaux
business strategy
stratégie (f) des
affaires
business transaction
transaction (f) *ou*
opération (f)
business trip voyage
(m) d'affaires
businessman *or*
businesswoman
homme d'affaires *ou*
femme d'affaires
busy (adj) *[work,*
phone] occupé(e)
buy (v) acheter
buy back racheter
buy for cash
acheter au comptant
buy forward
acheter à terme
buyer (n) *[for a*
store] acheteur
(-euse)
buyer *[client]*
acheteur (-euse)

buyer's market
marché (m) à la baisse
buying (n)
achat (m)
buying department
service (m) achats
by-product
sous-produit (m)

Cc

cable address
adresse (f) télégraphique
calculate (v)
calculer; estimer
calculation (n)
calcul (m)
calculator (n) calculatrice (f); calculette (f)
calendar month
mois (m) civil; mois complet
calendar year
année (f) civile

call (n) *[for money]*
demande (f) (de remboursement d'un prêt)
call (n) *[phone]*
appel (m) *ou* communication (f) (téléphonique)
call (n) *[Stock Exchange]* appel (m) de fonds
call (n) *[visit]*
visite (f)
call (v) *or* make a call *[phone]*
téléphoner à *ou* appeler (quelqu'un)
call (v) a meeting
convoquer une réunion *ou* une assemblée
call off (v) a deal
annuler un contrat
call off a strike
annuler un ordre de grève
call on (v) *[visit]*
visiter
call rate (n)
fréquence (f) des visites (d'un représentant)

callable bond
obligation (f)
remboursable par
anticipation
campaign (n)
campagne (f)
cancel (v) annuler;
décommander (un
rendez-vous)
cancel a cheque
annuler un chèque
cancel a contract
annuler *ou* résilier
un contrat
cancellation (n)
annulation (f); rési-
liation (f) [contrat]
cancellation clause
clause (f) résolutoire
cancellation of an
appointment
annulation (f) d'un
rendez-vous
candidate (n)
candidat(e)
canvass (v)
prospecter *ou* faire
du porte-à-porte
canvasser (n)
démarcheur (m) qui
fait du porte-à-porte

canvassing (n)
démarchage (m) *ou*
prospection (f)
canvassing tech-
niques techniques
(fpl) de démarchage
capable of capable de
capacity (n)
[ability] don (m)
ou capacité (f)
capacity *[production]*
capacité (f) *ou*
rendement (m)
capacity *[space]*
capacité (f) *ou*
volume (m)
capacity utilization
utilisation (f) de la
capacité
capital (n)
capital (m) *ou*
capitaux (mpl)
capital account
compte (m) de
capital
capital assets actif
(m) immobilisé *ou*
immobilisations (fpl)
capital equipment
biens (mpl)
d'équipement

capital expenditure (coût d') acquisition (f) d'immobilisations

capital gains plus-value (f)

capital gains tax impôt (m) sur les plus-values

capital goods biens (mpl) d'équipement

capital loss moins-value (f)

capital-intensive industry industrie à fort coefficient de capital

capitalization (n) capitalisation (f)

capitalization of reserves capitalisation des réserves

capitalize (v) doter en capital *ou* capitaliser

capitalize on profiter de *ou* exploiter

captive market marché (m) captif

capture (v) prendre le contrôle (de)

capture 10% of the market accaparer 10% du marché

carbon copy copie (f) carbone

carbon paper (papier) carbone (m)

carbonless (adj) sans carbone *ou* autocopiant(e)

card (n) *[business card]* carte (f) (professionnelle)

card *[material]* carton (m)

card *[membership]* carte (f) de membre

card *[postcard]* carte postale

card index (n) fichier (m)

card phone téléphone (m) à carte

card-index (v) mettre sur fiches

card-index file fichier (m)

card-indexing (n) mise (f) sur fiches

cardboard (n) carton (m) *[matérial]*

cardboard box
boîte (f) en carton
ou carton (m)
care of (c/o) aux
bons soins de *ou* chez
cargo (n)
cargaison (f)
cargo ship cargo (m)
carnet *[interna-*
tional document]
carnet (m) ATA
carriage transport
(m) *ou* port (m)
carriage forward
port dû *ou* en port dû
carriage free
franco de port *ou*
franc de port
carriage paid port
payé *ou* en port payé
carrier *[company]*
transporteur (m) *ou*
entreprise (f) de
transports
carrier *[vehicle]*
camion (m); *[ship]*
navire (m)
carry (v) *[approve*
in a vote] adopter
ou voter
carry *[have in stock]*
avoir en stock

carry *[produce*
interest] produire
(un intérêt)
carry *[transport]*
transporter;
acheminer
carry a line of
goods suivre une
ligne de produits
carry forward reporter
carry on a
business diriger
une entreprise
carry over a
balance reporter
un solde
cartel cartel (m)
carton *[box]* boîte
(f) en carton *ou*
carton (m)
carton *[material]*
carton (m)
case (n) *[box]*
caisse (f)
case (n) *[suitcase]*
valise (f)
case (v) *[put in*
boxes] emballer *ou*
mettre dans une boîte
cash (adv) (payer)
(au) comptant *ou*
(payer) cash

cash (n) *[money]*
argent (m)
comptant *ou* espèces
(fpl) *ou* liquide (m)
ou cash (m)
cash (v) a cheque
encaisser un chèque
ou remettre un chèque
à l'encaissement
cash account
compte (m) de caisse
cash (n) advance
avance (f) de caisse
cash and carry
libre-service (m) de
gros *ou* cash and
carry (m)
cash balance solde
(m) de trésorerie
cash book livre (m)
de caisse
cash card carte (f)
de retrait
cash deal
vente (f) au
comptant
cash deposit dépôt
(m) en espèces
cash desk caisse (f)
cash discount
escompte (m) de
caisse

cash dispenser dis-
tributeur (m) automa-
tique de billets (DAB)
ou billetterie (f)
cash float encaisse
(f) *ou* caisse (f)
cash flow marge (f)
brute d'auto-finance-
ment (MBA); flux
(m) de trésorerie
cash flow forecast
prévisions (fpl) de
trésorerie
cash flow statement
plan (m) de trésorerie
cash in hand avoir
(m) en caisse
cash offer offre (f)
en espèces *ou* offre
au comptant
cash on delivery
(c.o.d.) livraison (f)
contre remboursement
cash payment pai-
ement (au) comptant
cash price prix (m)
du comptant
cash purchase achat
(m) (au) comptant
cash register *[till]*
caisse (f)
(enregistreuse)

cash reserves
réserves (fpl) de
trésorerie
cash sale vente (f)
au comptant
cash terms paiement
(m) comptant
cash transaction
opération (f) au
comptant
cash voucher bon (m)
de caisse
cashable (adj)
encaissable *ou* qui
peut être encaissé(e)
cashier (n)
caissier (-ière)
cashier's check *[US]*
chèque (m) de banque
casting vote (n) voix
(f) prépondérante
casual work (n) tra-
vail (m) temporaire
casual worker
travailleur (-euse)
ou employé(e)
temporaire
catalogue
catalogue (m)
catalogue price
prix (m) catalogue

category catégorie (f)
cater for (v) fournir
caveat emptor aux
risques de l'acheteur
ceiling (n) plafond (m)
ceiling price prix (m)
plafond
cellular telephone
téléphone (m)
cellulaire
central (adj)
central(e)
central bank
banque (f) centrale
central purchasing
achats (mpl)
centralisés
centralization (n)
centralisation (f)
centralize (v)
centraliser
**centre *[important
town]*** centre (m)
**CEO (chief
executive officer)**
directeur (m) général
certificate (n)
certificat (m)
**certificate of
approval** certificat
d'homologation

certificate of deposit certificat de dépôt *ou* bon (m) de caisse

certificate of gua-rantee certificat de garantie

certificate of origin certificat d'origine

certificate of regis-tration certificat d'enregistrement

certificated (adj) certifié(e)

certificated bankrupt failli (m) concordataire

certified accountant expert-comptable (m) (diplômé)

certified cheque chèque certifié

certified copy copie certifiée conforme

certify (v) certifier

cession (n) cession (f)

chain (n) [of stores] chaîne (f) de magasins

chain store magasin (m) à succursales multiples

chairman [of committee] président(e)

chairman [of com-pany] président(e)

chairman and managing director président-directeur général (PDG)

Chamber of Commerce Chambre (f) de commerce et d'industrie

change (n) [cash] monnaie (f)

change (n) [differ-ence] changement (m)

change (v) [become different] changer

change (v) [money] changer (de l'argent)

change hands changer de propriétaire

change machine distributeur (m) de monnaie

channel (n) canal (m)

channel (v) canaliser

channels of distribution canaux (mpl) de distribution

charge (n) *[in court]* inculpation (f) *ou* accusation (f)
charge (n) *[money]* prix (m) *ou* droit (m) *ou* frais (mpl)
charge (n) *[on account]* débit (m); imputation (f)
charge (v) (in court] inculper *ou* accuser quelqu'un
charge (v) *[money]* demander *ou* faire payer *ou* facturer
charge a purchase mettre (un achat) sur un compte
charge account compte (m) d'achat
charge card carte (f) accréditive
chargeable (adj) imputable *ou* à la charge de
charges forward en port dû *ou* frais à payer
charter (n) affrètement (m) *ou* nolisage (m)

charter (v) affréter *ou* noliser
charter an aircraft affréter *ou* noliser un avion
charter flight vol (m) charter
charter plane avion (m) charter
charterer (n) affréteur (m)
chartering (n) affrètement (m) *ou* nolisage (m)
chase (v) *[an order]* relancer *ou* activer (le travail)
chase (v) *[follow]* poursuivre
cheap bon marché
cheap labour main-d'oeuvre (f) bon marché
cheap money argent (m) bon marché
cheap rate tarif (m) réduit
check (n) *[examination]* contrôle (m) *ou* vérification (f)

check (n) [stop]
arrêt (m) *ou*
interruption (f)
check (v) [examine]
contrôler *ou* vérifier
check (v) [stop]
arrêter *ou* interrompre
check in [at airport]
se présenter
à l'enregistrement
check in [at hotel]
arriver à l'hôtel;
s'inscrire à l'arrivée
(à l'hôtel)
check-in (n)
[at airport]
enregistrement (m)
check-in counter
enregistrement (m)
check-in time heure
(f) d'enregistrement
check out [of hotel]
quitter l'hôtel;
régler la note
d'hôtel au départ
checkout [in super-
market] caisse (f)
check sample échan-
tillon-témoin (m)
cheque (n)
chèque (m)

cheque (guarantee)
card carte (de
garantie) bancaire
cheque account or
(US) checking
account compte
(m) de chèques
cheque book carnet
(m) de chèques *ou*
chéquier (m)
cheque number
numéro (m) de chèque
cheque stub talon
(m) de chèque
cheque to bearer
chèque (m) au porteur
chief (adj)
principal(e)
chief clerk chef (m)
de bureau
chief executive
(officer) président-
directeur (m) général
(PDG)
choice (adj) de
choix *ou* de qualité
choice (n) [choosing]
choix (m)
choice (n) [items
to choose from]
choix (m)

choice (n) [thing chosen] choix (m)
choose (v) choisir
Christmas bonus treizième mois
chronic (adj) chronique (adj)
chronological order ordre (m) chronologique
c.i.f. (cost, insurance and freight) CAF (coût, assurance, fret)
circular (n) circulaire (f)
circular letter circulaire (f)
circular letter of credit lettre (f) de crédit circulaire
circulation (n) [money] circulation (f)
circulation [newspaper] tirage (m)
civil law code (m) civil ou droit (m) civil
claim (n) réclamation (f) ou revendication (f) ou demande (f)

claim (v) [insurance] réclamer (des dommages-intérêts)
claim (v) [right] réclamer
claim (v) [suggest] prétendre
claimant (n) requérant(e)
claims department service (m) des réclamations
claims manager chef (m) du service des réclamations
class (n) classe (f) ou catégorie (f)
classification (n) classification (f)
classified ads annonces classées ou petites annonces
classified advertisements annonces classées ou petites annonces
classified directory répertoire (m) d'adresses par professions
classify (v) classer

clause **(n)** clause
(f) *ou* article (m)
clawback (n)
récupération (f) *ou*
reprise (f)
clear (adj) *[com-*
plete] entier (-ière)
ou complet (-ète)
clear (adj) *[easy to*
understand] clair(e)
clear (v) *[stock]*
liquider
clear: to clear en
solde
clear (v) a cheque
compenser un chèque
clear (v) a debt
rembourser une
dette
clear (adj) profit
bénéfice (m) net
clearance certificate
[customs]
certificat (m) de
passage en
douane *ou* de
dédouanement
clearance of
a cheque
compensation (f)
d'un chèque

clearance sale
soldes (m&fpl)
clearing (n) *[paying]*
acquittement (m)
(d'une dette)
clearing bank
banque (f) de
compensation
clerical error erreur
(f) d'écriture
clerical staff per-
sonnel (m) de bureau
clerical work travail
(m) de bureau
clerk (n) employé(e)
de bureau
client (n) client(e)
clientele (n)
clientèle (f)
climb (v) grimper
clinch (v) (a deal)
conclure (un marché)
clipping service
agence (f) de
coupures de
presse
close (n) *[end]* fin
(f) *ou* clôture (f)
close (v) *[after*
work] fermer (après
le travail)

close a bank account
fermer un compte en
banque
close a meeting
lever la séance
close an account
fermer *ou* clôturer
un compte
close down fermer
(un magasin *ou* une
usine)
close to (adj) près de
closed fermé(e)
closed circuit TV
télévision (f) en
circuit fermé
closed market
marché d'exclusivité
closing (adj) final(e)
ou dernier (-ière)
closing (n)
fermeture (f)
closing balance bilan
(m) de fin d'exercice
closing bid
dernière enchère (f)
closing date date
(f) limite
closing price prix
(m) *ou* cours (m) de
clôture

closing stock stock
(m) en fin d'exercise
closing time heure (f)
de fermeture
closing-down sale
liquidation (f)
du stock
closure (n)
fermeture (f)
c/o (care of) aux
bons soins de
ou chez
co-creditor
cocréancier (-ière)
co-director
codirecteur (-trice)
co-insurance
coassurance (f)
co-operate (v) col-
laborer *ou* coopérer
co-operation (n)
coopération (f)
co-operative (adj)
coopératif (-ive)
co-operative (n)
coopérative (f)
[société]
co-opt (v) someone
coopter quelqu'un
co-owner (n)
copropriétaire (mf)

co-ownership (n)
copropriété (f)
**c.o.d. *or* COD (cash
on delivery)**
livraison (f) contre
remboursement
code (n) code (m)
code of practice
politique (f) générale
(de l'entreprise)
coding (n) codage
(m) *ou* chiffrage (m)
coin (n) pièce (f)
de monnaie
cold call (n) visite
(f) impromptue
(d'un représentant)
cold start (n)
démarrage (m) à *ou*
de zéro
cold storage (n)
conservation (f) en
chambre froide
cold store (n)
chambre (f) froide
ou entrepôt (m)
frigorifique
collaborate (v)
collaborer
collaboration (n)
collaboration (f)

collapse (n)
effondrement (m)
collapse (v) s'ef-
fondrer *ou* s'écrouler
collateral (adj) en
nantissement
collateral (n)
garantie (f) *ou*
nantissement (m)
collect (v) *[fetch]*
aller chercher
collect (v) *[money]*
percevoir
collect (v) a debt
recouvrer une créance
collect call *[US]*
appel (m) en PCV
**collection (n)
*[of goods]*** enlève-
ment (m)
collection *[of money]*
recouvrement (m) *ou*
perception (f)
collection *[postal]*
levée (f)
**collection charges
or collection rates**
frais (mpl)
d'enlèvement
collective (adj)
collectif (-ive)

collective owner-ship propriété (f) collective

collective wage agreement convention (f) collective sur les salaires

collector (n) percepteur (m) *ou* receveur (m)

commerce (n) commerce (m)

commercial (adj) commercial(e)

commercial (n) *[TV]* publicité (f) *ou* pub (f) *ou* message (m) publicitaire *[à la télévision]*

commercial attaché attaché(e) commercial(e)

commercial college école (f) supérieure de commerce

commercial course cours (m) de commerce

commercial direc-tory répertoire (m) d'entreprises

commercial district quartier (m) commerçant

commercial failure faillite (f) *ou* banqueroute (f)

commercial law droit (m) commercial

commercial traveller représentant(e) de commerce *ou* délégué(e) commer-cial(e) *ou* VRP (m)

commercial under-taking entreprise (f) commerciale

commercialization (n) commercialisa-tion (f)

commercialize (v) commercialiser

commercials (n) *[TV]* la publicité *[à la télévision]*

commission (n) *[com-mittee]* commission (f) (d'enquête)

commission *[money]* commission (f)

commission agent agent (m) à la commission

commission rep
représentant (m) à
la commission
commit (v) *[crime]*
commettre
**commit funds to a
project** affecter une
somme à un projet
commitments (n)
engagements (mpl)
financiers
commodity (n)
marchandise (f) *ou*
denrée (f)
**commodity
exchange** bourse
(f) de commerce *ou*
des matières
premières
commodity futures
opérations (fpl) à
terme sur les
matières premières
commodity market
marché (m) des
matières premières
common *[frequent]*
courant(e) *ou*
commun(e)
common *[belonging
to more than one]*
commun(e)

common carrier
entreprise (f) de
transports publics
Common Market
Marché (m) Commun
common ownership
propriété (f)
collective
common pricing
fixation (f)
concertée des prix
communicate (v)
communiquer
communication (n)
[general]
communication (f)
communication
[message]
message (m) *ou*
communication (f)
communications
communications (fpl)
community (n)
communauté (f) *ou*
collectivité (f)
commute (v)
[exchange] échanger
commute (v)
[travel] voyager
(chaque jour) entre
son domicile et son
lieu de travail

commuter (n) banlieusard (m) *[qui fait le trajet quotidien de son domicile à son lieu de travail]*
companies' register (n) registre (m) du commerce et des sociétés (RCS)
company (n) société (f) *ou* compagnie (f)
company director directeur (-trice); administrateur (-trice)
company law droit (m) des sociétés
company secretary secrétaire (mf) général(e)
comparability (n) comparabilité (f)
comparable (adj) comparable
compare (v) comparer
compare with (v) être comparable à
comparison (n) comparaison (f)

compensate (v) dédommager *ou* indemniser
compensation (n) compensation (f)
compensation for damage dédommagement (m) *ou* indemnisation (f)
compete (v) with someone *or* with a company faire concurrence à *ou* concurrencer quelqu'un *ou* une société
competing (adj) concurrentiel (-elle) *ou* en concurrence
competing firms entreprises (fpl) concurrentes
competing products produits (mpl) concurrentiels
competition (n) concurrence (f)
competitive (adj) concurrentiel (-elle) *ou* compétitif (-ive)

competitive price
prix (m)
concurrentiel *ou*
prix compétitif
competitive pricing
fixation (f) de prix
compétitifs
competitive
products produits
(mpl) concurrentiels
competitively
priced à (un) prix
compétitif
competitiveness (n)
compétitivité (f)
competitor (n)
concurrent(e)
complain (v)
(about)
se plaindre (de)
complaint (n)
réclamation (f)
complaints depart-
ment service (m)
des réclamations
complementary
(adj) complé-
mentaire
complete (adj)
complet (-ète) *ou*
achevé(e)

complete (v) exé-
cuter *ou* terminer
completion
exécution (f) *ou*
achèvement (m)
(de travaux, etc.)
completion
date date (f)
d'achèvement
(de travaux)
completion of a
contract signature
(f) d'un contrat
compliance (n)
acceptation (f)
complimentary
(adj) de faveur
complimentary
ticket billet (m)
gratuit *ou* billet de
faveur
compliments slip
carte (f)
professionnelle
(qui accompagne
un envoi)
comply with (v) se
conformer à
composition (n)
[with creditors]
accommodement (m)

compound interest
intérêts (mpl)
composés
comprehensive
(adj) global(e) *ou*
général(e)
comprehensive
insurance
assurance (f) tous
risques
compromise (n)
compromis (m)
compromise (v)
arriver à un
compromis
compulsory (adj)
obligatoire; forcé(e)
compulsory
liquidation liquida-
tion (f) forcée
compulsory
purchase
[of property]
expropriation (f)
computer (n)
ordinateur (m)
computer bureau
société (f) de servi-
ces et d'ingénierie
informatique (SSII)

computer depart-
ment service (m)
informatique
computer error
erreur (f)
d'ordinateur
computer file
fichier (m)
(informatique)
computer language
langage (m) de
programmation
computer listing
listing (m) *ou*
sortie (f)
d'imprimante
computer printer
imprimante (f)
(d'ordinateur)
computer printout
sortie (f)
d'imprimante *ou*
listing (m)
computer program
programme (m)
ou logiciel (m)
computer program-
mer programmeur
(-euse) *ou* infor-
maticien (-ienne)

computer programming programmation (f)
computer services services (mpl) informatiques
computer system système (m) informatique
computer terminal terminal (m) d'ordinateur
computer time temps (m) d'ordinateur
computer-readable en langage machine
computer-readable codes codes (mpl) en langage machine
computerize (v) informatiser
computerized (adj) informatisé(e)
concealment (n) of assets dissimulation (f) d'actif
concern (n) [business] enterprise (f) ou firme (f)

concern (n) [worry] préoccupation (f)
concern (v) concerner
concession (n) [reduction] réduction (f)
concession [right] concession (f) ou droit (m) exclusif de vente
concessionaire (n) concessionnaire (mf)
conciliation (n) conciliation (f)
conclude (v) [agreement] conclure
condition (n) [state] condition (f) ou état (m)
condition [terms] condition (f)
condition: on condition that à (la) condition que ou sous réserve de
conditional (adj) conditionnel (-elle)

conditions of employment condi-tions (fpl) d'emploi
conditions of sale conditions (fpl) de vente
conduct (v) negotiations mener des négociations
conference (n) [large] congrès (m)
conference [small] conférence (f)
conference phone téléphone (m) de conférence
conference room salle (f) de conférences *ou* de réunion
confidence (n) confiance (f)
confidential (adj) confidentiel (-elle)
confidential report rapport (m) confidentiel
confidentiality (n) confidentialité (f)
confirm (v) confirmer

confirm a booking confirmer une réservation
confirm by letter envoyer une lettre de confirmation
confirm someone in a job confirmer une embauche
confirmation confirmation (f)
conflict (n) of interest conflit (m) d'intérêts
conglomerate (n) conglomérat (m)
connect (v) lier *ou* relier
connecting flight correspondance (f)
connection lien (m) *ou* relation (f)
consider (v) examiner *ou* étudier
consign (v) consigner
consignee (n) destinataire (mf) *ou* consignataire (mf)
consignment (n) [sending] expédition (f) *ou* envoi (m)

consignment (n)
[things
sent,received] envoi
(m); arrivage (m)
consignment note
bordereau (m)
d'expédition
consignor (n)
expéditeur (m)
consist of (v)
consister en *ou*
comprendre
consolidate (v)
consolider
consolidate *[ship-*
ments] grouper
consolidated
consolidé(e)
consolidated
shipment envoi
(m) groupé
consolidation (n)
groupage (m)
(d'envois)
consortium (n)
consortium (m)
constant (adj)
constant(e)
consult (v)
consulter
consultancy
assistance (f)

consultancy firm
cabinet-conseil (m)
consultant (n)
expert (m) *ou*
consultant (m)
consulting engineer
ingénieur conseil (m)
consumables (n)
produits (mpl) de
consommation
consumer (n)
consommateur
(-trice)
consumer credit
crédits (mpl) à la
consommation
consumer durables
biens (mpl) de con-
sommation durables
consumer goods
biens (mpl) de
consommation
consumer panel
panel (m) de
consommateurs
consumer price
index indice (m)
des prix à la
consommation
consumer protection
protection (f) du
consommateur

consumer research
recherche (f) des
besoins des
consommateurs
consumer spending
dépenses (fpl) des
consommateurs
consumption (n)
consommation (f)
contact (n) [general]
contact (m)
contact (n) [person]
relation (f) *ou*
contact (m)
contact (v)
contacter *ou* joindre
contain (v) contenir
**container (n) [box,
tin]** contenant (m)
**container (n) [for
shipping]**
conteneur (m)
container port port
(m) pour
porte-conteneurs
container ship
porte-conteneurs (m)
container terminal
terminal (m)
maritime (pour
porte-conteneurs)

**containerization
(n) [putting into
containers]**
conteneurisation (f)
ou mise (f) en
conteneurs
**containerization
[shipping in
containers]**
transport (m) par
conteneurs
**containerize (v)
[put into
containers]**
conteneuriser *ou*
mettre (des
marchandises) en
conteneurs
**containerize [ship
in containers]**
expédier (des
marchandises) par
conteneurs
content (n)
contenu (m) *ou*
teneur (f)
**contents (n)
[things contained]**
contenu (m)
contested takeover
rachat (m) contesté

contingency (n)
imprévu (m) *ou*
éventualité (f)
contingency fund
fonds (m) de
prévoyance
contingency
plan plan (m)
d'urgence
continual (adj)
continuel (-elle)
continually (adv)
continuellement *ou*
sans cesse
continuation (n)
continuation (f) *ou*
poursuite (f)
continue (v)
continuer
continuous (adj)
continu(e)
continuous feed
[paper] alimenta-
tion (f) en continu
continuous
stationery papier
(m) en continu *ou*
papier listing
contra account
compte (m) de
contrepartie

contra an entry
contrepasser une
écriture
contra entry
écriture (f) de
contrepartie *ou*
contrepassation (f)
contract (n)
contrat (m);
engagement (m)
contract (v)
contracter
contract law droit
(m) des contrats et
des obligations
contract note avis
(m) d'exécution
contract of
employment
contrat (m) de
travail
contract work
travail (m)
contractuel
contracting party
partie (f)
contractante
contractor (n)
entrepreneur (m)
contractual (adj)
contractuel (-elle)

contractual liability
responsabilité (f)
contractuelle
contractually (adv)
conformément à un
contrat
contrary (n)
contraire (m)
contrast (n)
contraste (m)
contribute (v)
contribuer (une
somme) *ou* cotiser
contribution
contribution (f)
**contribution of
capital** versement
(m) au capital
**contributor (n) *[of
money]*** donateur
(-trice)
**contributor (n)
*[of work, etc.]*** collaborateur (-trice)
control (n) *[check]*
contrôle (m) *ou*
vérification (f) *ou*
surveillance (f)
control (n) *[power]*
contrôle (m) *ou*
maîtrise (f)

control (v) *[check]*
contrôler *ou* vérifier
ou surveiller
**control (v) *[have
power]*** contrôler *ou*
maîtriser
**control (v) a
business** diriger
une entreprise
**control (n) key
*[computer key-
board]*** touche (f)
de contrôle
control systems
tests (mpl) et
diagnostics
controlled economy
économie (f) dirigée
controller *[US]*
chef comptable (m)
**controller *[who
checks]*** contrôleur
(m) *ou*
vérificateur (m)
controlling (adj)
qui contrôle
convene (v)
convoquer
convenient (adj)
pratique *ou*
commode

conversion (n)
conversion (f)
conversion of funds
[embezzlement]
détournement (m)
de fonds
conversion price or
conversion rate taux
(m) de conversion
convert (v)
changer de l'argent
convertibility (n)
convertibilité (f)
convertible
currency monnaie
(f) convertible
convertible loan
valeurs (f)
convertibles
conveyance (n)
acte (m) de cession
conveyancer (n)
notaire (mf) (qui
rédige un acte de
cession)
conveyancing (n)
rédaction (f) d'un
acte de cession
cooling off period
(after purchase)
délai (m) de réflexion

cooperative society
société (f)
coopérative ou
coopérative (f)
copartner (n)
coassocié(e)
copartnership (n)
coparticipation (f)
cope (v) se
débrouiller ou s'en
tirer
copier (n)
photocopieur (m) ou
photocopieuse (f)
copy (n) [book]
exemplaire (n)
copy (n)
[document]
document (m)
copy (n) [duplicate]
copie (f)
copy (n) [newspaper]
exemplaire (m) ou
numéro (m)
copy (v) faire une
copie ou reproduire
copying machine
photocopieur (m) ou
photocopieuse (f)
corner (n) [angle]
coin (m) ou angle (m)

corner (n)
[monopoly]
situation (f) de
monopole
corner shop
magasin (m) du coin
corner (v) the
market accaparer
le marché
corporate (adj)
image image (f) de
marque (de la
société)
corporate name
raison (f) sociale
corporate plan
plan (m) de
développement de
la société
corporate planning
planification (f)
dans l'entreprise
corporate profits
bénéfices (mpl)
d'une société
corporation (n)
société (f)
corporation tax
impôt (m) sur les
bénéfices des
sociétés

correct (adj) cor-
rect(e) *ou* exact(e)
correct (v) corriger
correction (n)
correction (f)
correspond (v)
with someone
[write] correspon-
dre avec quelqu'un
correspond with
something *[fit]*
correspondre à
quelque chose
correspondence (n)
correspondance (f)
correspondent (n)
[journalist]
correspondant(e)
ou journaliste (mf)
correspondent (n)
[who writes letters]
correspondant(e)
cost (n) coût (m)
ou frais (mpl) *ou*
prix (m)
cost (v) coûter;
valoir
cost accountant
responsable (mf) de
la comptabilité
analytique

cost accounting
comptabilité (f)
analytique
cost analysis
analyse (f) des coûts
cost centre centre
(m) de coût
cost factor facteur
(m) (de) coût
cost of living coût
(m) de la vie
cost of sales coût
(m) de revient (des
marchandises
vendues)
cost plus coût (m)
majoré
cost price prix (m)
coûtant
**cost, insurance and
freight (c.i.f.)**
coût, assurance, fret
(CAF)
**cost-benefit
analysis** étude (f)
du rapport
coût-bénéfice
cost-cutting (n)
réduction (f) des frais
cost-effective (adj)
rentable

**cost-effectiveness
(n)** rentabilité (f)
**cost-of-living
allowance**
indemnité (f)
de vie chère
**cost-of-living
bonus** prime (f) de
vie chère
**cost-of-living
increase** augmen-
tation (f) indexée
sur le coût de la vie
cost-of-living index
indice (m) du coût
de la vie
cost-push inflation
inflation (f) par les
coûts
costing (n) calcul
(m) du prix de
revient
costly (adj) cher
(chère) *ou* onéreux
(-euse)
costs (n) frais
(mpl) *[de procès]*
counsel (n)
avocat-conseil (m)
count (v) *[add]*
compter

count (v) *[include]*
inclure
counter (n) comptoir
(m); rayon (m)
counter staff
vendeurs (-euses)
ou préposé(e)s
au(x) comptoir(s)
counter-claim (n)
demande (f)
reconventionnelle
counter-claim (v)
opposer une
demande
reconventionnelle
counter-offer
contre-proposition (f)
counterbid (n)
surenchère (f)
counterfeit (adj)
faux (fausse)
counterfeit (v)
contrefaire
counterfoil (n)
talon (m) *ou* souche
(f) *[chéquier, etc.]*
countermand (v)
annuler *[rendez-
vous, réunion]*
countersign (v)
contresigner

**country (n) *[not
town]*** campagne
(f); province (f);
région (f)
country *[state]*
pays (m)
country of origin
pays (m) d'origine
coupon bon (m)
coupon ad
publicité (f) avec
coupon-réponse
courier (n) *[guide]*
accompagnateur
(-trice)
courier *[messenger]*
coursier (m)
court (n) cour (f)
ou tribunal (m)
court case
procès (m)
covenant (n)
engagement (m)
contractuel
covenant (v)
s'engager (à verser
une somme d'argent
déterminée)
cover (n) *[insurance]*
garantie (f) *ou*
couverture (f)

cover (n) [protective cover] housse (f)

cover (v) [expenses] couvrir (ses dépenses)

cover (v) [put on top] couvrir ou recouvrir

cover (v) costs couvrir les coûts de production

cover (v) a risk être assuré contre un risque

cover charge (n) [in restaurant] couvert (m)

cover note (n) attestation (f) provisoire d'assurance

covering letter or note lettre (f) d'accompagnement

crash (n) [accident] accident (m)

crash (n) [financial] crise (f) (financière); krach (m)

crash (v) [fail] faire faillite ou s'effondrer

crash (v) [hit] s'écraser contre

crate (n) caisse (f)

crate (v) mettre (des marchandises) en caisse(s)

credit (n) crédit (m)

credit: in credit [account] créditeur (-trice) (adj)

credit: on credit à crédit

credit (v) (an account) créditer (un compte)

credit account [in shop] compte (m) d'achat

credit agency agence (f) de notation financière

credit balance solde (m) créditeur

credit bank banque (f) de crédit

credit card carte (f) de crédit

credit card sale vente (f) réglée avec (une) carte de crédit

credit ceiling
plafond (m) de crédit
credit column
colonne (f) des
crédits
credit control
contrôle (m) de crédit
ou encadrement (m)
du crédit
credit entry
écriture (f) au crédit
credit facilities
facilités (fpl) de
crédit
credit freeze
restriction (f) *ou*
encadrement (m) du
crédit
credit limit
plafond (m) *ou*
limite (f) de crédit
credit note
facture (f) d'avoir
ou note (f) de crédit
credit policy
politique (f) en
matière de crédit
credit rating
notation (f) *ou* note
(f) financière

credit side
colonne (f) des
crédits *ou* côté (m)
crédit
credit-worthy (adj)
solvable
creditor (n)
créancier (m)
**cross (v) a
cheque** barrer un
chèque
cross off (v)
radier (quelque
chose d'une liste)
cross out (v)
barrer
cross rate
taux (m)
(de change) croisé
crossed cheque
chèque (m) barré
cubic (adj) cube
cubic measure
mesure (f) de
volume
cum avec
cum coupon
coupon attaché
cum dividend
avec dividende

cumulative (adj)
cumulatif (-ive)
cumulative interest
intérêts (mpl)
composés
cumulative
preference share
action (f) privilégiée
cumulative
currency (n) devise
(f) (étrangère)
currency
conversion
conversion (f) en
devises étrangères
currency note
billet (m) de banque
currency reserves
réserves (fpl) de
devises
current (adj)
courant(e)
current account
compte (m) courant
current assets
actif (m) circulant
current cost
accounting
méthode (f) des
coûts courants

current liabilities
dettes (fpl) à court
terme *ou* passif (m)
exigible
current price prix
(m) courant *ou* actuel
current rate of
exchange taux (m)
de change en
vigueur
current yield
rendement (m)
courant *ou* taux (m)
de rendement
(d'une action)
curriculum vitae
(CV) curriculum
(m) vitae (CV)
curve courbe (f)
custom (n)
clientèle (f)
custom-built *or*
custom-made (fait)
sur mesure *ou* sur
commande
customer (n)
client(e)
customer appeal
facteur (m) de
séduction du client

customer loyalty
fidélité (f) de la
clientèle
**customer
satisfaction**
satisfaction (f)
du client
**customer service
department** service
(m) clients
customs douane (f)
Customs and Excise
Administration (f)
des douanes
customs barrier
barrière (f)
douanière
customs broker
agent (m) en
douane
customs clearance
dédouanement (m)
**customs
declaration**
déclaration (f)
en douane
**customs
declaration form**
formulaire (m)
de déclaration
en douane

customs duty droit
(m) de douane
**customs entry
point** poste (m)
frontière
**customs examina-
tion** contrôle (m)
douanier
customs formalities
formalités (fpl) de
douane *ou* formalités
douanières
**customs officer *or*
customs official**
douanier (m)
customs receipt
récépissé (m) des
douanes
customs seal
plomb (m) de la
douane
customs tariff
tarif (m) douanier
**customs
union** union (f)
douanière
cut (n)
réduction (f)
cut (v) réduire *ou*
diminuer *ou*
supprimer

cut down on expenses réduire les dépenses

cut price (n) prix (m) réduit

cut-price (adj) à prix réduit *ou* au rabais

cut-price goods marchandises à prix sacrifiés

cut-price petrol essence à prix réduit

cut-price store magasin à prix réduits *ou* de discount

cut-throat competition concurrence (f) féroce

CV (curriculum vitae) curriculum (m) vitae (CV)

cycle cycle (m)

cyclical (adj) cyclique

cyclical factors facteurs (mpl) conjoncturels

Dd

daily journalier (-ière) *ou* quotidien (-ienne)

daisy-wheel printer imprimante (f) à marguerite

damage (n) dommage (m) *ou* dégâts (mpl)

damage (v) abîmer *ou* endommager

damage survey expertise (f) des dégâts

damage to property dommages (mpl) matériels

damaged endommagé(e) *ou* abîmé(e)

damages dommages-intérêts (mpl) *ou* dommages et intérêts

data (n)
données (fpl)
data processing
traitement (m) de
données *ou*
informatique (f)
data retrieval
recherche (f)
d'information
database base (f)
de données
date (n) date (f)
date (v) dater
date of receipt
date (f) de réception
date stamp *[device]*
timbre (m) dateur
dated (adj)
daté(e) (de)
day (n) *[24 hours]*
jour (m)
day *[working day]*
jour (m) *ou* journée
(f) (de travail)
day shift équipe (f)
de jour
day-to-day
ordinaire *ou*
courant(e) *ou* au
jour le jour

dead (adj) *[person]*
mort(e) *ou*
décédé(e)
dead account
compte (m)
oisif *ou* compte
qui dort
dead loss perte (f)
sèche
deadline (n) date
(f) limite
deadlock (n)
impasse (f)
deadlock (v)
arriver à une
impasse
deadweight
charge (f)
en lourd
deadweight
cargo port (m)
en lourd
deadweight
tonnage charge (f)
en lourd
deal (n) marché
(m) *ou* accord (m)
ou contrat (m)
deal in (v) faire le
commerce de

deal with (v) an order s'occuper d'une commande *ou* exécuter une commande

deal with someone faire affaire *ou* traiter avec quelqu'un

dealer (n) négociant(e) *ou* marchand(e)

dealing (n) [commerce] commerce (m)

dealing [Stock Exchange] opération (f) boursière *ou* de Bourse

dear (adj) [costly] cher (chère) *ou* coûteux (-euse)

dear (adj) [starting a letter] cher (chère)

Dear Madam; Dear Sir Madame; Monsieur

debenture (n) obligation (f) (émise par une société)

debenture holder obligataire (mf)

debit (n) débit (m)

debit (v) an account débiter un compte

debit balance solde (m) débiteur

debit column colonne (f) des débits

debit entry écriture (f) au débit

debit note note (f) de débit

debits and credits débit et crédit *ou* passif et actif

debt (n) dette (f)

debt collection recouvrement (m) de créances

debt collection agency agence (f) de recouvrement (de créances)

debt collector
agent (m) de
recouvrement (de
créances)
debtor (n)
débiteur (m)
debtor side
colonne (f) des
débits
debts due créances
(fpl) exigibles
decentralization (n)
décentralisation (f)
decentralize (v)
décentraliser
decide (v) décider
de; se décider à
**decide on a course
of action** arrêter un
plan d'action
deciding (adj)
décisif (-ive)
deciding factor
facteur (m) décisif
decimal (n)
décimale (f)
decimal (adj) point
virgule (f)
(décimale)
decision (n)
décision (f)

decision maker
décideur (m)
decision making
prise (f) de décision
**decision-making
processes**
processus (m) de
prise de décision
deck (n) *[ship]*
pont (m) (d'un
navire)
deck cargo
pontée (f)
declaration (n)
déclaration (f)
**declaration of
bankruptcy**
jugement (m)
déclaratif de faillite
**declaration of
income** déclaration
(f) de revenus
declare (v)
déclarer
**declare goods to
customs** déclarer
des marchandises à
la douane
**declare someone
bankrupt** déclarer
quelqu'un en faillite

declared
déclaré(e)
declared value
valeur (f) déclarée
decline (n)
baisse (f) *ou*
ralentissement (m)
decline (v) [fall]
être en baisse *ou*
diminuer
decontrol (v)
libérer
decrease (n)
baisse (f) *ou*
diminution (f)
decrease (v)
baisser *ou* diminuer
decrease (n) in
price baisse (f)
de prix
decrease (n) in
value diminution
(f) *ou* perte (f) de
valeur
decreasing (adj)
décroissant(e) *ou* en
baisse
deduct (v) déduire
ou retenir
deductible (adj)
déductible

deduction (n)
déduction (f) *ou*
retenue (f)
deed (n) acte (m)
deed of assignment
acte (m) de cession
(de créance)
deed of covenant
engagement (m)
contractuel (à
verser une somme
déterminée)
deed of partnership
contrat (m)
d'association
deed of transfer
acte (m) de cession
(de propriété)
deeds (of a house)
acte (m) de
propriété
default (n)
manquement (m) *ou*
défaillance (f)
default (v) ne pas
faire face à ses
engagements
default on
payments se
trouver en cessation
de paiements

defaulter (n)
témoin (m)
défaillant; partie (f)
défaillante
defect (n) défaut
(m) *ou* vice (m) de
fabrication
defective [faulty]
défectueux (-euse)
**defective [not
valid]** non valable
ou non valide
defence (n) [legal]
défense (f)
**defence [protec-
tion]** défense (f)
defence counsel
avocat (m) de la
défense
defend (v)
défendre
defend a lawsuit se
défendre en justice
defendant (n)
défendeur (défend-
eresse) *ou* accusé(e)
ou prévenu(e)
defer (v) différer
ou remettre
defer payment
différer le paiement

deferment (n)
ajournement (m) *ou*
remise (f)
**deferment of
payment** délai (m)
de paiement
deferred reporté(e)
ou différé(e)
deferred creditor
créancier (m)
différé
deferred payment
paiement (m)
différé
deficit (n)
déficit (m)
deficit financing
financement (m) du
déficit budgétaire
deflation (n)
déflation (f)
deflationary (adj)
déflationniste
defray (v) [costs]
défrayer *ou* couvrir
des frais
**defray someone's
expenses**
rembourser les frais
de quelqu'un
del credere ducroire

del credere agent
commissionnaire
(m) ducroire
delay (n)
retard (m)
delay (v) être en
retard *ou* retarder
delegate (n)
délégué(e)
delegate (v)
déléguer
delegation (n)
[action] délégation
(f) (de pouvoirs)
delegation *[people]*
délégation (f)
delete (v) rayer *ou*
supprimer
deliver (v)
livrer
delivered price prix
tout compris *[port*
et emballage inclus]
delivery (n)
[goods] livraison
(f) *ou* envoi (m)
delivery date date
(f) de livraison
delivery note
bulletin (m) de
livraison

delivery of a bill of
exchange transfert
(m) *ou* cession (f)
d'une traite
delivery of goods
livraison (f) de
marchandises
delivery order
instructions (fpl)
pour la livraison
delivery time délai
(m) de livraison
delivery van camion
(m) *ou* camionnette
(f) de livraison
deliveryman (n)
livreur (m)
demand (n) *[for*
payment] demande
(f) *ou* réclamation (f)
demand (n) *[need]*
demande (f)
demand: on
demand à vue *ou* à
présentation
demand (v)
réclamer
demand bill traite
(f) à vue
demand deposit
dépôt (m) à vue

**demand-led infla-
tion** inflation (f)
liée à la demande
demerge (v)
effectuer une (opéra-
tion de) scission
demerger (n)
scission (f)
demonstrate (v)
faire une démon-
stration
demonstration (n)
démonstration (f)
**demonstration
model** modèle (m)
ou appareil (m) de
démonstration
demonstrator (n)
démonstrateur (-trice)
demurrage (n)
surestarie (f)
**department (n) [in
government]**
ministère (m)
**department [in
office]** service (m)
ou bureau (m)
**department [in
shop]** rayon (m)
department store
grand magasin

departmental (adj)
départemental(e)
**departmental man-
ager [shop]** chef
(m) de rayon [d'un
magasin]
**departure (n)
[going away]**
départ (m)
**departure [new
venture]** nouveau
départ *ou* nouvelle
orientation
**departure lounge
[airport]** salle (f)
d'embarquement
**departures (n) [at
airport, etc.]**
départs (mpl)
depend on (v)
dépendre de *ou*
compter sur
depending on
suivant *ou* en
fonction de
**deposit (n) [in
bank]** dépôt (m)
**deposit (n) [paid in
advance]** acompte
(m) *ou* provision (f)
ou arrhes (fpl)

deposit (v) verser de l'argent (sur un compte)

deposit account compte (m) de dépôt(s) *ou* compte sur livret

deposit slip *[bank]* bordereau (m) de versement

depositor (n) déposant(e)

depository (n) *[place]* dépôt (m)

depot (n) dépôt (m) *ou* entrepôt (m)

depreciate (v) *[amortize]* amortir

depreciate (v) *[lose value]* diminuer de valeur *ou* se déprécier

depreciation (n) *[amortizing]* amortissement (m) *ou* dépréciation (f)

depreciation (n) *[loss of value]* moins-value (f) *ou* dévaluation (f)

depreciation rate taux (m) d'amortissement

depression (n) dépression (f)

dept (= depart- ment) deputize (v) for someone assurer l'intérim de quelqu'un

deputy (n) suppléant(e) *ou* adjoint(e)

deputy manager directeur (-trice) adjoint(e)

deputy managing director directeur général adjoint *ou* directrice générale adjointe

deregulation (n) déréglementation (f)

describe (v) décrire

description (n) description (f)

design (n) conception (f) *ou* étude (f) *ou* design (m)

design (v) dessiner
ou concevoir
design department
bureau (m) d'études
desk (n)
bureau (m)
desk diary agenda
(m) de bureau
desk-top
publishing (DTP)
publication (f)
assistée par
ordinateur (PAO)
despatch
(= dispatch)
destination (n)
destination (f)
detail (n) détail
(m) *ou* précision (f)
detail (v)
détailler
detailed
détaillé(e)
detailed account
compte (m) détaillé
determine (v)
déterminer *ou* fixer
Deutschmark (n)
mark (m) (allemand)
ou Deutschemark (m)

devaluation (n)
dévaluation (f)
devalue (v) dévaluer
develop (v) *[build]*
aménager
develop *[plan]*
développer *ou*
mettre au point
developing country
pays (m) en
développement (PED)
development (n)
développement (m)
device (n)
dispositif (m) *ou*
système (m)
diagram (n)
diagramme (m) *ou*
schéma (m) *ou*
graphique (m)
dial (v) faire *ou*
composer un numéro
dial (v) a number
composer un numéro
(de téléphone)
dial (v) direct
appeler en direct
dialling (n) composi-
tion (f) d'un numéro
(de téléphone)

dialling code
indicatif (m)
(téléphonique)
dialling tone
tonalité (f) (du
téléphone)
diary (n)
agenda (m)
dictate (v) dicter
dictating machine
Dictaphone (m)
dictation (n)
dictée (f)
differ (v) différer
difference (n)
différence (f)
differences in price
différences (fpl)
de prix
different (adj)
différent(e)
differential (adj)
différentiel (-ielle)
differential tariffs
tarifs (mpl)
différentiels
digit (n) chiffre (m)
dilution of equity
dilution (f) du
capital

direct (adj)
direct(e)
direct (adv)
directement
direct (v) diriger
ou mener
direct cost coût
(m) direct
direct debit
prélèvement (m)
automatique
direct mail
publicité (f)
directe *ou*
publipostage (m)
direct selling
vente (f) par
correspondance
direct tax impôt
(m) direct
direct taxation
impôt(s) direct(s)
ou imposition (f)
directe
direct-mail
advertising
publicité (f) directe
ou publipostage (m)
direction (n)
direction (f)

directions for use
mode (m) d'emploi
directive (n)
directive (f)
director (n)
administrateur
(-trice); directeur
(-trice)
directorship (n)
directorat (m) *ou*
poste (m) de
directeur
directory (n)
[addresses]
répertoire (m)
d'adresses
**directory *[tele-
phone]*** annuaire
(m) (des
téléphones)
disburse (v)
débourser
**discharge (n) *[of
debt]*** règlement
(m) d'une dette
**discharge (v)
*[employee]*** ren-
voyer *ou* congédier
**discharge (v) a
debt** régler *ou*
acquitter une dette

disclaimer (n)
déni (m) de
responsabilité
disclose (v)
révéler *ou* divulger
**disclose a piece of
information**
divulguer un
renseignement
disclosure (n)
révélation (f) *ou*
divulgation (f)
discontinue (v)
cesser (la
fabrication *ou* la
vente d'un produit)
discount (n)
réduction (f) *ou* remise
(f) *ou* escompte (m)
ou rabais (m)
discount (v)
vendre au rabais
**discount house
*[bank]*** banque (f)
d'escompte
**discount house
*[shop]*** magasin (m)
de discount *ou* dis-
counter (m)
discount price prix
(de) discount

discount rate
[bank] taux
d'escompte
discount store
magasin (m) de
discount *ou*
discounter (m)
discountable (adj)
escomptable
discounted cash
flow (DCF) cash-
flow (m) actualisé
discounted value
valeur (f) actualisée
discounter (n) mag-
asin (m) de discount
ou discounter (m)
discrepancy (n)
erreur (f) *ou*
écart (m)
discuss (v) discuter
discussion (n)
discussion (f)
diseconomies (n) of
scale déséconomies
(fpl) d'échelle
dishonour (v) a bill
ne pas honorer une
traite
disinflation (n)
désinflation (f)

disinvest (v)
désinvestir
disinvestment
(n) désinvestisse-
ment (m)
disk (n) disque (m)
disk drive lecteur
(m) de disques *ou*
de disquettes
diskette (n)
disquette (f)
dismiss (v) (an
employee)
licencier (un
employé)
dismissal (n)
licenciement (m)
dispatch (n) *[goods*
sent] envoi (m)
dispatch (n)
[sending]
envoi (m) *ou*
expédition (f)
dispatch (v) *[send]*
expédier (des
marchandises)
dispatch depart-
ment service (m)
des livraisons *ou*
service des
expéditions

dispatch note
bordereau (m)
d'expédition
display (n) présenta-
tion (f) *ou* étalage (m)
display (v)
présenter
display case vitrine (f)
display material
matériel (m)
publicitaire
display pack
emballage (m) de
présentation; condi-
tionnement (m)
display stand
présentoir (m) *ou*
étalage (m)
display unit
présentoir (m);
gondole (f)
disposable (adj) à
jeter après usage
disposal (n) *[sale]*
vente (f)
dispose (v) of
excess stock *[sell]*
écouler le surplus
de stock
dissolve (v)
dissoudre

dissolve a partner-
ship dissoudre une
association
distress merchan-
dise marchandises
vendues en catastro-
phe *ou* à tout prix
distress sale vente
(f) forcée
distributable profit
bénéfice (m)
distribuable
distribute (v)
[goods] distribuer
(des marchandises)
distribute *[share]*
distribuer
distribution (n)
distribution (f);
[books] diffusion (f)
distribution chan-
nels canaux (mpl)
de distribution
distribution costs
frais (mpl) de distri-
bution *ou* de diffusion
distribution
manager
responsable (mf) de
la distribution *ou* de
la diffusion

**distribution
network** réseau
(m) de distribution
distributor (n) dis-
tributeur (m); con-
cessionnaire (m);
[books] diffuseur (m)
distributorship (n)
concession (f) *[pour
la distribution de
certains produits]*
diversification (n)
diversification (f)
diversify (v)
diversifier *ou*
varier
dividend (n)
dividende (m)
dividend cover
couverture (f) des
dividendes
dividend warrant
chèque (m) de
dividende
dividend yield taux
(m) de rendement
d'une action
division (n) *[part
of a company]*
division (f) *ou*
secteur (m)

division *[part of a
group]* division (f)
dock (n) bassin (m)
dock (v) *[remove
money]* retenir
(une somme)
dock (v) *[ship]*
arriver à quai *ou*
accoster
docket (n) fiche (f)
(de contenu)
doctor's certificate
certificat (m)
médical
document (n)
document (m)
documentary (adj)
documentaire
**documentary
evidence *or* proof**
(document)
justificatif (m) *ou*
pièce (f)
justificative
documentation (n)
documentation (f)
documents
documents (mpl);
dossier (m)
dole (n) indemnité
(f) de chômage

dollar (n)
[American] dollar
(m) (américain) *ou*
le billet vert
dollar area zone (f)
dollar
dollar balance
balance (f) commer-
ciale en dollars
dollar crisis crise
(f) du dollar
dollar stocks
actions (fpl) en
dollars
domestic (adj)
intérieur(e) *ou*
domestique *ou*
national(e)
domestic market
marché (m) intérieur
domestic
production produc-
tion (f) intérieure
domestic sales
ventes (fpl)
intérieures
domestic trade com-
merce (m) intérieur
domicile
domicile (m)
door (n) porte (f)

door-to-door
porte-à-porte (m)
door-to-door sales-
man démarcheur (m)
door-to-door sell-
ing *[canvassing]*
démarchage (m) *ou*
porte-à-porte (m)
dormant account
compte (m) oisif *ou*
qui dort
dossier (n)
dossier (m)
dot-matrix printer
imprimante (f)
matricielle
double (adj) double
double (v) doubler
double taxation
double imposition (f)
double taxation
agreement
convention (f) entre
deux pays sur la
double imposition
double-book (v)
surréserver *ou* faire
du surbooking
double-booking (n)
surréservation (f)
ou surbooking (m)

down en bas *ou* vers le bas

down payment acompte (m)

down time temps (m) d'arrêt *ou* temps improductif

down-market bas de gamme

downside factor facteur (m) pessimiste *ou* négatif

downtown (adv) au centre de la ville

downtown (n) centre(-)ville (m)

downturn (n) repli (m) *ou* baisse (f) *ou* recul (m)

downward vers le bas *ou* en baisse

dozen (n) douzaine (f)

draft (n) *[money]* traite (f) *ou* lettre (f) de change

draft (n) *[rough plan]* esquisse (f) *ou* ébauche (f) *ou* avant-projet (m)

draft (v) esquisser *ou* ébaucher

draft a contract faire une ébauche de contrat

draft a letter faire un brouillon de lettre

draft plan *or* draft project esquisse (f) *ou* ébauche (f) *ou* avant-projet (m)

draw (v) *[a cheque]* tirer un chèque *[sur une banque]*

draw *[money]* tirer *ou* retirer *[de l'argent]*

draw up (v) rédiger

draw up a contract rédiger un contrat

drawee (n) tiré (m)

drawer (n) tireur (m)

drawing account compte (m) courant

drive (n) *[campaign]* campagne (f)

drive (n) *[energy]* energie (f)

drive (n) *[part of machine]*
commande (f)
drive (v) *[a car]*
conduire (une voiture)
driver (n)
conducteur (-trice)
drop (n) chute (f) *ou* baisse (f)
drop (v) chuter *ou* baisser
drop in sales chute (f) des ventes
dud (adj) cheque chèque (m) sans provision
due (adj) *[awaited]* attendu(e)
due (adj) *[owing]* dû (due)
dues (n) *[orders of items not yet on the market]* commandes (fpl) en attente *ou* anticipées
duly *[in time]* en temps voulu
duly *[legally]* dûment

dummy (n)
maquette (f)
dummy pack emballage (m) factice *ou* boîte (f) factice
dump bin (n)
présentoir (m) de produits en vrac
dump (v) goods on a market faire du dumping
dumping (n)
dumping (m)
duplicate (n) double (m) *ou* duplicata (m) *ou* copie (f)
duplicate (v)
copier *ou* faire une copie; polycopier
duplicate (v) a letter faire une copie d'une lettre
duplicate receipt *or* **duplicate of a receipt** duplicata (m) d'une quittance
duplication (n)
reproduction (f)
durable goods
biens (mpl) durables

duty (n) [tax] taxe (f) *ou* droit (m)
duty-free [article] hors taxe *ou* exempt(e) de droits
duty-free shop boutique (f) hors taxe
duty-paid goods marchandises (fpl) dédouanées

Ee

e. & o.e. (errors and omissions excepted) sauf erreur ou omission
early (adj & adv) tôt *ou* de bonne heure
earmark (v) funds for a project affecter des fonds à un projet
earn (v) [interest] rapporter; être rémunéré

earn [money] gagner
earning capacity niveau (m) de salaire possible
earnings [profit] bénéfice (m)
earnings [salary] salaire (m) *ou* revenu (m)
earnings per share *or* **earnings yield** rendement (m) *ou* revenu (m) d'une action
earnings-related pension retraite (f) proportionnelle (au salaire)
easy (adj) facile
easy terms facilités (fpl) de paiement
ECGD (Export Credit Guarantee Department) bureau (m) d'assurance crédit à l'exportation
e-commerce (n) commerce (m) électronique *ou* commerce en ligne

economic (adj) [general] économique
economic [profitable] rentable
Economic and Monetary Union (EMU) Union (f) économique et monétaire (UEM)
economic cycle cycle (m) économique
economic development développement (m) économique
economic growth croissance (f) économique
economic indicators indicateurs (mpl) économiques
economic model modèle (m) économique
economic planning planification (f) économique
economic trends tendances (fpl) économiques *ou* conjoncture (f) économique

economical (adj) économique; avantageux (-euse)
economics (n) [profitability] côté (m) économique *ou* rentabilité (f)
economics [study] économie (f) (politique)
economies of scale économies (fpl) d'échelle
economist (n) économiste (mf)
economize (v) économiser *ou* faire des économies
economy (n) [saving] économie (f)
economy [system] économie (f) *ou* régime (m) économique
economy class [travel] classe (f) touriste
economy size format (m) économique
effect (n) résultat (m) *ou* effet (m)

effect (v)
effectuer
effective (adj)
efficace
effective date
date (f) d'entrée en
vigueur
effective demand
demande (f) effective
effective yield ren-
dement (m) effectif
effectiveness (n)
efficacité (f)
efficiency (n)
efficacité (f) *ou*
performance (f)
efficient (adj)
efficace *ou*
performant(e); com-
pétent(e) *[personne]*
effort (n)
effort (m)
elasticity (n)
élasticité (f)
elect (v) élire *ou*
choisir
election (n)
élection (f)
**electronic mail *or*
email** courrier (m)
électronique

**electronic point of
sale (EPOS)** point
(m) de vente
électronique
**elevator (n)
*[goods]***
monte-charge (m)
elevator *[grain]*
silo (m)
**email (n)
(electronic mail)**
courrier (m)
électronique
**email (n) *[
message]*** message
(m) électronique *ou*
e-mail (m)
email (v) envoyer
par courrier
électronique
embargo (n)
embargo (m)
embargo (v) met-
tre l'embargo sur
embark (v) embar-
quer *ou* monter à
bord (d'un navire)
embark on (v)
entreprendre
embarkation (n)
embarquement (m)

embarkation card
carte (f)
d'embarquement
embezzle (v)
détourner des fonds
embezzlement (n)
détournement (m)
de fonds
embezzler (n)
escroc (m)
emergency (n)
urgence (f);
situation (f) critique
emergency reserves
réserves (fpl) de
secours *ou* fonds
(m) de secours
employ (v)
employer
employed (adj) *[in
*job]*** employé(e)
employed (adj)
[money] investi(e)
employed (adj)
[used] employé(e)
ou utilisé(e)
employee (n)
employé(e) *ou*
salarié(e)
employer (n)
employeur (m)

employment (n)
emploi (m)
employment
agency agence (f)
ou bureau (m) de
placement
empty (adj) vide
empty (v) vider
EMS (European
Monetary System)
SME (système
monétaire
européen)
encash (v)
toucher un chèque
ou encaisser un
chèque
encashment (n)
encaissement (m)
enclose (v) joindre
enclosure (n)
(encl. *or* enc.)
pièce (f) jointe (p.j.)
end (n) fin (f)
end (v) prendre fin
ou finir *ou* se terminer
end of season sale
vente (f) de fin de
saison
end product
produit (m) fini

end user utilisateur (m) (final) *ou* consommateur (m)

endorse (v) a cheque endosser un chèque

endorsee (n) endossataire (mf)

endorsement (n) *[action]* endossement (m)

endorsement *[on insurance]* avenant (m)

endorser (n) endosseur (m)

energy (n) *[electricity]* énergie (f)

energy *[human]* énergie (f) *ou* dynamisme (m)

energy-saving (adj) qui économise l'énergie

enforce (v) faire exécuter *ou* faire observer

enforcement (n) application (f) *ou* mise (f) en vigueur

engage (v) employer *ou* embaucher

engaged (adj) *[telephone]* occupé(e)

engaged tone tonalité 'occupé'

enquire se renseigner

enquiry demande (f) (officielle)

enter (v) *[go in]* entrer

enter *[write in]* inscrire *ou* enregistrer *ou* noter

enter into *[discussion]* entamer (des discussions)

enterprise (n) entreprise (f)

entertainment allowance indemnité (f) de représentation

entitle (v) (someone to) autoriser (quelqu'un) *ou* donner le droit (à quelqu'un de)

entitlement (n) droit (m)

entrepot port
(port) entrepôt (m)
entrepreneur (n)
entrepreneur (m)
**entrepreneurial
(adj)** d'entrepre-
neur; dynamique
mais risqué
entrust (v) confier
entry (n) [going in]
entrée (f)
entry [writing]
écriture (f)
entry visa
visa (m) d'entrée
envelope (n)
enveloppe (f)
**environmentally
friendly (adj)**
écologique
**epos or EPOS
(electronic point
of sale)** point (m)
de vente élec-
tronique
equal (adj) égal(e)
ou même
equal (v) égaler
equalization (n)
égalisation (f)
equip (v) équiper

equipment (n)
équipement (m) ou
matériel (m)
equities (n) actions
(fpl) ordinaires
equity (n) droit
(m) de participation
**equity or sharehold-
ers' equity** capitaux
(mpl) propres
equity capital
capital (m) social
**ERM (Exchange
Rate Mechanism)**
mécanisme (m) de
change (du SME)
erode (v)
éroder ou réduire
error (n)
erreur (f)
error rate
taux (m) d'erreur
**errors and
omissions excepted
(e. & o.e.)** sauf
erreur ou omission
escalate (v)
monter rapidement
escape clause
clause (f)
échappatoire

escrow account
compte (m) bloqué
escrow: in escrow
à la garde d'un tiers
essential (adj)
essentiel (-elle)
establish (v) établir
ou ouvrir *ou* fonder
establishment (n)
[business]
établissement (m)
ou maison (f) de
commerce
establishment *[staff]*
personnel (m)
estimate (n) *[cal-
culation]* évaluation
(f) *ou* estimation (f)
estimate (n)
[quote] devis (m)
estimate (v)
estimer
estimated (adj)
estimé(e) *ou*
estimatif (-ive)
estimated figure
chiffre (m) estimatif
estimated sales esti-
mation (f) des ventes
estimation (n)
estimation (f)

EU (European
Union) UE (Union
européenne)
euro euro (m)
Eurocheque (n)
eurochèque (m)
Eurocurrency (n)
eurodevise (f)
Eurodollar (n)
eurodollar (m)
Euromarket (n)
Euromarché (m)
European (adj)
européen (-éenne)
European
Investment Bank
(EIB) Banque
Européenne d'Inves-
tissement (BEI)
European Monetary
System (EMS)
système monétaire
européen (SME)
European Union
(EU) Union
européenne (UE)
eurozone (n)
eurozone (f)
evade (v)
se soustraire à *ou*
échapper à

evade tax frauder le fisc
evaluate (v) évaluer
evaluate costs évaluer les coûts
evaluation (n) évaluation (f)
evasion (n) évasion (f)
ex coupon coupon détaché
ex dividend ex-dividende
ex-directory *[telephone]* sur la liste rouge
exact (adj) exact(e)
exactly exactement
examination (n) *[inspection]* examen (m) *ou* contrôle (m)
examination *[test]* examen (m)
examine (v) examiner
exceed (v) excéder *ou* dépasser
excellent (adj) excellent(e)

except excepté *ou* sauf *ou* à l'exception de
exceptional (adj) exceptionnel (-elle)
exceptional items postes (mpl) exceptionnels
excess (n) excédent (m) *ou* surplus (m)
excess baggage excédent (m) de bagages
excess capacity surcapacité (f)
excess profits bénéfices (mpl) exceptionnels
excessive (adj) excessif (-ive) *ou* démesuré(e)
excessive costs frais (mpl) excessifs
exchange (n) *[currency]* change (m)
exchange (v) *[currency]* changer de l'argent
exchange (v) *[one thing for another]* échanger

exchange control contrôle (m) des changes

exchange rate taux (m) de change

exchangeable (adj) échangeable

Exchequer Ministère (m) des Finances

excise (v) *[cut out]* supprimer

excise duty droits (mpl) de régie

Excise officer receveur (m) des contributions indirectes

exclude (v) exclure

excluding à l'exception de

exclusion (n) exclusion (f)

exclusion clause clause (f) d'exclusion

exclusive agreement contrat (m) d'exclusivité

exclusive of non compris(e)

exclusive of tax hors taxe

exclusivity (n) exclusivité (f)

execute (v) exécuter

execution (n) exécution (f)

executive (adj) exécutif (-ive)

executive (n) directeur (-trice) *ou* dirigeant (m) *ou* cadre (m)

executive director administrateur (m) dirigeant; cadre (m) supérieur

exempt (adj) exempté(e) *ou* exonéré(e)

exempt (v) exempter *ou* exonérer

exempt from tax exonéré(e) d'impôt

exemption (n) exemption (f) *ou* dispense (f)

exemption from tax exonération (f) d'impôt

exercise (n) exercice (m)

exercise (v)
exercer
exercise an option
lever une option
exercise of an
option levée (f)
d'une option
exhibit (v)
exposer
exhibition (n)
exposition (f)
exhibition hall hall
(m) *ou* pavillon (m)
d'exposition
exhibitor (n)
exposant(e)
expand (v)
augmenter *ou*
développer; se
développer
expansion (n)
croissance (f) *ou*
développement (m)
expenditure (n)
dépense (f)
expense (n) dépense
(f) *ou* frais (mpl)
expense account
note (f) de frais;
frais (mpl) de
représentation

expenses (n)
dépenses (fpl) *ou*
frais (mpl)
expensive (adj)
cher (chère) *ou*
coûteux (-euse)
experienced (n)
expérimenté(e) *ou*
compétent(e)
expertise (n)
compétence (f)
expiration (n)
expiration (f)
expire (v) expirer
ou prendre fin *ou*
venir à expiration
expiry (n) termi-
naison (f) *ou*
expiration (f)
expiry date date
(f) d'expiration
explain (v)
expliquer *ou* donner
une raison
explanation (n)
explication (f) *ou*
raison (f)
exploit (v) exploiter
explore (v)
explorer *ou* étudier
ou examiner

export (n) exporta-
tion (f) *ou* export (m)
export (v)
exporter
**Export Credit
Guarantee
Department (ECGD)**
bureau (m)
d'assurance-crédit à
l'exportation
export department
service (m) des
exportations *ou*
service export
export duty taxe
(f) à l'exportation *ou*
droit (m) de sortie
export house mai-
son (f) d'exportation
**export licence *or*
export permit**
licence (f) *ou* permis
(m) d'exportation
export manager chef
du service export
export trade
commerce (m)
d'exportation
exporter (n) expor-
tateur (m) *ou* société
(f) exportatrice

exporting (adj) qui
exporte *ou*
exportateur (-trice)
exports (n)
exportations (fpl)
ou marchandises
(fpl) exportées
exposure (n) *[risk]*
risque (m)
express (adj) *[fast]*
rapide *ou* express
express (adj) *[stated
clearly]* explicite *ou*
exprès (-esse)
express (v) *[send
fast]* expédier rapide-
ment *ou* par express
express (v) *[state]*
exprimer
express delivery
livraison (f) express
express letter
lettre (f) express *ou*
prioritaire
extend (v) *[grant]*
accorder
extend *[make
longer]* prolonger
extended credit
crédit (m) à long
terme

extension (n)
[making longer]
prolongation (f)
extension
[telephone] poste
(m) (téléphonique)
external (adj) *[for-
eign]* extérieur(e)
ou étranger (-ère)
external *[outside a
company]* externe
external account
[bank] compte (m)
extérieur *ou* compte
de non-résident
external audit
audit (m) externe
external auditor
auditeur (m) externe
external growth
croissance (f)
externe
external trade com-
merce (m) extérieur
extra (adj) en plus
ou en sus *ou*
supplémentaire
extra charges
supplément (m) *ou*
frais (mpl)
supplémentaires

extraordinary (adj)
extraordinaire
**extraordinary
items** postes (mpl)
exceptionnels
extras (n)
frais (mpl)
supplémentaires

Ff

face value valeur
(f) nominale
facilities (n)
installations (fpl);
locaux (mpl)
facility *[building]*
bâtiment (m)
facility *[ease]*
facilité (f)
**fact-finding
mission** mission (f)
d'enquête
factor (n) *[influ-
ence]* facteur (m)

factor (n) *[person, company]* factor (m) *ou* société (f) d'affacturage *ou* de factoring
factor (v) faire de l'affacturage
factoring affacturage (m) *ou* factoring (m)
factoring charges commission (f) d'affacturage
factors of production facteurs (mpl) de production
factory (n) usine (f) *ou* fabrique (f)
factory inspector inspecteur (m) du travail
factory outlet magasin (m) d'usine
factory price prix (m) départ usine
fail (v) *[go bust]* faire faillite
fail *[not to do something]* omettre de
fail *[not to succeed]* échouer
failing that à défaut *ou* sinon

failure (n) *[lack of success]* échec (m)
failure (n) *[machine]* panne (f) *ou* arrêt (m) *ou* défaillance (f)
failure to pay non-paiement (m) (d'une facture)
fair (adj) honnête *ou* correct(e)
fair dealing *or* trading transactions (fpl) honnêtes
fair price prix (m) raisonnable *ou* équitable
fair trade accord (m) de réprocité (internationale)
fair wear and tear usure (f) normale
fake (n) faux (m)
fake (v) falsifier
faked documents documents (mpl) *ou* papiers falsifiés
fall (n) chute (f) *ou* baisse (f) *ou* effondrement (m)

fall (v) *[go lower]*
baisser *ou* diminuer
fall (v) *[on a date]*
avoir lieu *ou* tomber
**fall behind *[be in a
worse position]*** se
laisser distancer
fall behind *[be late]*
être en retard *ou*
prendre du retard
fall due venir à
échéance
fall off diminuer *ou*
chuter
fall through
échouer *ou* ne pas
avoir lieu
falling (adj) en
baisse
false (adj)
faux (fausse) *ou*
incorrect(e)
false description
description (f)
mensongère
false pretences
moyens (mpl)
frauduleux
false weight faux
poids (m) *ou* poids
inexact

falsification (n)
falsification (f)
falsify (v) falsifier
ou truquer
family company
société (f) familiale
**FAO (= for the
attention of)** à
l'attention de
fare (n) prix (m)
du billet
farm out (v) work
sous-traiter
fast (adj) rapide
fast (adv) rapidement
fast-selling items
articles qui se
vendent rapidement
fault (n) *[blame]*
faute (f)
fault *[mechanical]*
défaut (m)
faulty equipment
matériel (m)
défectueux
favourable (adj)
avantageux (-euse)
**favourable balance
of trade** balance (f)
commerciale bénéfi-
ciaire *ou* excédentaire

fax (n) fax (m) *ou* télécopie (f)
fax (n) (machine) fax (m) *ou* télécopieur (m)
fax (v) faxer *ou* envoyer par fax *ou* par télécopie
feasibility (n) faisabilité (f)
feasibility report rapport (m) de faisabilité
fee (n) *[admission]* droit (m) d'entrée
fee *[for services]* honoraires (mpl) *ou* rémunération (f)
feedback (n) information (f) (en retour) *ou* réaction (f)
ferry (n) ferry (m)
fiddle (n) combine (f)
fiddle (v) trafiquer
field (n) champ (m)
field sales manager responsable (mf) d'une équipe de représentants régionaux

field work enquête (f) sur le terrain
FIFO (first in first out) PEPS (premier entré, premier sorti)
figure (n) chiffre (m); montant (m)
figures chiffres (mpl); résultat (m) (quantitatif)
file (n) *[computer]* fichier (m)
file (n) *[documents]* dossier (m)
file (v) *[request]* déposer une requête
file (v) a patent application déposer une demande de brevet
file (v) documents classer (des documents)
filing (n) *[action]* classement (m)
filing cabinet classeur (m)
filing card fiche (f)
fill (v) a gap combler un manque

final (adj) final(e)
ou dernier (-ière)
final demand
dernier rappel
final discharge
paiement (m)
libératoire
final dividend dernier
dividende *ou* solde
(m) de dividende
final result
[accounts] résultat
(m) net
finalize (v) mettre
au point
finance (n)
finance (f)
finance (v)
financer
finance an
operation financer
une opération
finance company
société (f) de crédit
ou de financement
finance director
directeur financier
finances (n) *[funds]*
finances (fpl)
financial (adj)
financier (-ière)

financial adviser
conseiller financier
financial asset
actif (m) financier
financial crisis
crise (f) financière
financial institution
institution (f)
financière
financial position
position (f) *ou*
situation (f)
financière
financial resources
ressources (fpl)
financières
financial risk
risque (m) financier
financial statement
état (m) financier
financial year
exercice (m)
financier
financially
financièrement
financing (n)
financement (m)
fine (adj) *[very*
good] très bien
fine (adj) *[very*
small] fin(e)

fine (n) amende (f)
fine (v) condamner quelqu'un à une amende
fine tuning réglage (m) plus fin *ou* plus précis (de l'économie)
finished (adj) fini(e)
finished goods produits (mpl) finis
fire (n) feu (m) *ou* incendie (m)
fire damage dégâts (mpl) causés par le feu
fire insurance assurance (f) incendie *ou* assurance contre l'incendie
fire regulations consignes (fpl) en cas d'incendie
fire risk risque (m) d'incendie
fire-damaged goods marchandises (fpl) abîmées au cours d'un incendie

firm (adj) ferme *ou* définitif (-ive) *ou* soutenu(e)
firm (n) firme (f) *ou* maison (f) *ou* société (f) *ou* entreprise (f)
firm (v) se maintenir
firm price prix (m) ferme
first (adj) premier (-ière)
first in first out (FIFO) premier entré, premier sorti (PEPS)
first option en première option
first quarter premier trimestre (m)
first-class de première qualité
fiscal (adj) fiscal(e)
fiscal measures mesures (fpl) fiscales
fittings (n) accessoires (mpl); équipement (m)

fix (v) *[arrange]*
fixer *ou* établir
fix (v) *[mend]* réparer
fix a meeting
for 3 p.m. fixer une
réunion à 15h
fixed (adj)
fixe *ou* établi(e)
fixed assets actif
(m) immobilisé
fixed costs
coûts (mpl) fixes
fixed deposit dépôt
(m) à terme fixe
fixed exchange
rate taux (m) de
change fixe
fixed income
revenu (m) fixe
fixed interest
intérêt (m) fixe
fixed scale of
charges barème
(m) fixe *ou* échelle
(f) de prix fixe
fixed-interest
investments
investissements
(mpl) à intérêt fixe
fixed-price
agreement contrat
(m) forfaitaire

fixed-term contract
contrat (m) à durée
déterminée
fixing (n) détermina-
tion (f) *ou* fixation (f)
flat (adj) *[dull]*
terne
flat (adj)
[fixed] fixe
flat (n)
appartement (m)
flat rate taux (m)
fixe *ou* forfait (m)
flexibility (n)
souplesse (f) *ou*
flexibilité (f)
flexible (adj)
souple *ou* adaptable
ou flexible
flexible prices prix
(mpl) flexibles
flexible pricing
policy politique (f)
de fixation souple
des prix
flight (n) *[of*
money] fuite (f)
(d'argent)
flight *[of plane]*
vol (m)
flight of capital
fuite (f) de capitaux

flip chart tableau (m) à feuilles mobiles

float (n) [cash] avance (f) (de caisse)

float (n) [of company] lancement (m) d'une société (en Bourse)

float (v) [a currency] laisser flotter une devise

float (v) a company lancer une société (en Bourse)

floating (adj) flottant(e)

floating exchange rates taux (m) de change flottants

floating (n) of a company lancement (m) d'une société (en Bourse)

flood (n) inondation (f)

flood (v) inonder

floor (n) [level] étage (m)

floor [surface] sol (m) ou plancher (m)

floor manager chef (m) de rayon

floor plan plan (m) d'ensemble

floor space surface (f) au sol

flop (n) échec (m) ou ratage (m) ou fiasco (m)

flop (v) échouer ou rater

flotation (n) lancement (m) d'une société en Bourse

flourish (v) prospérer

flourishing (adj) prospère ou florissant(e)

flourishing trade commerce (m) prospère

flow (n) flux (m) ou mouvement (m)

flow (v) s'écouler

flow chart or flow diagram graphique (m) d'évolution

fluctuate (v) fluctuer ou osciller

fluctuating (adj) variable ou qui fluctue

fluctuation (n)
fluctuation (f)
**FOB *or* f.o.b. (free
on board)** franco à
bord (FAB)
follow (v) suivre
follow up (v)
[examine further]
suivre *ou* poursuivre
ou exploiter
follow-up letter
lettre (f) de relance
for sale à vendre
forbid (v) défendre
ou interdire
force majeure
force (f) majeure
**force (v) prices
down** faire baisser
les prix
force prices up
faire monter les prix
forced (adj)
forcé(e)
forced sale liquida-
tion (f) forcée *ou*
vente (f) forcée
forecast (n)
prévisions (fpl)
forecast (v)
prévoir

forecasting (n)
prévision (f) *ou*
estimation (f)
foreign (adj)
étranger (-ère)
foreign currency
devises (fpl)
(étrangères)
foreign exchange
[currency]
change (m)
foreign exchange
[rate of exchange]
(cours du) change (m)
**foreign exchange
broker** cambiste (mf)
**foreign exchange
dealing** opération
(f) de change
**foreign exchange
market** marché (m)
des changes
foreign investments
investissements
(mpl) à l'étranger
**foreign money
order** mandat (m)
international
foreign trade
commerce (m)
extérieur

forfeit (n)
confiscation (f)
forfeit (v) perdre
par confiscation
forfeit a deposit
perdre des arrhes
forfeiture (n)
confiscation (f)
(d'un bien)
forge (v) falsifier
ou contrefaire
forgery (n) *[action]*
falsification (f)
forgery *[copy]*
contrefaçon (f)
fork-lift truck char-
iot (m) élévateur
form (n) *[paper]*
formulaire (m)
form (v) former *ou*
constituer *ou* créer
formal (adj)
officiel (-elle)
formality (n)
formalité (f)
forward à l'avance
ou à terme
forward buying
achat (m) à terme
forward dealing
opération (f) à terme

forward market
marché (m) à terme
forward rate taux
(m) de change à
terme
forward sales
ventes (fpl) à terme
forwarding (n)
acheminement (m)
ou expédition (f)
forwarding address
adresse (f) de réex-
pédition
forwarding agent
transitaire (m)
**forwarding
instructions**
instructions (fpl)
relatives à
l'expédition
fourth quarter qua-
trième trimestre (m)
fragile (adj) fragile
franc (n) *[Swiss
currency]* franc (m)
franchise (n)
franchise(f)
franchise (v)
accorder une
franchise *ou*
franchiser

franchisee (n)
franchisé (m)
franchiser (n)
franchiseur (m)
franchising (n)
franchisage (m)
franco (adv) franco
frank (v) affranchir
(une lettre)
franking machine
machine (f) à
affranchir
fraud (n) fraude (f)
fraudulent (adj)
frauduleux (-euse)
**fraudulent transac-
tion** transaction
frauduleuse
fraudulently
frauduleusement
free (adj) *[no pay-
ment]* gratuit(e)
free (adj) *[no
restrictions]* libre
free (adj) *[not
busy]* libre
free (adj) *[not
occupied]* libre
free (adv) *[no pay-
ment]* gratuitement
ou sans payer

free (v) libérer
free delivery livrai-
son gratuite *ou* colis
expédié franc de port
free gift prime (f)
freelance (adj)
freelance
freelance (n) *or*
freelancer collabo-
rateur (-trice)
indépendant(e)
**free market
economy** économie
(f) de marché *ou*
économie libérale
free of charge gra-
tuit(e); gratuitement
free of duty
exempt(e) de taxe
ou hors taxe
free of tax
exonéré(e) d'impôt
free on board
(f.o.b.) franco à
bord (FAB)
free on rail
franco wagon
free port
port (m) franc
free sample échan-
tillon (m) gratuit

free trade libre-échange (m)

free trade agreement accord (m) de libre-échange

free trade area zone (f) de libre-échange

free trade zone zone franche

free trial essai (m) gratuit

free zone zone (f) franche

freeze (n) gel (m) *ou* blocage (m)

freeze (v) *[prices]* bloquer *ou* geler

freeze (v) credits geler *ou* limiter les crédits

freeze wages and prices bloquer les salaires et les prix

freight (n) *[carriage]* fret (m) *ou* prix (m) du transport

freight car wagon (m) de marchandises

freight costs port (m) *ou* frais (mpl) de transport

freight depot dépôt (m) *ou* entrepôt (m) de marchandises

freight forward (en) port dû

freight plane avion-cargo (m)

freight rates tarifs (mpl) d'expédition

freight train train (m) de marchandises

freightage (n) frais (mpl) de transport

freighter (n) *[plane]* avion-cargo (m)

freighter *[ship]* cargo (m)

freightliner (n) train (m) de marchandises en conteneurs

frequent (adj) fréquent(e)

frozen (adj) gelé(e)

frozen account compte (m) gelé

frozen assets actifs (mpl) gelés *ou* fonds (mpl) bloqués

frozen credits
crédits (mpl) gelés
fulfil (v) an order
exécuter une
commande
fulfilment (n)
exécution (f)
full (adj) plein(e)
ou complet (-ète)
**full discharge of a
debt** pour acquit
full payment
règlement (m) total
full price
prix (m) fort
full refund rem-
boursement (m) total
full-scale (adj)
total(e) *ou*
complet (-ète)
full-time (adj) à
temps complet *ou* à
plein temps
**full-time employ-
ment** travail (m) à
plein temps
fund (n)
fonds (mpl)
fund (v)
financer
**funding (n) *[financ-
ing]*** financement (m)

funding *[of debt]*
consolidation (f)
(d'une dette)
further to suite à
ou en réponse à
future delivery
livraison (f) future
futures (n)
opérations
(fpl) à terme *[en
Bourse]*

Gg

gain (n)
[getting bigger]
accroissement (m)
ou augmentation (f)
**gain (n) *[increase in
value]*** augmenta-
tion (f) (de valeur)
**gain (v) *[become
bigger]*** augmenter;
gagner
gain (v) *[get]*
acquérir *ou* obtenir
gap (n) vide (m)

gap in the market
créneau (m) sur le
marché
**GDP (gross
domestic product)**
PIB (produit
intérieur brut)
gear adapter *ou*
ajuster
gearing (n) effet
(m) de levier *ou* ratio
(m) d'endettement
general (adj)
général(e)
general audit véri-
fication (f) générale
des comptes
general average
avarie (f) commune
general insurance
assurance (f)
multirisque
general manager
directeur (-trice)
général(e)
general meeting
assemblée (f)
générale
general office
siège (m) social
general post office
poste (f) centrale

general strike
grève (f) générale
**gentleman's agree-
ment** gentleman's
agreement (m)
genuine (adj)
véritable *ou*
authentique
genuine purchaser
acheteur (m) sérieux
get (v) recevoir
get along
se débrouiller
get back
[something lost]
récupérer
get into debt
s'endetter
**get rid of
something** se
débarrasser de
quelque chose
**get round (a
problem)** éviter *ou*
contourner (une
difficulté)
get the sack être
renvoyé *ou* licencié
ou mis à la porte
get through to
[telephone] joindre
[au téléphone]

gift (n) cadeau (m)
gift coupon bon
(m) d'achat
gift shop boutique
(f) de souvenirs
gift voucher
chèque-cadeau (m)
**gilt-edged securi-
ties (n) or gilts (n)**
titres (mpl) d'état
ou obligations (fpl)
d'état
giro account
compte (m) de vire-
ment (à la Girobank)
giro cheque chèque
(m) de virement
giro system
système (m) de
virement bancaire
give (v) *[as gift]*
offrir
give *[pass]* donner
give away *[free]*
offrir (en prime)
give away (n)
cadeau (m)
(publicitaire) gratuit
giveaway price prix
défiant toute
concurrence

glut (n) surplus (m)
ou surabondance (f)
glut (v) surcharger
ou encombrer
**GNP (gross
national product)**
PNB (produit
national brut)
go (v) aller
go into business se
lancer dans les
affaires
go-ahead (adj)
dynamique *ou*
entreprenant(e)
go-slow (n) grève
(f) du zèle *ou* grève
perlée
**going (adj) *[rate,
price]*** actuel (-elle)
ou courant(e)
going rate
tarif en vigueur
good (adj)
bon (bonne)
good buy
bonne affaire
good management
bonne gestion
good quality
bonne qualité

good value (for money) aubaine (f); rapport qualité/prix excellent

goods (n) marchandises (fpl)

goods depot dépôt (m) *ou* entrepôt (m)

goods in transit marchandises (fpl) en transit

goods train train (m) de marchandises

goodwill goodwill (m)

government (n) gouvernement (m) *ou* Etat (m)

government (adj) gouvernemental(e) *ou* du gouvernement *ou* de l'Etat

government bonds bons (mpl) du Trésor

government contractor fournisseur (m) du gouvernement

government stock titres (mpl) d'Etat

government-backed avec l'aval du gouvernement

government-controlled contrôlé(e) par l'Etat; d'Etat

government-regulated réglementé(e) par l'Etat

government-sponsored subventionné(e) par l'Etat

graded advertising rates tarifs (mpl) publicitaires dégressifs

graded hotel hôtel (m) classé

graded tax impôt (m) progressif

gradual (adj) progressif (-ive)

graduate trainee stagiaire (mf) diplômé(e)

graduated (adj) progressif (-ive)

graduated income tax impôt (m) progressif

**gram *or* gramme
(n)** gramme (m)
grand total total
(m) général *ou*
somme (f) globale
grant (n)
subvention (f);
bourse (f)
grant (v) accorder
ou octroyer
gratis gratis *ou*
gratuitement
grid (n) grille (f)
grid structure
structure (f) en grille
gross (adj) brut(e)
ou sans déductions
gross (n) (= 144)
douze douzaines *ou*
grosse (f)
gross (v) rapporter
brut *ou* faire un
profit brut
**gross domestic
product (GDP)**
produit (m)
intérieur brut (PIB)
gross earnings
revenu (m) brut
gross income
salaire (m) brut

gross margin
marge (f) brute
**gross national
product (GNP)**
produit (m) national
brut (PNB)
gross profit
bénéfice (m) brut
gross salary
salaire (m) brut
gross tonnage
jauge (f) brute
gross weight poids
(m) brut
gross yield rende-
ment (m) brut
**group (n) *[of
businesses]*** groupe
(m) (industriel)
group *[of people]*
groupe (m)
growth (n)
croissance (f)
growth index indice
(m) de croissance
growth rate taux
(m) de croissance
guarantee (n)
garantie (f)
guarantee (v)
garantir

Hh

**guarantee a
bill of exchange**
avaliser une traite
guarantee a debt
se porter garant
d'une dette
**guarantee: go guar-
antee for someone**
se porter garant de
quelqu'un
**guaranteed for six
months [product]**
garanti(e) six mois
**guaranteed mini-
mum wage** salaire
(m) minimum
garanti
guarantor (n)
avaliste (m) *ou*
garant (m)
guideline (n) ligne
(f) de conduite *ou*
directive (f)
guild guilde (f) *ou*
corporation (f)

haggle (v)
marchander
half (adj) demi(e)
half (n) moitié (f)
ou demie (f)
**half a dozen *or* a
half-dozen**
demi-douzaine (f)
half-price sale solde
(m) à moitié prix
half-year semestre
(m) (comptable)
**half-yearly
accounts** comptes
(mpl) semestriels
**half-yearly pay-
ment** paiement (m)
semestriel
**half-yearly state-
ment** relevé (m)
semestriel
hand in (v) remettre
hand luggage
bagages (mpl)
à main
hand over (v)
remettre

handle (v) *[deal with]* s'occuper de *ou* traiter
handle (v) *[sell]* vendre
handling (n) manutention (f)
handling charge frais (mpl) de manutention
handwriting (n) écriture (f)
handwritten (adj) écrit(e) à la main *ou* manuscrit(e)
handy (adj) pratique
harbour (n) port (m)
harbour dues droits (mpl) de port
harbour facilities installations (fpl) portuaires
hard bargain affaire (f) difficile
hard bargaining tractations (fpl) difficiles
hard copy copie (f) (sur) papier *ou* imprimé (m)

hard currency devise (f) forte
hard disk disque (m) dur
hard sell (n) vente (n) agressive
hard selling (politique de) vente (f) agressive
harmonization (n) *[of prices, etc.]* harmonisation (f)
haulage (n) transport (m) routier
haulage contractor entrepreneur (m) de transports routiers
haulage costs *or* **haulage rates** frais (mpl) de transport (routier)
head (n) of department chef (m) de service
head office siège (m) social *ou* bureau (m) central
headquarters (HQ) siège (m) social
heads of agreement protocole (m) d'accord

health (n) santé (f)
health insurance
assurance (f)
maladie
healthy profit béné-
fice (m) substantiel
heavy (adj) *[impor-*
tant] lourd(e) *ou*
important(e) *ou*
massif (-ive)
heavy *[weight]*
lourd(e)
heavy costs *or*
heavy expenditure
frais (mpl)
importants
heavy equipment
matériel (m) lourd
heavy goods
vehicle (HGV)
poids lourd (m)
heavy industry
industrie (f) lourde
heavy machinery
installations (fpl)
lourdes *ou* matériel
(m) lourd
hectare (n)
hectare (m)
hedge (n)
couverture (f)

hedging (n)
opérations (fpl) de
couverture
HGV (heavy goods
vehicle) poids
lourd (m)
hidden asset bien
(m) masqué
hidden reserves
caisse (f) noire *ou*
réserves (fpl)
occultes
high interest
intérêt (m) élevé
high rent loyer (m)
élevé
high taxation taux
(m) d'imposition
élevé
high-quality (adj)
de première qualité
high-quality
goods
marchandises (fpl)
de première qualité
highest bidder le
plus offrant
highly motivated
sales staff
personnel (m) de
vente très motivé

highly qualified
hautement
qualifié(e)
highly-geared company société qui a
un fort coefficient
d'endettement
highly-paid qui
perçoit un salaire
élevé
highly-priced
onéreux (-euse) *ou*
coûteux (-euse)
hire (n) location (f)
hire (v) a car louer
une voiture
hire car voiture de
location
hire purchase (HP)
achat (m) à crédit
ou à tempérament
hire (v) staff
embaucher du
personnel
**hire-purchase
company** société
(f) de crédit
historic(al) cost
prix (m) d'origine
ou coût (m)
historique

historical figures
chiffres (mpl)
d'origine
hive off (v)
décentraliser
hoard (v)
faire des réserves
ou amasser
**hoarding (n) *[for
posters]*** panneau
(m) d'affichage
hoarding *[of goods]*
accumulation (f) de
provisions
**hold (n) *[ship,
plane]*** cale (f)
(d'un navire); soute
(f) (d'un avion)
hold (v) *[contain]*
contenir
hold (v) *[keep]*
détenir *ou* garder
**hold a meeting *or* a
discussion** tenir
une réunion *ou* une
discussion
hold out for
maintenir sa
position
hold over remettre
ou ajourner

**hold the line
please** *or* **please
hold** *[phone]* ne
quittez pas, s'il vous
plaît!
hold up (v) *[delay]*
retarder
hold-up (n) *[delay]*
retard (m)
holder (n) *[person]*
titulaire (mf) *ou*
détenteur (-trice)
holder *[thing]*
support (m); étui (m)
holding (n)
portefeuille (m)
d'actions
holding company
holding (m)
holiday pay salaire
(m) payé pendant
les vacances
home address
adresse (f)
personnelle
home consumption
consommation (f)
domestique
home market
marché (m)
intérieur

home sales ventes
(fpl) intérieures
**homeward
freight** fret (m) de
retour
homeward journey
voyage (m) de
retour
homeworker (n)
travailleur (-euse)
ou ouvrier (-ière) à
domicile
honorarium (n)
honoraires (mpl)
honour (v) a bill
honorer *ou* acquitter
une traite
**honour one's
signature** honorer
sa signature
**horizontal (adj)
communication**
communication (f)
horizontale
**horizontal integra-
tion** intégration (f)
horizontale
hotel (n) hôtel (m)
**hotel accommoda-
tion** chambre (f)
d'hôtel

hotel bill note (f) d'hôtel

hotelier (n) hôtelier (m)

hotel manager directeur (-trice) d'hôtel

hotel staff personnel (m) hôtelier

hour heure (f)

hourly (adv) à l'heure ou horaire

hourly rate tarif (m) horaire

hourly wage salaire (m) horaire

hourly-paid workers ouvriers payés à l'heure

house (n) [company] maison (f) ou firme (f) ou entreprise (f)

house [for family] maison (f); résidence (f)

house insurance assurance-habitation (f)

house magazine journal (m) de l'entreprise

house-to-house porte-à-porte (m)

house-to-house selling vente (f) à domicile ou porte-à-porte (m) ou démarchage (m)

HP (= hire purchase) achat (m) à crédit ou à tempérament

HQ (=headquarters) siège (m) social

human resources ressources (fpl) humaines

hurry up (v) [order] activer ou accélérer [une commande]

hype (n) publicité (f) excessive

hype (v) lancer (un produit) à grand renfort de publicité

hypermarket (n) hypermarché (m) [grande surface]

Ii

illegal (adj)
illégal(e)
illegality (n)
illégalité (f)
illegally (adv)
illégalement
illicit (adj) illicite
ILO (International Labour Organization)
OIT (Organisation Internationale du Travail)
IMF (International Monetary Fund) FMI (Fonds Monétaire International)
imitation (n)
imitation (f)
immediate (adj)
immédiat(e)
immediately
tout de suite *ou* immédiatement
imperfect (adj)
défectueux (-euse); imparfait(e); de second choix

imperfection (n)
imperfection (f)
implement (n)
outil (m) *ou* instrument (m)
implement (v)
appliquer *ou* mettre en pratique; exécuter
implement (v) an agreement
appliquer un accord
implementation (n)
exécution (f) *ou* application (f)
import (n)
importation (f) *ou* import (m)
import (v) importer
import ban
interdiction (f) d'importer
import duty *or* import levy taxe (f) à l'importation
import licence *or* import permit
licence (f) d'importation
import quota quota (m) d'importation

import restrictions
limitations (fpl) des
importations
import surcharge
surtaxe (f) à
l'importation
import-export
(n & adj) (d')
import-export (m)
importance (n)
importance (f)
important (adj)
important(e)
importation (n)
importation (f)
importer (n)
importateur (-trice)
importing (adj)
importateur (-trice)
importing (n)
importation (f)
imports
importations (fpl)
impose (v) imposer
impulse buyer
acheteur impulsif
impulse purchase
achat (m) impulsif
ou achat
d'impulsion

in-house dans l'en-
treprise *ou* dans la
maison
in-house training
formation (f) dans
l'entreprise
incentive (n)
incitation (f)
incentive bonus *or*
incentive payment
prime (f)
d'incitation au
travail
incidental (adj)
expenses faux
frais (mpl)
include (v) inclure
ou comprendre
inclusive (adj)
inclus(e) *ou*
compris(e)
inclusive charge
tarif (m) tout
compris
inclusive of tax
taxe (f) comprise *ou*
toutes taxes
comprises (TTC)
income (n)
revenu (m)

income tax impôt
(m) sur le revenu
incoming call
[phone] appel (m)
venant de l'extérieur
incoming mail cour-
rier (m) à l'arrivée
incompetent (adj)
incompétent(e)
incorporate (v)
incorporer *ou*
intégrer
incorporate *[a com-*
pany] constituer;
immatriculer
(une société)
incorporation (n)
constitution (f);
immatriculation (f)
d'une société
incorrect (adj)
incorrect(e)
incorrectly
incorrectement
increase (n)
augmentation (f) *ou*
hausse (f)
increase (n) *[higher*
salary] augmenta-
tion (f) (de salaire)

increase (v)
augmenter *[le prix*
d'un article]
increase (v) in price
augmenter de prix
ou coûter plus cher
increasing (adj) en
augmentation *ou* de
plus en plus grand
increment (n)
augmentation (f) de
salaire automatique
incremental (adj)
qui augmente
régulièrement
incremental cost
coût (m) marginal
incremental scale
échelle (f) mobile
des salaires
incur (v) *[costs]*
engager (des
dépenses)
incur (v) *[risk]*
courir (le risque de)
incur debts con-
tracter des dettes
indebted (adj) qui
a une dette *ou* qui
doit de l'argent

indebtedness (n)
endettement (m)
indemnification (n)
indemnisation (f) *ou*
dédommagement (m)
indemnify (v)
indemniser *ou*
dédommager
indemnify someone
for a loss indem-
niser quelqu'un
d'une perte
indemnity (n)
indemnité (f)
independent (adj)
indépendant(e)
independent
company société
(f) indépendante
index (n)
[alphabetical]
index (m)
index (n) *[of*
prices] indice (m)
(des prix)
index (v) indexer
index card fiche (f)
[de fichier]
index number
numéro (m) de
référence; indice (m)

index-linked (adj)
indexé(e) (sur l'indice
du coût de la vie)
indexation (n)
indexation (f)
indicator (n)
indicateur (m)
indirect indirect(e)
indirect labour
costs charges (fpl)
indirectes
indirect tax impôt
(m) indirect
indirect taxation
imposition (f)
indirecte *ou* impôts
(mpl) indirects
induction (n)
initiation (f)
induction courses
or induction
training cours
(mpl) d'initiation
industrial (adj)
industriel (-elle)
industrial accident
accident (m) du travail
industrial (arbitra-
tion) tribunal
conseil (m) de
prud'hommes

industrial capacity
capacité (f)
industrielle
industrial centre
centre (m) industriel
industrial design
esthétique (f) indus-
trielle *ou* dessin (m)
industriel
industrial disputes
conflits (mpl) du
travail
**industrial espi-
onage** espionnage
(m) industriel
**industrial
estate** zone (f)
industrielle
**industrial
expansion**
développement (m)
industriel
**industrial
processes** procédés
(mpl) industriels
industrial relations
relations (fpl) entre
employeurs et
employés
industrialist (n)
industriel (m)

industrialization (n)
industrialisation (f)
industrialize (v)
industrialiser
**industrialized
societies** pays
(mpl) industrialisés
industry (n)
[companies]
industrie (f)
industry *[general]*
industrie (f)
inefficiency (n)
inefficacité (f);
incompétence (f)
[personne]
inefficient (adj)
inefficace;
incompétent(e)
[personne]
inexpensive (adj)
bon marché; peu *ou*
pas cher (chère)
inflated currency
monnaie (f)
inflationniste
inflated prices prix
(mpl) gonflés
(artificiellement)
inflation (n)
inflation (f)

inflationary (adj)
inflationniste
influence (n)
influence (f)
influence (v)
influencer
inform (v)
informer *ou*
renseigner
information (n)
renseignement(s)
(m(pl))
information bureau
bureau (m) de
renseignements
information officer
responsable (mf) de
l'information
infrastructure (n)
infrastructure (f)
infringe (v)
transgresser
infringe a patent
contrefaire un
produit protégé par
un brevet
infringement (n) of
customs regula-
tions non respect
(m) des formalités
douanières

infringement of
patent contrefaçon
(f) (d'un produit
breveté)
initial (adj)
initial(e)
initial (v) parapher
ou signer de ses
initiales
initial capital
capital (m) initial *ou*
capital
d'investissement
initials (n) *[letters]*
initiales (fpl)
initiate (v)
commencer
initiate discussions
entamer des
discussions
initiative (n)
initiative (f)
inland (adj)
intérieur(e)
Inland Revenue
le fisc
innovate (v) innover
innovation (n)
innovation (f)
innovative (adj)
innovateur (-trice)

innovator (n)
innovateur (-trice)
input (v)
information saisir
ou introduire des
données
input tax TVA
exigible (sur biens
et services)
inquire (v)
se renseigner
inquiry (n)
demande (f) (de
reseignement(s))
insider (n) initié(e)
insider dealing or
trading délit (m)
d'initié(s)
insolvency (n)
insolvabilité (f)
insolvent (adj)
insolvable
inspect (v)
inspecter *ou* vérifier
ou contrôler
inspection (n)
inspection (f) *ou*
vérification (f) *ou*
contrôle (m)
instalment (n)
versement (m)

instant (adj)
[current] courant
ou de ce mois
instant (adj)
[immediate]
instantané(e) *ou*
immédiat(e)
instant credit
crédit (m) immédiat
institute (n)
institut (m)
institute (v)
instituer *ou* engager
institution (n)
institution (f)
institutional (adj)
institutionnel (-elle)
institutional
investors
investisseurs (mpl)
institutionnels
instruction (n)
ordre (m) *ou*
instruction (f)
instrument (n)
[device] instrument
(m) *ou* appareil (m)
instrument *[docu-*
ment] acte (m) *ou*
document (m) *ou*
instrument (m)

insufficient funds
[US] (compte)
insuffisamment
approvisionné
insurable (adj)
assurable
insurance (n)
assurance (f)
insurance agent
agent (m)
d'assurances
insurance broker
courtier (m)
d'assurances
insurance claim déc-
laration (f) de sinistre
insurance company
compagnie (f)
d'assurances
insurance contract
contrat (m)
d'assurance
insurance cover
garantie (f) *ou* couver-
ture (f) d'assurance
insurance policy
police (f) d'assurance
insurance premium
prime (f) d'assurance
insurance rates tar-
ifs (mpl) d'assurance

insurance salesman
agent (m)
d'assurances
insure (v) assurer
insurer (n)
assureur (m) *ou*
compagnie (f)
d'assurances
intangible (adj)
incorporel (-elle)
intangible assets
immobilisations
(fpl) incorporelles
interest (n)
[investment]
participation (f)
interest (n) *[paid
on investment, on
loan]* intérêt (m)
interest (v)
intéresser
(quelqu'un)
interest charges
intérêts (mpl) (à
payer) *ou* frais
(mpl) financiers
interest rate taux
(m) d'intérêt
**interest-bearing
deposits** dépôts
(mpl) rémunérés

interest-free credit
crédit (m) gratuit
interface (n)
interface (f)
interface (v)
connecter *ou* relier
(par interface)
interim dividend
dividende (m)
intérimaire
interim payment
paiement (m)
intérimaire *ou*
acompte (m)
interim report rap-
port (m) intérimaire
intermediary (adj)
intermédiaire (m)
internal (adj)
[inside a company]
interne
internal *[inside a*
country]
intérieur(e)
internal audit
audit (m) interne
internal auditor
auditeur (m) interne
internal telephone
téléphone (m)
interne *ou* intérieur

international (adj)
international(e)
international call
[phone] appel (m)
(téléphonique)
international
international direct
dialling système (m)
téléphonique automa-
tique international
International
Labour Organization
(ILO) Organisation
(f) Internationale du
Travail (OIT)
international law
droit (m)
international
International
Monetary Fund
(IMF) Fonds (m)
Monétaire
International (FMI)
international trade
commerce (m)
international
Internet (n)
Internet (m)
interpret (v)
interpréter *ou* servir
d'interprète

interpreter (n)
interprète (mf)
intervention price
prix (m)
d'intervention
interview (n)
interview (m)
interview (n)
[for a job]
entretien (m)
interview (v)
interviewer
interview (v)
[for a job] avoir un
entretien avec (un
candidat)
interviewee (n)
interviewé(e)
interviewer (n)
interviewer (m)
introduce (v)
présenter
introduction (n)
[bringing into use]
introduction (f)
introduction
[letter] lettre (f)
d'introduction
introductory offer
offre (f) de
lancement

invalid (adj) non
valable *ou* non
valide; périmé(e)
invalidate (v)
invalider *ou* annuler
invalidation (n)
invalidation (f) *ou*
annulation (f)
invalidity (n)
invalidité (f)
inventory (n) *[list
of contents]*
inventaire (m)
inventory (n) *[US:
stock]* stock (m)
inventory (v)
inventorier *ou* faire
l'inventaire
inventory control
contrôle (m)
des stocks *ou* ges-
tion (f) des stocks
invest (v) investir *ou*
placer (de l'argent)
investigate (v)
enquêter *ou* examiner
investigation (n)
enquête (f)
investment (n)
investissement (m)
ou placement (m)

investment income
revenus (mpl) de
placements
investor (n)
investisseur (m)
invisible assets biens
(mpl) incorporels
invisible earnings
revenus (mpl)
invisibles
invisible trade com-
merce (m) invisible
invitation (n)
invitation (f)
invite (v) inviter
quelqu'un à *ou*
demander à
quelqu'un de
invoice (n) facture
(f) *ou* note (f)
invoice (v)
facturer; envoyer
une facture
invoice number
numéro (m) de
facture
invoice value
montant (m) (total)
de la facture
invoicing (n)
facturation (f)

**invoicing depart-
ment** service (m)
de la facturation
IOU (= I owe you)
reconnaissance (f)
de dette
irrecoverable debt
dette (f)
irrécouvrable
irredeemable bond
obligation (f) non
remboursable
irregular (adj)
irrégulier (-ière)
irregularities (n)
irrégularités (fpl)
irrevocable (adj)
irrévocable
**irrevocable accept-
ance** acceptation
(f) irrévocable
**irrevocable lettre
of credit** lettre (f)
de crédit irrévocable
issue (n) *[maga-
zine]* numéro (m)
issue (n) *[of shares]*
émission (f) d'ac-
tions nouvelles
issue (v) *[shares]*
émettre (des actions)

**issue a letter of
credit** émettre une
lettre de crédit
issue instructions
donner des
instructions
issuing bank banque
(f) émettrice *ou*
banque d'émission
item (n) *[accounts]*
poste (m)
item *[on agenda]*
question (f)
[à l'ordre du jour]
item *[thing for sale]*
article (m)
itemize (v)
détailler
itemized account
compte (m) détaillé
itemized invoice
facture (f) détaillée
itinerary (n)
itinéraire (m)

Jj

**job (n) *[employ-
ment]*** emploi (m)
ou travail (m)
job *[piece of work]*
travail (m) *ou*
tâche (f)
job analysis analyse
(f) des tâches *ou* de
la fonction
job application
candidature (f) à un
emploi *ou* demande
(f) d'emploi
job cuts suppres-
sion (f) d'emplois
job description
description (f) de la
fonction *ou* profil
(m) de poste
job satisfaction sat-
isfaction (f) au travail
job security sécu-
rité (f) de l'emploi
job specification
description (f) de la
fonction *ou* profil
(m) de poste

job title titre (m)
join (v) joindre *ou*
relier
joint (adj)
commun(e) *ou*
conjoint(e); mixte
joint account
compte (m) joint
joint discussions
discussions (fpl)
collectives *[dans
l'entreprise]*
joint management
codirection (f) *ou*
cogestion (f)
**joint managing
director** codirecteur
(-trice) général(e)
ou directeur (-trice)
général(e) adjoint(e)
joint owner
copropriétaire (mf)
joint ownership
copropriété (f) *ou*
propriété (f) en
commun
joint signatory
cosignataire (mf)
**joint-stock com-
pany** société (f)
anonyme par actions

joint venture
joint-venture (f) *ou*
coentreprise (f)
jointly
conjointement
journal (n)
[accounts book]
journal (m) *ou*
livre-journal (m)
journal *[magazine]*
revue (f) *ou*
journal (m)
judge (n) juge (m)
ou magistrat (m)
judge (v) juger *ou*
estimer
**judgement (n) *or*
judgment**
jugement (m)
judgment debtor
débiteur condamné
à rembourser une
dette
judicial processes
procédures (fpl)
juridiques
jump (v) the queue
resquiller dans une
queue
junior (adj) subal-
terne; débutant(e)

junior clerk
employé(e)
subalterne
junior executive *or*
junior manager
cadre (m) débutant
ou jeune cadre
junior partner
simple associé(e)
junk bonds
obligations (fpl)
d'une société en
cours d'OPA *ou* junk
bonds (mpl)
junk mail
prospectus (mpl)
publicitaires *[par la
poste]*
jurisdiction (n)
juridiction (f)

Kk

**keen (adj) competi-
tion** compétition (f)
acharnée *ou* concur-
rence (f) vive
keen demand
demande (f) forte
keen prices prix
(mpl) compétitifs
keep (v) a promise
tenir une promesse
keep back (v)
retenir
keep up (v)
maintenir
**keep up with the
demand** satisfaire à
la demande
**key (n) *[on key-
board]*** touche (f)
key *[to door]* clef
(f) *ou* clé (f)
**key *[very
important]*** clé
key factor facteur
(m) clé
key industry
industrie (f) clé

key personnel *or*
key staff personnel
(m) clé
key post
poste (m) clé
keyboard (n)
clavier (m)
keyboard (v) saisir
(sur clavier) *[des
données]*
keyboarder (n) clav-
iste (mf) *ou* opéra-
teur (-trice) de saisie
keyboarding (n)
saisie (f) (de
données sur clavier)
kilo *or* **kilogram (n)**
kilo (m) *ou* kilo-
gramme (m)
knock down (v)
[price] baisser
(un prix)
knock off (v)
[reduce price]
baisser un
prix de *ou*
faire un rabais de
knock off
[stop work] arrêter
le travail *ou*
débrayer

knock-on effect
réaction (f) en
chaîne *ou*
répercussion (f)
knockdown prices
prix (mpl) sacrifiés
krona (n) *[currency
in Sweden and
Iceland]* couronne (f)
krone (n) *[currency
in Denmark and
Norway]* couronne (f)

Ll

label (n) étiquette
(f) *ou* label (m)
label (v) étiqueter
labelling (n)
étiquetage (m)
labour (n) travail (m)
labour costs coût (m)
de la main-d'oeuvre
labour disputes
conflits (mpl) du
travail

labour force
main-d'oeuvre (f)
**labour-intensive
industry** industrie
(f) à forte densité
de main-d'oeuvre
labour laws légis-
lation (f) du travail
labour relations
relations (fpl) entre
employeurs et
employés
labour union syndi-
cat (m) (ouvrier)
lack (n) of funds
manque (m) de fonds
land (n) terre (f)
ou terrain (m)
land (v) *[of plane]*
atterrir
land (v)
[passengers, cargo]
débarquer
**land goods at a
port** débarquer des
marchandises dans
un port
landed costs prix
(m) à quai
landing card carte
(f) de débarquement

landing charges
frais (mpl) de
débarquement
landlord (n) *or*
landlady (n)
propriétaire (m)
*[d'un logement
locatif]*
lapse (v) expirer
ou n'être plus valide
laser printer
imprimante (f) laser
**last in first out
(LIFO)** dernier
entré, premier sorti
(DEPS)
last quarter dernier
trimestre (m)
late (adv) en
retard
late-night opening
nocturne (m)
latest (adj) le
dernier *ou* la
dernière; le plus
récent *ou* la plus
récente
launch (n)
lancement (m)
launch (v) lancer
(un produit)

launching (n)
[action]
lancement (m)
launching costs
coûts (mpl) de
lancement
launching date date
(f) de lancement
launder (money)
blanchir
(des capitaux)
law (n) *[rule]* loi (f)
law *[study]*
droit (m)
law courts cour (f)
de justice *ou*
tribunal (m) *ou*
tribunaux (mpl)
**law of diminishing
returns** loi (f) des
rendements décrois-
sants
**law of supply and
demand** loi (f) de
l'offre et de la
demande
lawful (adj)
légal(e) *ou* licite *ou*
légitime
lawful trade
commerce (m) licite

lawsuit (n)
procès (m)
lawyer (n) avocat(e)
lay off (v) workers
mettre à pied *ou*
licencier des ouvriers
**LBO (= leveraged
buyout)** rachat
d'une société avec
des capitaux garan-
tis par l'actif de la
société
**L/C (= letter of
credit)** lettre (f) de
crédit
leader (n)
[person] chef (m)
ou leader (m)
lead time délai (m)
de livraison *ou*
d'exécution
leaflet (n)
prospectus (m) *ou*
feuillet (m)
leakage (n) coulage
(m) *ou* fuite (f)
lease (n) bail (m)
ou location-bail (f)
**lease (v) *[of
landlord, of tenant]***
louer (à bail)

lease back (v)
faire une opération
de cession-bail
lease-back (n)
cession-bail (m)
lease (v) equipment
louer du matériel en
crédit-bail
leasing (contrat
de) location (f)
leave (n) congé (m)
leave (v) *[go away]*
quitter *ou* partir
leave (v) *[resign]*
démissionner *ou* partir
leave of absence
autorisation (f) d'ab-
sence *ou* congé (m)
ledger (n) registre
(m) *ou* grand livre
left (adj) *[not
right]* gauche; de
gauche
left luggage office
consigne (f)
legal (adj)
[according to law]
légal(e) *ou* licite
legal *[referring to
law]* légal(e) *ou*
juridique

legal advice
conseils (mpl)
juridiques
legal adviser
conseiller (m)
juridique
legal costs *or* **legal
charges** frais (mpl)
de justice *ou* frais
juridiques
legal department
service (m) du
contentieux
legal expenses
frais (mpl) de justice
ou frais juridiques
legal proceedings
poursuites (fpl)
judiciaires
legal status
situation (f) légale
ou statut légal
legal tender
monnaie (f) légale
legislation (n)
législation (f)
lend (v) prêter
lender (n) prêteur
(-euse)
lending (n) prêt
(m) *ou* crédit (m)

lending limit pla-
fond (m) de crédit
lessee (n) locataire
(mf) à bail
lessor (n) bailleur,
bailleresse
let (n) (période de)
location (f)
let (v) louer
let (v) an office
louer un bureau
[donner à bail]
letter (n) lettre (f)
**letter of applica-
tion** lettre (f) de
candidature *ou* de
demanded'emploi
**letter of appoint-
ment** lettre (f)
d'embauche; (lettre
de) nomination (f)
letter of complaint
lettre (f) de
réclamation
letter of credit (L/C)
lettre (f) de crédit
letter of intent
lettre (f) d'intention
letter of reference
lettre (f) de
recommandation

letters patent brevet
(m) d'invention
letting agency
agence (f) immobil-
ière *ou* de location
level (n) niveau (m)
**level off *or* level
out (v)** se stabiliser
leverage (n) ratio
(m) d'endettement;
effet (m) de levier
**leveraged buyout
(LBO)** rachat d'une
société avec des
capitaux garantis
par l'actif de la
société
levy (n) impôt (m)
ou contribution (f)
levy (v) lever *ou*
percevoir (un impôt)
liabilities (n)
dettes (fpl) *ou*
passif (m)
liability (n)
responsabilité
(f) *[obligation
légale]*
liable for (adj)
responsable de
[légalement]

liable to (adj)
passible de *ou*
assujetti(e) à
licence (n)
autorisation (f)
ou permis (m)
license (v)
autoriser; octroyer
un permis
licensee (n)
titulaire (mf) d'une
licence
licensing (n) octroi
(m) *ou* concession
(f) de licence
lien (n) droit (m)
de retention
life assurance *or*
life insurance
assurance-vie (f)
life interest
jouissance (f) à vie
ou usufruit (m)
LIFO (last in first
out) DEPS (dernier
entré, premier sorti)
lift (n) ascenseur (m)
lift (v) *[remove]*
lever
lift (v) an embargo
lever l'embargo

lift (v) credit
restrictions désen-
cadrer le crédit
limit (n) limite (f)
limit (v) limiter
limitation (n)
limitation (f) *ou*
limite (f)
limited (adj)
limité(e)
limited (liability)
company (Ltd)
société (f) à
responsabilité
limitée (S.A.R.L.)
limited market
marché (m)
restreint
limited partnership
société (f) en
commandite
simple (SCS)
line (n) ligne (f)
line management
or **line organization**
organisation (f)
hiérarchique *ou*
verticale
line printer
imprimante (f) ligne
à ligne

liquid assets
disponibilités (fpl)
ou liquidités (fpl)
liquid: go liquid
réaliser son actif
liquidate (v) a
company liquider
une entreprise
liquidate stock
liquider du stock
liquidation (n)
liquidation (f) d'un
société
liquidator (n)
liquidateur (m)
liquidity (n)
liquidité (f)
liquidity crisis
crise (f) de liquidité
ou problème (m) de
trésorerie
lira (n) *[currency in*
Turkey] lire (f)
list (n) liste (f)
list (n) *[catalogue]*
catalogue (m)
list (v) faire *ou*
dresser *ou* établir
une liste
list price prix (m)
catalogue

listed company
société (f) cotée en
Bourse
litre (n) litre (m)
Lloyd's register
registre (m)
maritime Lloyd
load (n) charge (f)
ou chargement (m)
load (v) embarquer
ou charger
load (v) *[computer*
program] charger
(un programme)
load a lorry
***or* a ship** charger
un camion *ou* un
navire
load factor
coefficient (m) de
remplissage *[avion]*
loading bay aire (f)
de chargement
loading ramp
plateforme (f) de
chargement
loan (n) *[borrow-*
ing] emprunt (m)
loan
[lending] prêt (m)
loan (v) prêter

loan capital capital (m) d'emprunt

loan stock emprunt obligataire

lobby (n) groupe (m) de pression

local (adj) local(e)

local call [phone] communication (f) urbaine

local government municipalités (fpl)

local labour main-d'oeuvre (f) locale

lock (n) serrure (f)

lock (v) fermer à clé

lock up a shop or an office fermer (un magasin ou un bureau à la fin de la journée)

lock up capital bloquer ou immobiliser des capitaux

lock-up premises magasin (m) sans logement

log (v) enregistrer

log calls [phone] enregistrer le nombre et la durée des appels

logo (n) logo (m)

long (adj) long (longue)

long credit crédit (m) à long terme

long-dated bill effet (m) à longue échéance

long-range à longue portée ou à long terme

long-standing de longue date

long-standing agreement accord (m) de longue date

long-term à long terme

long-term debts dettes (fpl) à long terme

long-term forecast prévisions (fpl) à long terme

long-term liabilities dettes (fpl) à long terme

long-term loan prêt (m) ou emprunt (m) à long terme

long-term objectives objectifs (mpl) à long terme
long-term planning planification (f) à long terme
loophole (n) faille (f)
loose (adj) *[goods]* en vrac
lorry (n) camion (m)
lorry driver camionneur (m)
lorry-load charge (f) complète d'un camion
lose (v) (some-thing) perdre
lose *[fall to a lower level]* chuter
lose an order perdre une commande
lose money perdre de l'argent
loss (n) *[not a profit]* déficit (m) *ou* perte (f)
loss *[of something]* perte (f)
loss of an order perte d'une commande

loss of earnings perte de salaire *ou* manque (m) à gagner
loss-leader produit (m) d'appel *ou* article-réclame (m)
lot (n) *[of items]* lot (m)
low (adj) bas (basse)
low (n) niveau (m) très bas
low sales ventes (fpl) médiocres
low-grade (item) de qualité inférieure
low-level de bas niveau *ou* peu important
low-quality de qualité inférieure *ou* médiocre
lower (adj) moindre *ou* moins élevé(e) *ou* inférieur(e)
lower (v) baisser *ou* diminuer
lower prices baisser les prix
lowering (n) réduction (f) *ou* diminution (f)

Ltd (limited liability company) S.A.R.L. (société à responsabilité limitée)

luggage (n) bagages (mpl)

lump sum (n) montant (m) *ou* versement (m) unique; versement forfaitaire

luxury goods *or* items articles (mpl) de luxe

Mm

machine (n) machine (f) *ou* appareil (m)

macro-economics (n) macro-économie (f)

magazine (n) revue (f) *ou* magazine (m) *ou* périodique (m)

magazine insert encart (m) publicitaire

magazine mailing envoi (m) de revues par la poste *ou* mailing (m) de revues

magnetic tape *or* mag tape bande (f) magnétique

mail (n) *[letters sent or received]* courrier (m)

mail (n) *[postal system]* poste (f)

mail (v) poster; expédier *ou* envoyer par la poste

mail shot mailing (m)

mail-order vente (f) par correspondance (VPC)

mail-order business *or* mail-order maison (f) de vente par correspondance

mail-order catalogue catalogue (m) de vente par correspondance

mailing (n) envoi (m) par la poste

mailing list fichier (m) d'adresses

mailing piece prospectus (m) *ou* imprimé (m) publicitaire *[envoyé par la poste]*

mailing shot mailing (m) *ou* publipostage (m)

main (adj) principal(e)

main building bâtiment (m) principal

main office siège (m) social

maintain (v) *[keep at same level]* maintenir *ou* conserver

maintain *[keep going]* maintenir *ou* entretenir

maintenance (n) *[keeping in working order]* entretien (m) *ou* maintenance (f)

maintenance *[keeping things going]* maintien (m)

maintenance of contacts maintien (m) *ou* entretien (m) de relations

maintenance of supplies maintien (m) du stock de fournitures

major (adj) important(e) *ou* majeur(e)

major shareholder actionnaire (m) important

majority (n) majorité (f)

majority shareholder actionnaire (m) majoritaire

make (v) faire

make good *[a defect, a loss]* compenser *ou* réparer

make money faire un gain *ou* un profit

make out *[invoice]* rédiger *ou* établir

make provision for prévoir *ou* prendre des dispositions

make-ready time
temps de mise en
marche d'une machine
**make up for [com-
pensate]** compenser
ou dédommager
(une perte, etc.)
**maladministration
(n)** mauvaise
gestion (f)
man (n) [worker]
homme (m) *ou*
ouvrier (m)
man (v) assurer
une permanence *[à
un stand, etc.]*
man-hour
heure/homme (f) *ou*
heure travaillée
manage (v) gérer
ou diriger
manage property
gérer une propriété
manage to arriver
à *ou* réussir à
manageable (adj)
qui peut être
contrôlé *ou* géré
**management (n)
[action]** gestion (f)
ou management (m)
ou direction (f)

**management [man-
agers]** la direction
ou l'administration
(f); les cadres (mpl)
**management
accounts** comptes
(mpl) de gestion
**management buy-
out (MBO)** rachat
(m) de l'entreprise
par ses salariés
**management con-
sultant** conseiller
(m) en gestion
d'entreprise
management course
cours (m) de
management *ou* de
gestion d'entreprise
management team
équipe (f) dirigeante
ou équipe de direction
**management
techniques**
techniques (fpl) de
gestion
**management
trainee** jeune cadre
en stage
**management train-
ing** formation (f) en
gestion d'entreprise

manager (n) [of branch, shop] directeur (-trice) d'agence; gérant(e)
manager [of department] directeur (-trice) ou chef (m) (de service) ou manager (m)
managerial (adj) de gestion
managerial staff personnel (m) de direction; les cadres (mpl)
managing director (MD) directeur (-trice) général(e)
mandate (n) mandat (m)
manifest (n) manifeste (m)
manned (adj) avec du personnel en service
manning (n) effectifs (mpl)
manning levels besoins (mpl) en effectifs
manpower (n) main-d'oeuvre (f)

manpower forecasting prévisions (fpl) des besoins en main-d'oeuvre
manpower planning planification (f) de la main-d'oeuvre
manpower requirements besoins (mpl) en main-d'oeuvre
manpower shortage pénurie (f) de main-d'oeuvre
manual (adj) manuel (-elle)
manual (n) manuel (m) ou livret (m)
manual work travail (m) manuel
manual worker manoeuvre (m) ou travailleur (m) manuel
manufacture (n) fabrication (f) ou usinage (m)
manufacture (v) fabriquer ou manufacturer ou usiner
manufactured goods produits (mpl) manufacturés

manufacturer (n)
fabricant (m) *ou*
constructeur (m)
manufacturer's
recommended price
(MRP) prix (m) de
vente conseillé
manufacturing (n)
fabrication (f);
transformation (f)
manufacturing
capacity capacité
(f) de production
manufacturing
costs coûts (mpl)
ou frais (mpl) de
fabrication
manufacturing
overheads frais
(mpl) de fabrication
margin [profit]
marge (f)
margin of error
marge (f) d'erreur
marginal (adj)
marginal(e) *ou* faible
marginal cost coût
(m) marginal
marginal pricing
méthode (f) de
coûts marginaux

marine (adj)
maritime
marine insurance
assurance (f) maritime
marine underwriter
assureur (m)
maritime
maritime (adj)
maritime
maritime law droit
(m) maritime
maritime lawyer
spécialiste (mf) en
droit maritime
maritime trade com-
merce (m) maritime
mark (n) [stamp]
marque (f);
estampille (f)
mark (v) marquer
ou noter
mark down (v)
réduire (le prix d'un
article) *ou* démar-
quer (un article)
mark-down (n)
réduction (f) de prix
ou rabais (m)
mark up (v) aug-
menter *ou* majorer
(le prix d'un article)

mark-up (n)
[action] augmenta-
tion (f) *ou* majora-
tion (f) (de prix)
mark-up *[profit
margin]* marge (f)
bénéficiaire
marker pen
marqueur (m) *ou*
surligneur (m)
market (n) *[place]*
marché (m)
market (n)
[possible sales]
marché (m)
market (n) *[where
a product might
sell]* marché (m)
market (v) vendre
ou commercialiser
market analysis
analyse (f) du marché
market analyst
analyste (m) de
marché
market capitaliza-
tion capitalisation
(f) boursière
market economist
économiste (m)
financier

market forces
tendances (fpl) du
marché
market forecast
prévisions (fpl) du
marché
market leader N° 1
du marché *ou*
leader (m)
market opportunity
créneau (m)
market penetration
pénétration (f) du
marché
market price prix
(m) du marché
market rate cours
(m) du marché
market research
étude (f) de marché
market share part
(f) du marché
market trends
tendances (fpl) du
marché
market value
valeur (f)
marchande
market value
[stockmarket]
valeur (f) à la cote

marketable (adj)
[product] facile à
commercialiser *ou* à
vendre
marketing (n)
marketing (m) *ou*
commercialisation (f)
marketing agree-
ment accord (m) de
commercialisation
marketing
department *or*
division service
(m) (du) marketing
marketing manager
directeur (-trice) du
marketing
marketing strategy
stratégie (f)
commerciale
marketing
techniques
techniques (fpl) de
marketing
marketplace (n) [in
town] place (f) du
marché
marketplace
[place where
something is sold]
marché (m)

mass (n) [of
people] foule (f)
mass [of things]
grande quantité
mass market
product produit
(m) grand public
mass marketing
distribution (f)
grand public
mass media
médias (mpl)
mass production
production (f) *ou* fab-
rication (f) en série
mass-produce (v)
fabriquer en série
mass-produce cars
fabriquer des
voitures en série
Master's degree in
Business Admini-
stration (MBA)
maîtrise (f) de ges-
tion d'entreprise
material (n) [for
building, etc.]
matériau (m)
material (n) [four-
niture] matériel (m)
ou équipement (m)

materials control
contrôle (m) des four-
nitures *ou* des matéri-
aux (en magasin)
materials handling
manutention (f) du
matériel
maternity leave
congé (m) de
maternité
matter (n)
[problem] sujet (m)
ou problème (m)
matter (n) *[to be
discussed]* point
(m) *ou* question (f)
matter (v) avoir de
l'importance *ou*
importer
mature (v) venir *ou*
arriver à échéance
mature economy
maturité (f)
économique
maturity date date
(f) d'échéance
maximization (n)
maximalisation (f)
maximize (v)
maximaliser *ou*
maximiser

maximum (adj)
maximum *ou*
maximal(e)
maximum (n)
maximum (m)
maximum price
prix (m) maximum
**MBA (Master in
Business
Administration)**
maîtrise (f) de ges-
tion d'entreprise
**MBO (management
buyout)** rachat (m)
de l'entreprise par
ses salariés
**MD (managing
director)** directeur
(-trice) général(e)
mean (adj) moyen
(-enne)
mean (n)
moyenne (f)
**mean annual
increase** augmen-
tation annuelle
moyenne
means *[money]*
moyens (mpl)
means *[ways]* moyen
(m) *ou* façon (f)

means test
enquête (f) sur les
ressources (d'une
personne)
measure (n)
mesure (f)
measure (v)
mesurer
**measurement (n) of
profitability** analyse
(f) de la rentabilité
ou mesure (f) du
rendement
measurements (n)
mesures (fpl) *ou*
dimensions (fpl)
media coverage
couverture (f)
médiatique
median (n)
médiane (f)
mediate (v)
intervenir comme
médiateur
mediation (n)
médiation (f) *ou*
intervention (f)
mediator (n)
médiateur (-trice)
medium (adj)
moyen (-enne)

medium (n)
moyen (m)
medium-sized (adj)
moyen (-enne)
medium-term à
moyen terme
meet (v)
[expenses] faire
face (aux dépenses)
meet (v) *[require-
ments]* satisfaire
ou convenir (à)
meet (v) *[some-
one]* rencontrer
(quelqu'un); se
rencontrer *ou* se
réunir
meet a deadline
respecter un délai
meet a demand
satisfaire *ou* répon-
dre à la demande
meet a target
atteindre un objectif
meeting (n)
réunion (f) *ou*
assemblée (f)
meeting place lieu
(m) de réunion
member (n) *[of a
group]* membre (m)

membership (n) *[all members]* ensemble (m) des membres d'un groupe
membership *[being a member]* apparte-nance (f) *ou* adhésion (f) *ou* affiliation (f)
memorandum (n) or memo (n) note (f) *ou* mémorandum (m)
memory (n) *[computer]* mémoire (f)
merchandise (n) marchandise (f)
merchandize (v) commercialiser
merchandize (v) a product commer-cialiser un produit
merchandizer (n) spécialiste (mf) des techniques marchandes *ou* marchandiseur (m)
merchandizing (n) techniques (fpl) marchandes *ou* marchandisage (m) *ou* mer-chandising (m)

merchant (n) marchand(e) *ou* négociant(e)
merchant *[whole-saler]* grossiste (mf)
merchant bank banque (f) d'affaires
merchant navy marine (f) marchande
merchant ship or merchant vessel navire (m) marc-hand *ou* cargo (m)
merge (v) fusionner
merger (n) fusion (f)
merit (n) mérite (m)
merit award or merit bonus prime (f) d'encouragement
message (n) message (m)
messenger (n) commissionnaire (m) *ou* coursier (m)
micro-economics (n) micro-économie (f)
microcomputer (n) micro-ordinateur (m)
mid-month accounts comptes (mpl) de quinzaine

mid-week en
milieu de semaine
middle management
cadres (mpl) moyens
**middle-sized com-
pany** entreprise (f)
de taille moyenne
middleman (n)
intermédiaire (m)
million (n)
million (m)
millionaire (n)
millionnaire (m)
minimarket (n)
supérette (f)
minimum (adj) min-
imum *ou* minimal(e)
minimum (n)
minimum (m)
minimum dividend
dividende (m)
minimum
minimum payment
paiement (m)
minimum
minimum wage
salaire (m)
minimum (garanti)
minor shareholders
petits actionnaires
(mpl)

minority (n)
minorité (f)
minority shareholder
actionnaire (m)
minoritaire
minus moins *ou* sans
minus factor facteur
(m) négatif
minute (n) [time]
minute (f)
minute (v)
enregistrer *ou*
prendre note de
**minutes (n) [of
meeting]** procès-
verbal (m)
misappropriate (v)
détourner des fonds
misappropriation (n)
détournement (m) de
fonds
miscalculate (v)
faire une erreur de
calcul
miscalculation (n)
erreur (f) de calcul
**miscellaneous
(adj)** divers(e) *ou*
varié(e)
miscellaneous items
articles (mpl) divers

mismanage (v)
mal gérer
mismanagement (n)
mauvaise gestion
**miss (v) *[not to hit,
not to meet]*** manquer *ou* rater
miss an instalment
être en retard d'un
versement
miss a target ne
pas atteindre un
objectif *ou* manquer
son but
miss a train, a plane
manquer *ou* rater un
train, un avion
mistake (n) erreur
(f) *ou* faute (f)
**misunderstanding
(n)** malentendu (m)
mixed (adj) *[different sorts]* mixte
**mixed *[neither good
nor bad]*** mitigé(e)
mixed economy
économie (f) mixte
mobile phone téléphone (m) mobile
mobility (n)
mobilité (f)

mobilize (v)
mobiliser
mobilize capital
mobiliser des capitaux
mock-up (n)
maquette (f)
mode (n) mode (m)
mode of payment
modalités (fpl) de
paiement
model (n) *[person]*
mannequin (m)
model *[small copy]*
modèle (m) réduit
ou maquette (f)
model *[style of product]* modèle (m)
**model (v)
*[clothes]*** présenter
des modèles de
collection
model (adj) agreement accord-type (m)
modem (n)
modem (m)
moderate (adj)
modéré(e)
moderate (v)
modérer *ou* limiter
monetary (adj)
monétaire

monetary base
base (f) monétaire
monetary unit
unité (f) monétaire
money (n)
argent (m)
money changer
courtier (m) de
change *ou* bureau
(m) de change
money markets
marchés (mpl)
monétaires
money order man-
dat (m) postal *ou*
mandat-poste (m)
money rates taux
(m) d'intérêt de
l'argent
money supply
masse (f) monétaire
money up front ava-
nce (f) *ou* paiement
(m) d'avance
money-making
(adj) qui rapporte
moneylender (n)
prêteur (-euse)
monitor (n)
[screen] écran (m)
(d'ordinateur)

monitor (v) con-
trôler *ou* vérifier
monopolization (n)
monopolisation (f)
monopolize (v)
monopoliser
monopoly (n)
monopole (m)
month (n) mois (m)
month end
fin (f) de mois
month-end accounts
comptes (mpl) de fin
de mois
monthly (adj)
mensuel (-elle)
monthly (adv)
mensuellement *ou*
chaque mois
monthly payments
paiements (mpl)
mensuels *ou* mensu-
alités (fpl)
monthly state-
ment relevé (m)
mensuel
moonlight (v)
travailler au noir
moonlighter (n)
travailleur (-euse)
au noir

moonlighting (n)
travail (m) au noir
more than plus de;
supérieur(e) à
moratorium (n)
moratoire (m)
mortgage (n)
hypothèque (f)
ou prêt (m)
hypothécaire
mortgage (v)
prêter sur
hypothèque
mortgage payments
remboursements
(mpl) de prêt
(hypothécaire)
mortgagee (n)
prêteur (m) (sur
hypothèque)
mortgager or
mortgagor (n)
emprunteur (m)
(sur hypothèque)
most-favoured
nation nation (f) la
plus favorisée
motivated (adj)
motivé(e)
motivation (n)
motivation (f)

motor insurance
assurance (f)
automobile
mount up (v) aug-
menter *ou* monter
ou flamber
mounting (adj)
grandissant(e)
move (v) *[be sold]*
se vendre
move *[house, office]*
déménager
move *[propose]*
déposer
(une motion)
movement
mouvement (m) *ou*
fluctuation (f)
movements of capi-
tal mouvements
(mpl) de capitaux
MRP (manu-
facturer's recom-
mended price)
prix (m) de vente
conseillé
multicurrency
operation opèration
(f) multidevise
multilateral (adj)
multilatéral(e)

**multilateral agree-
ment** accord (m)
multilatéral
multilateral trade
commerce (m)
multilatéral
multidedia (n)
multimédia
multinational (adj)
multinational(e)
multinational (n)
multinationale (f)
multiple (adj)
multiple
multiple entry visa
visa (m) permanent
(bon pour plusieurs
entrées)
multiple ownership
propriété (f) collective
multiple store
magasin (m) à suc-
cursales multiples
multiplication (n)
multiplication (f)
multiply (v)
multiplier
mutual (adj) com-
mun(e) *ou* mutuel
(-elle) *ou* réciproque
**mutual (insurance)
company** mutuelle (f)

Nn

**NAFTA (North
American Free
Trade Agreement)**
Aléna (Accord de
libre-échange
nord-américain)
national (adj)
national(e)
**national
advertising**
publicité (f) à
l'échelon national
nationalization (n)
nationalisation (f)
nationalize (v)
nationaliser
**nationalized
industry** industrie
(f) nationalisée
nationwide (adj)
national(e) *ou* à
l'échelon national
natural resources
ressources (fpl)
naturelles
**natural wastage
*[workers]*** départs
(mpl) naturels

**near letter-quality
(NLQ)** *[printer]*
qualité (f) courrier
necessary (adj)
nécessaire *ou*
indispensable
negative cash flow
cash-flow (m) négatif
ou trésorerie (f)
négative
neglected business
entreprise (f) mal
gérée
neglected shares
valeurs (fpl)
négligées
negligence (n)
négligence (f)
negligent (adj)
négligent(e)
negligible (adj)
négligeable
negotiable (adj)
négociable
**negotiable instru-
ment** effet (m)
négociable
negotiate (v) négocier
negotiation (n)
négociation (f)
negotiator (n)
négociateur (-trice)

net (adj) net (nette)
net (v) toucher *ou*
gagner net
**net assets or net
worth** actif (m)
net; valeur (f) nette
**net earnings or net
income** profit (m)
net; revenu (m) net
**net income or net
salary** salaire (m) net
net loss
perte (f) nette
net margin marge
(f) nette
net price
prix (m) net
net profit
bénéfice (m) net
ou gain (m) net
net receipts
recettes (fpl) nettes
net sales
ventes (fpl) nettes
net weight
poids (m) net
net worth
valeur (f) nette
net yield rendement
(m) net
network (n)
réseau (m)

**network (v) [com-
puters]** connecter
en réseau
**networking (n) [mak-
ing business contacts]**
exploitation (f) des
contacts d'affaires
news agency
agence (f) de presse
newspaper (n)
journal (m)
niche (n) créneau
(m) (sur le marché)
night (n) nuit (f)
night rate tarif (m)
de nuit *ou* tarif réduit
night shift
équipe (f) de nuit
nil (noun) néant
(m) *ou* zéro (m)
nil return
état (m) néant
**NLQ (near letter-
quality)** qualité (f)
courrier
**no-claims bonus [ins-
urance]** bonus (m)
**no-strike agreement
or no-strike clause**
clause (f) interdisant
la grève

nominal capital
capital (m) nominal
nominal ledger grand
livre (m) général
nominal rent loyer (m)
symbolique
nominal value
valeur (f) nominale
nominee (n) per-
sonne (f) désignée
nominee account
compte confié à un
fondé de pouvoir
non-delivery
non-livraison (f)
**non-executive
director** administra-
teur (m) non
dirigeant
non-feasance
délit (m) par
abstention
**non-negotiable
instrument** effet (m)
non négociable
**non-payment (n)
[of a debt]** non-
paiement (m)
non profit-making
non lucratif (-ive)
ou sans but lucratif

non-recurring items postes (mpl) exceptionnels
non-refundable deposit arrhes (fpl) non remboursables
non-returnable packing emballage (m) perdu *ou* non consigné
non-stop sans arrêt; sans escale *ou* non-stop *[vol]*
non-taxable income revenu (m) non imposable
non-voting shares actions (fpl) sans droit de vote
norm (n) norme (f)
North American Free Trade Agreement (NAFTA) Accord de libre-échange nord-américain (Aléna)
notary public notaire (mf)
note (n) avis (m) *ou* note (f)
note (v) *[write down]* noter

note (n) of hand billet (m) à ordre
notice (n) *[piece of information]* notice (f) *ou* note (f) (d'information)
notice *[that worker is leaving his job]* préavis (m)
notice *[time allowed]* préavis (m)
notification (n) notification (f) *ou* avis (m)
notify (v) notifier
null (adj) nul (nulle)
number (n) *[figure]* numéro (m)
number (v) numéroter
numbered account compte (m) numéroté
numeric *or* numerical (adj) numérique
numeric keypad *[on keyboard]* clavier (m) *ou* pavé (m) numérique

Oo

objective (adj)
objectif (-ive)
objective (n)
objectif (m)
obligation (n) [debt]
dette (f)
obligation [duty]
obligation (f)
obsolescence (n)
obsolescence (f)
obsolescent (adj)
obsolescent(e)
obsolete (adj)
obsolète *ou* qui
n'est plus en usage
obtain (v) obtenir
ou se procurer
obtainable (adj)
disponible *ou* qu'on
peut se procurer
occupancy (n)
occupation (f)
occupancy rate
taux (m)
d'occupation
occupant (n)
occupant (m)

occupational (adj)
professionnel (-elle)
**occupational acci-
dent** accident (m)
du travail
**odd (adj) [not a
pair]** dépareillé(e)
odd [not even]
impair(e)
odd numbers nom-
bres (mpl) impairs
**off [away from
work]** absent(e)
off [cancelled]
annulé(e)
off [reduced by]
avec réduction
off-peak en dehors
des heures de pointe
off-season
morte-saison (f)
off the record
officieusement *ou*
en privé
off-the-job training
formation (f) pro-
fessionnelle dans un
centre spécialisé
offer (n) offre (f)
offer (v) [to buy]
offrir *ou* proposer

offer (v) *[to sell]*
mettre en vente
offer for sale offre
(f) publique de vente
(OPV)
offer price *[shares]*
prix (m) d'émission
(d'une action)
office (n) bureau (m)
office equipment
équipement (m) *ou*
matériel (m) de
bureau
office furniture
meubles (mpl) de
bureaux
office hours heures
(fpl) de bureau
office security
mesures (fpl) de
sécurité dans les
bureaux
office space local
(m) pour bureaux
office staff person-
nel (m) de bureau
office stationery
fournitures (fpl) de
bureau
offices to let
bureaux (mpl) à louer

official (adj)
officiel (-elle)
official (n)
fonctionnaire (m)
official receiver
administrateur (m)
judiciaire
official return déc-
laration (f) officielle
officialese (n) jar-
gon (m) administratif
offset (v) losses
against tax déduire
ses pertes des impôts
off-shore (adj)
offshore
off-shore bank
banque (f) offshore
off-shore fund
placement (m) dans
un paradis fiscal
oil *[petroleum]*
pétrole (m)
oil price prix (m)
du pétrole
oil-exporting
countries pays
(mpl) exportateurs
de pétrole
old (adj) vieux, vieil
(vieille)

old-established (adj)
établi(e) depuis
longtemps
old-fashioned (adj)
démodé(e)
ombudsman (n)
médiateur (m) *ou*
ombudsman (m)
omission (n)
omission (f)
omit (v) oublier *ou*
omettre (de faire
quelque chose)
**on a short-term
basis** à court terme
on account
en acompte
on agreed terms aux
termes le l'accord
on an annual basis
chaque année *ou* sur
une base annuelle
on average en
moyenne
on approval à l'essai
ou à condition
on behalf of
au nom de
on board à bord
on business pour
affaires

on condition that à
(la) condition que
ou sous réserve de
on credit à crédit
on demand à vue
ou à présentation
on duty de service
on favourable terms
à des conditions
avantageuses *ou*
exceptionnelles
on line *or* online
en ligne
on request
sur demande
on sale en vente
on the increase qui
va en augmentant
on time à l'heure
on-the-job training
formation (f) dans
l'entreprise *ou* sur
le tas *ou* sur le
terrain
one-off isolé(e) *ou*
unique
one-off item article
(m) unique *ou* non
suivi
one-sided (adj)
unilatéral(e)

one-sided agreement accord (m) unilatéral
one-way fare tarif (m) d'un aller simple
one-way trade commerce (m) unilatéral
OPEC (Organization of Petroleum Exporting Countries) OPEP (Organisation des pays exportateurs de pétrole)
open (adj) *[not closed]* ouvert(e)
open (v) *[begin]* démarrer *ou* entamer
open (v) *[start new business]* ouvrir
open a bank account ouvrir un compte en banque
open a line of credit autoriser *ou* ouvrir une ligne de crédit
open a meeting ouvrir la séance
open (adj) account compte (m) ouvert
open (v) an account ouvrir un compte

open cheque chèque (m) non barré
open credit découvert (m) autorisé *ou* crédit (m) à découvert
open market marché (m) libre
open (v) negotiations entamer des négociations
open (adj) ticket billet (m) open
open (adj) to offers ouvert à toute proposition
open-ended agreement accord (m) flexible *ou* non limité
open-plan office bureau (m) à modules *ou* bureau paysager
opening (adj) initial(e)
opening (n) ouverture (f)
opening balance bilan (m) initial
opening bid offre (f) d'ouverture *ou* première mise (f)

opening hours
heures (fpl)
d'ouverture
opening price *[auction]* mise (f) à prix
opening price
[shares] prix (m) *ou*
cours (m) d'ouverture
opening stock
stock (m) initial *ou*
stock d'ouverture
opening time
heure(s) (f(pl))
d'ouverture
operate (v) être en
vigueur
operate (v)
[machine] (faire)
fonctionner
operating budget
budget (m)
opérationnel
operating costs *or*
operating expenses
coûts (mpl) opéra-
tionnels *ou* coûts
d'exploitation
operating manual
manuel (m)
d'utilisation

operating profit
bénéfice (m)
commercial
operating system
système (m)
d'exploitation
operation (n)
[business]
exploitation (f) *ou*
opération (f)
operation (n)
[dealing] opération
(f) (boursière)
operational (adj)
opérationnel (-elle)
operational budget
budget (m)
opérationnel
**operational
costs** coûts (mpl)
opérationnels
operative (adj)
en vigueur;
opérationnel (-elle)
operative (n)
opérateur (-trice)
[d'une machine]
operator (n)
opérateur (-trice)
[d'une machine]

operator (n)
[telephone]
standardiste (mf)
ou opératrice (f)
opinion poll
sondage (m)
d'opinion
opportunity (n)
opportunité (f)
ou occasion (f)
option to purchase
option (f) d'achat
optional (adj)
facultatif (-ive) ou
en option ou
optionnel (-elle)
optional extras
accessoires (mpl) en
option
order (n) [certain
way] ordre (m)
order (n) [for goods]
commande (f)
order (n) [instruc-
tion] ordre (m)
ou instruction (f)
order (n) [money]
mandat (m)
order (v) [goods]
commander

order (v) [put in
order] classer ou
ordonner
order (n) book
carnet (m) de
commandes
order fulfilment
exécution (f) de
commande(s)
order number
numéro (m) de
commande
order picking
sélection (f) des
différents éléments
d'une commande
order processing
traitement (m)
de commande(s)
order: on order
commandé ou en
commande
ordinary (adj)
ordinaire
ordinary shares
actions (fpl)
ordinaires
organization (n)
[institution]
organisation (f)

organization *[way of arranging]* organisation (f)

organization and methods organisation et méthodes

organization chart organigramme (m)

Organization of Petroleum Exporting Countries (OPEC) Organisation des pays exportateurs de pétrole (OPEP)

organizational (adj) relatif à l'organisation *ou* à la structure

organize (v) organiser

origin (n) origine (f) *ou* provenance (f)

original (adj) original(e) *ou* d'origine

original (n) original (m)

OS (= outsize) grande taille (f)

out of date démodé(e) *ou* dépassé(e)

out-of-pocket expenses débours (mpl)

out of pocket: be out of pocket en être de sa poche

out of stock épuisé(e) *[article]*

out of stock en rupture de stock *[marchand]*

out of work au *ou* en chômage

outbid (v) surenchérir

outgoing (adj) sortant(e)

outgoing mail courrier (m) au départ

outgoings (n) sorties (fpl) *ou* dépenses (fpl)

outlay (n) dépense (f)

outlet (n) point (m) de vente

output (n) *[computer]* sortie (f) *ou* données (fpl) de sortie

output (n) *[goods]*
production (f) *ou*
rendement (m)
output (v)
[computer] sortir
output tax TVA sur
les prestations de
service
outright (adv)
[completely]
complètement *ou*
totalement
outright (adj)
[purchase]
au comptant
outside (adj)
extérieur(e) *ou* à
l'extérieur
outside director
administrateur (m)
externe
outside line
[phone] ligne (f)
(téléphonique)
extérieure
**outside office
hours** en dehors
des heures de
bureau
outsize (OS)
grande taille (f)

outstanding (adj)
[exceptional]
exceptionnel (-elle)
outstanding *[unpaid]*
à payer; impayé(e)
outstanding debts
dettes (fpl) à payer;
les impayés (mpl)
outstanding orders
commandes (fpl) en
attente
overall (adj)
global(e) *ou*
général(e)
overall plan plan
(m) global
overbook (v)
surréserver *ou* faire
un surbooking
overbooking (n)
surréservation (f)
ou surbooking (m)
**overbought (mar-
ket)** marché (m)
surévalué
overcapacity (n)
surcapacité (f)
overcharge (n)
trop-perçu (m)
overcharge (v)
faire payer trop cher

overdraft (n)
découvert (m)
overdraft facility
autorisation (f) de
découvert
overdraw (v) tirer
à découvert
overdrawn account
compte (m) à
découvert
overdue (adj)
en retard
overestimate (v)
surestimer
overhead budget
budget (m) des frais
généraux
overheads (n) *or*
overhead costs
frais (mpl) généraux
ou d'administration
générale
overmanning (n)
excédent (m) de
personnel
overpayment (n)
trop-perçu (m)
overproduce (v)
produire en excé-
dent *ou* surproduire

overproduction (n)
surproduction (f)
overseas (adj) à l'é-
tranger *ou* outre-mer
overseas (n)
l'étranger *ou* les
pays étrangers
overseas markets
marchés (mpl)
étrangers
overseas trade com-
merce (m) extérieur
overspend (v)
trop dépenser
overspend one's
budget dépasser
son budget
overstock (v) avoir
un excédent de stock
overstocks (n) excé-
dents (m) de stock
overtime (n) heures
(f) supplémentaires
overtime ban
refus (m) de faire
des heures
supplémentaires
overtime pay tarif
(m) des heures
supplémentaires

overvalue (v)
surévaluer
overweight: to be
overweight être
trop lourd
owe (v) devoir
owing (adj)
dû (due)
owing to
en raison de *ou* à
cause de
own (v) posséder
ou détenir
own brand goods
or own label goods
produits (mpl)
à marque du
distributeur
owner (n)
propriétaire (mf)
ownership (n)
propriété (f)

Pp

p & p (postage and
packing) frais
(mpl) de port et
d'emballage
PA (personal assis-
tant) secrétaire (f)
ou assistante de
direction
pack (n) paquet (m)
pack (v) emballer
ou empaqueter
pack (v) goods into
cartons emballer
des marchandises
dans des cartons
pack (n) of
envelopes paquet
(m) d'enveloppes
package (n) *[of
goods]* paquet (m)
ou colis (m)
package
[of services]
contrat (m) global
package deal contrat
(m) global; forfait (m)

package holiday
forfait-vacances
(m); voyage (m)
organisé
packaging (m)
[action] emballage
(m) *ou* condition-
nement (m)
**packaging
(material)**
emballage (m) *ou*
conditionnement (m)
packer (n)
emballeur (-euse)
packet (n)
paquet (m)
packet of cigarettes
paquet (m) de
cigarettes
packing (n) *[action]*
emballage (m)
packing (material)
emballage (m)
packing case
caisse (f)
packing charges
frais (mpl)
d'emballage
packing list *or*
packing slip liste
(f) de colisage

paid (adj) *[for
work]* payé(e)
ou rémunéré(e)
paid *[invoice]*
payé(e) *ou* réglé(e)
pallet (n) palette (f)
palletize (v) met-
tre sur palette(s)
panel (n)
panneau (m)
panel (n) (of
experts) groupe
(m) (d'experts)
panic buying achat
(m) de précaution
paper bag sac (m)
ou pochette (f)
en papier
paper feed alimen-
tation (f) en papier
paper loss
[accounts] perte (f)
théorique
paper profit
[accounts] bénéfice
(m) théorique *ou*
gain (m) théorique
paperclip (n)
trombone (m)
papers (n)
documents (mpl)

paperwork (n)
paperasserie (f)
par (adj) au pair *ou*
à la parité
par value valeur (f)
nominale *ou* valeur
au pair
parcel (n) paquet
(m) *ou* colis (m)
parcel (v)
empaqueter
parcel post service
(m) colis (postaux)
parent company
maison (f) mère *ou*
société (f) mère
parity (n) parité
(f) *ou* égalité (f)
part (n) part (f) *ou*
partie (f)
part exchange
reprise (f)
(contre achat)
part-owner
copropriétaire (mf)
part-ownership
copropriété (f)
part-time (adj &
adv) temps (m)
partiel *ou*
mi-temps (m)

part-time work *or*
part-time employ-
ment travail (m) à
temps partiel *ou* à
mi-temps
part-timer (n)
employé(e) à temps
partiel *ou* à mi-temps
partial loss sinistre
(m) partiel
partial payment
acompte (m)
particulars (n)
détails (mpl) *ou*
coordonnées (fpl)
partner (n) associé(e)
partnership (n)
association (f)
ou société (f)
party (n) partie (f)
[juridique]
patent (n) brevet (m)
patent agent agent
(m) en brevets
patent (v) an inven-
tion faire breveter
une invention
patent applied for
or **patent pending**
demande (f) de
brevet déposée

patented (adj)
breveté(e)
pay (n) [salary]
salaire (m) *ou* paie
(f) *ou* traitement (m)
ou rémunération (f)
pay (v) [bill] payer
ou verser (de l'argent)
pay (v) [worker]
payer *ou* rémunérer
pay a bill régler *ou*
payer une note
pay a dividend
verser un dividende
pay an invoice
régler une facture
pay back
rembourser
pay by cheque
régler *ou* payer
par chèque
pay by credit card
régler *ou* payer avec
une carte de crédit
pay cash payer
comptant
pay (n) cheque
chèque (m) de salaire
pay desk caisse (f)
pay (v) in advance
payer d'avance

pay in instalments
payer par verse-
ments échelonnés
pay interest
verser un intérêt
pay money down
verser un acompte
ou une provision
pay off (v) [debt]
rembourser
pay off [worker]
congédier *ou*
licencier (avec paie)
pay out (v) verser
de l'argent
pay phone télé-
phone (m) public
pay (n) rise
augmentation (f)
de salaire
pay (n) slip
bulletin (m) de
salaire *ou* feuille (f)
de paie
pay the bill [at
restaurant] payer
l'addition
pay up (v)
régler une dette
payable (adj)
payable

payable at sixty days payable à soixante jours
payable in advance payable à l'avance
payable on delivery payable à la livraison *ou* livraison contre remboursement
payable on demand payable à vue *ou* sur présentation
payables (n) comptes (mpl) fournisseurs
payback (n) remboursement (m)
payback clause clause (f) de remboursement (d'un prêt)
payback period délai (m) de remboursement *ou* d'amortissement
payee (n) bénéficiaire (mf)
payer (n) payeur (m)
paying (adj) qui rapporte *ou* lucratif (-ive) *ou* rentable

paying (n) paiement (m)
paying-in slip bordereau (m) de versement
payload (n) *[lorry]* charge (f) utile
payment (n) paiement (m) *ou* règlement (m); versement (m)
payment by cheque règlement (m) par chèque
payment by credit card règlement avec carte de crédit
payment by results paiement (m) au rendement *ou* salaire (m) au rendement
payment in cash paiement (m) en espèces *ou* au comptant *ou* cash
payment in kind paiement (m) en nature
payment on account acompte (m)

**PC (personal com-
puter)** ordinateur
(m) personnel
**P/E ratio
(price/earnings
ratio)** PER (m) (coef-
ficient de capitalisa-
tion des résultats)
peak (n) maximum
(m) *ou* record (m)
peak (v) culminer;
atteindre un record
ou un niveau élevé
peak output
production (f)
record
peak period heures
(fpl) de pointe
peg (v) prices
bloquer les prix
penalize (v)
pénaliser *ou*
sanctionner
penalty (n)
amende (f) *ou*
pénalité (f) *ou*
sanction (f)
penalty clause
clause (f) pénale
pending (adj) en
attente

**penetrate (v) a
market** pénétrer un
marché *ou* s'implanter
sur un marché
pension (n)
pension (f) de retraite
pension fund
caisse (f) de retraite
pension scheme
régime (m) de retraite
per par *ou* pour
**per annum *or* per
year** par année
per capita par per-
sonne *ou* par tête
per cent [%]
pour cent [%]
per day par jour
per head par per-
sonne *ou* par tête
per hour (de)
l'heure; à l'heure
per week par
semaine
per year par année
percentage (n)
pourcentage (m);
taux (m)
**percentage dis-
count** pourcentage
(m) de remise

percentage increase taux (m) d'augmentation

percentage point un pour cent

performance (n) performance (f)

performance rating évaluation (f) du rendement

period (n) période (f) *ou* durée (f)

period of notice délai (m) de préavis *ou* délai-congé (m)

period of validity durée (f) *ou* période (f) de validité

periodic or periodical (adj) périodique

periodical (n) périodique (m) *ou* revue (f)

peripherals (n) *[computer]* périphériques (mpl) (d'ordinateur)

perishable (adj) périssable

perishable goods or perishables (n) denrées (fpl) périssables

permanent contract contrat (m) à durée indéterminée

permission (n) permission (f) *ou* autorisation (f)

permit (n) permis (m)

permit (v) autoriser quelqu'un à faire quelque chose

personal (adj) privé(e) *ou* personnel (-elle)

personal allowances *[income tax]* abattement (m); revenu (m) exonéré d'impôt

personal assets biens (mpl) meubles

personal assistant (PA) secrétaire (f) *ou* assistante de direction

personal computer (PC) ordinateur (m) personnel

personalized (adj)
personnalisé(e)
**personalized
cheques** chèques
personnalisés
personnel (n) *[staff]*
personnel (m)
**personnel depart-
ment** service (m)
du personnel
**personnel manage-
ment** gestion (f)
du personnel
personnel manager
chef (m) du personnel
petty (adj) peu
important
petty cash petite
caisse (f)
petty cash box
caisse (f)
petty expenses
petites *ou* menues
dépenses (fpl)
phase in (v) intro-
duire graduellement
phase out (v)
mettre fin
graduellement (à)
phone (n)
téléphone (m)

phone (v) télé-
phoner *ou* appeler
phone back (v)
rappeler
phone call appel
(m) (téléphonique)
ou coup (m) de fil
phone card
télécarte (f)
**phone for (some-
thing)** demander
ou commander
par téléphone
phone number
numéro (m) de
téléphone
photocopier
photocopieur (m)
photocopy (n)
photocopie (f)
photocopy (v)
photocopier
photocopying (n)
(action de faire des)
photocopies (fpl)
**photocopying
bureau** service (m)
de reproduction
picking list
inventaire (m)
de position

pie chart (n)
diagramme (m)
circulaire *ou*
camembert (m)
piece (n) pièce (f)
piece rate *[rate of
**pay]* tarif (m) unitaire
piecework (n)
travail (m) à la
pièce *ou* aux pièces
pilferage *or* pilfering
(n) chapardage (m)
pilot (adj) pilote
ou modèle
pilot (n) *[person]*
pilote (m)
pilot scheme pro-
gramme (m) pilote
pioneer (n)
pionnier (m) *ou*
novateur (-trice)
pioneer (v) innover
place (n) *[in a*
competition] place
(f) *ou* rang (m)
place (n) *[job]*
poste (m) *ou*
emploi (m)
place (n) *[situa-*
tion] endroit (m)
ou lieu (m)

place (v) placer
place an order passer
une commande
place (n) of work
lieu (m) de travail
plaintiff (n) partie
(f) plaignante
plan (n) *[drawing]*
plan (m)
plan (n) *[project]*
plan (m) *ou* projet (m)
plan (v) planifier;
projeter
plan (v) investments
faire des plans
d'investissement
plane (n) avion (m)
planner (n)
planificateur (-trice)
planning (n)
planification (f)
plant (n) *[factory]*
usine (f)
plant (n) *[machin-*
ery] machines (fpl)
plant-hire firm
société (f) de loca-
tion de matériel
platform (n) *[rail-*
way station] quai
(m) (de la gare)

PLC *or* plc (Public Limited Company) Société anonyme (S.A.) *[cotée en Bourse]*

plug (n) *[electric]* fiche (f)

plug (v) *[block]* arrêter

plug (v) *[publicize]* faire de la publicité

plummet (v) chuter

plus plus

plus factor atout (m)

pocket (n) poche (f)

pocket (v) gagner (net) *ou* empocher

pocket calculator calculatrice (f) de poche

point (n) point (m)

point of sale (p.o.s. *or* POS) point (m) de vente

point of sale material (POS material) matériel (m) de publicité sur le lieu de vente (PLV)

policy (n) politique (f)

pool (n) pool (m)

pool (v) resources mettre les ressources en commun

poor (adj) *[not rich]* pauvre

poor quality qualité (f) inférieure

poor service service (m) médiocre

popular (adj) populaire

popular prices prix (mpl) à la portée de tous

port (n) *[computer]* port (m)

port (n) *[harbour]* port (m)

port authority autorités (fpl) portuaires

port charges *or* port dues droits (mpl) de bassin

port of call port (m) d'escale

port of embarkation port (m) d'embarquement

port of registry
port (m) d'attache
[d'un navire]
portable (adj)
portatif (-ive) *ou*
portable
portfolio (n)
portefeuille (f)
(d'actions)
**portfolio manage-
ment** gestion (f) de
portefeuilles
**POS *or* p.o.s. (point
of sale)** point (m)
de vente
**POS material (point
of sale material)**
matériel (m) de
publicité sur le lieu
de vente (PLV)
position (n) *[job]*
poste (m)
**position *[state of
affairs]*** position (f)
positive (adj)
positif (-ive)
positive cash flow
trésorerie (f)
positive
possess (v)
posséder

possibility (n)
possibilité (f)
possible (adj)
possible
post (n) *[job]*
poste (m) *ou*
emploi (m)
post (n) *[letters]*
courrier (m)
**post (n) *[postal sys-
tem]*** poste (f) *ou*
service (m) postal
post (v) poster *ou*
mettre à la poste
post (v) an entry
passer une écriture
post (n) free
franco de port *ou*
franc de port
postage (n) tarif
(m) postal; affran-
chissement (m)
**postage and
packing (p & p)**
frais (mpl) de port
et d'emballage
postage paid
port (m) payé
postage stamp
timbre-poste (m) *ou*
timbre (m)

postal (adj)
postal(e)
postal charges *or*
postal rates tarifs
(mpl) postaux
postal order
mandat-poste (m)
postcode (n) code
(m) postal
postdate (v)
postdater
poste restante
poste restante
postmark (n) cachet
(m) de la poste
postmarked (adj)
timbré(e) (de)
postpaid (adj)
port (m) payé
postpone (v)
remettre à plus tard
ou reporter
postponement
renvoi (m) *ou*
remise (f) à
plus tard
potential (adj)
potentiel (-elle)
ou possible
potential (n)
potentiel (m)

**potential cus-
tomers** clients
(mpl) potentiels *ou*
prospects (mpl)
potential market
marché (m) potentiel
pound (n) *[currency]*
livre (f) (sterling)
pound (n) *[weight:
0.45kg]* livre (f)
pound sterling
livre (f) sterling
power of attorney
procuration (f)
**PR (public rela-
tions)** relations
(fpl) publiques
pre-empt (v)
devancer *ou* prévenir
pre-financing (n)
préfinancement (m)
prefer (v) préférer
preference (n)
préférence (f) *ou*
priorité (f)
preference shares
actions (fpl)
privilégiées
preferential (adj)
privilégié(e) *ou*
prioritaire

preferential creditor créancier (m) prioritaire
preferential duty *or* **preferential tariff** tarif (m) privilégié
preferred creditor créancier (m) prioritaire
premises (n) locaux (mpl)
premises: on the premises sur place
premium (n) *[extra charge]* plus-value (f) *[du change]*
premium *[insurance]* prime (f) (d'assurance)
premium *[on lease]* reprise (f)
premium offer prime (f) *ou* cadeau (m)
premium quality première qualité *ou* qualité (f) extra
premium: at a premium *[shares, etc.]* au-dessus du pair

prepack (v) *or* **prepackage (v)** préemballer *ou* conditionner
prepaid (adj) payé(e) d'avance
prepay (v) payer d'avance
prepayment (n) paiement (m) d'avance
present (adj) *[being there]* présent(e)
present (adj) *[now]* actuel (-elle)
present (n) *[gift]* cadeau (m)
present (v) *[give]* offrir
present (v) *[show a document]* présenter
present a bill for acceptance présenter une traite à l'acceptation
present a bill for payment présenter une traite au recouvrement
present (adj) value valeur (f) actuelle

presentation (n)
[exhibition]
présentation (f)
presentation [show-
ing a document]
présentation (f)
press (n) presse (f)
press conference
conférence (f) de
presse
press release
communiqué (m)
de presse
prestige (n)
prestige (m)
prestige product
produit (m) de luxe
pretax profit
bénéfice (m)
avant impôts
prevent (v)
empêcher
prevention (n)
prévention (f)
preventive (adj)
préventif (-ive)
previous (adj)
antérieur(e) *ou*
précédent(e)
price (n) prix (m)
price (v) fixer *ou*
déterminer un prix

price ceiling pla-
fond (m) des prix
price control con-
trôle (m) des prix
price differential
écart (m) de prix
price/earnings ratio
(P/E ratio) coeffi-
cient (m) de capital-
isation des résultats
ou PER (m)
price ex quay prix
(m) à quai *ou* franco
à quai
price ex warehouse
prix ex-entrepôt
price ex works prix
départ usine
price label éti-
quette (f) de prix
price list catalogue
(m) *ou* tarif (m) *ou*
liste (f) de prix
price range
fourchette (f) de prix
price reduction
réduction (f) de prix
ou rabais (m)
price-sensitive
product produit (m)
sensible aux change-
ments de prix

price stability stabilité (f) des prix

price tag *or* **price ticket** étiquette (f) de prix *ou* ticket (m) de prix

price war *or* **price-cutting war** guerre (f) des prix

pricing (n) fixation (f) d'un prix

pricing policy politique (f) (de fixation) des prix

primary (adj) de base

primary industry industrie (f) de base *ou* secteur (m) primaire

prime (adj) de base

prime cost prix (m) coûtant de base

prime rate taux (m) de base bancaire

principal (adj) principal(e)

principal (n) *[money]* capital (m)

principal (n) *[person]* chef (m) *ou* directeur (-trice)

principle (n) principe (m)

print (v) imprimer

print out (v) imprimer

printer (n) *[company]* imprimeur (m)

printer *[machine]* imprimante (f)

printout (n) sortie (f) d'imprimante

prior (adj) antérieur(e) *ou* préalable

private (adj) privé(e); privatif (-ive)

private enterprise entreprise (f) privée

private limited company société (f) anonyme (S.A.) *[ordinaire]*

private ownership propriété (f) privée

private property propriété (f) privée

private sector secteur (m) privé *ou* le privé

privatization (n) privatisation (f)

privatize (v)
privatiser
pro forma (n)
(invoice) facture
(f) pro forma
pro rata (adj &
adv) au prorata
probation (n)
période (f) d'essai
probationary (adj)
à l'essai *ou* d'essai
problem (n)
problème (m)
problem area
secteur (m) difficile
problem solving
solution (f) de
problèmes
procedure (n)
procédure (f) *ou*
méthode (f)
proceed (v) (se)
poursuivre *ou*
continuer
process (n)
procédé (m)
process (v) *[deal*
with] traiter *ou*
exécuter
process (v) *[raw*
materials] traiter

process figures
analyser des chiffres
processing (n) of
information *or* **of**
statistics traitement
(m) de données *ou*
de statistiques
produce (n) *[food]*
produits (mpl)
maraîchers
produce (v) *[bring*
out] produire *ou*
présenter
produce (v) *[inter-*
est] rapporter
produce (v) *[make]*
produire *ou* fabriquer
producer (n)
producteur (-trice)
product (n)
produit (m)
product advertising
publicité (f) de
produit
product design
conception (f) de
produit
product development
développement (m)
de nouveau(x)
produit(s)

product engineer
ingénieur (m) produit
product line
gamme (f) *ou* ligne
(f) de produits
product mix éven-
tail (m) *ou* gamme
(f) de produits
production (n)
[making] fabrication
(f) *ou* production (f)
production *[show-
ing]* présentation (f)
production cost
coût (m) de produc-
tion *ou* prix (m) de
revient
**production depart-
ment** service (m)
de la production *ou*
de la fabrication
production line
chaîne (f) de
production
**production man-
ager** directeur de la
production *ou* chef
(m) de la fabrication
**production stan-
dards** niveau (m) de
qualité de production

production targets
objectifs (mpl) de
production
production unit
unité (f) *ou* centre
(m) de production
productive (adj)
productif (-ive)
**productive
discussions**
discussions (fpl)
productives
productivity (n)
productivité (f) *ou*
rendement (m)
**productivity agree-
ment** contrat (m)
de productivité
**productivity
bonus** prime (f) de
rendement
**professional
(adj)** *[expert]*
professionnel (-elle)
professional (n)
[expert] spécialiste
(m) *ou* expert (m)
**professional
qualifications**
qualifications (fpl)
professionnelles

profit (n) profit
(m) *ou* bénéfice (m)
ou gain (m)
profit after tax
bénéfice (m) après
impôts
**profit and loss
account** compte
(m) de résultat;
compte de pertes et
profits
profit before tax
bénéfice (m) avant
impôts
profit centre cen-
tre (m) de profit
profit margin marge
(f) bénéficiaire
profit-making (adj)
rentable
**profit-oriented
company** société
(f) à but lucratif
**profit-sharing
(scheme)**
intéressement (m)
ou participation (f)
aux bénéfices
profitability (n)
[making a profit]
rentabilité (f)

profitability *[ratio
of profit to cost]*
coefficient (m)
de rentabilité
profitable (adj)
rentable
**program (v) a com-
puter** programmer
un ordinateur
programme (n) *[plan]*
programme (m)
programme (n) *or*
program (n) *[com-
puter]* programme
(m) *ou* logiciel (m)
programming (n)
[computer]
programmation (f)
**programming lan-
guage** langage (m)
de programmation
progress (n)
progrès (m) *ou*
avancement (m)
progress (v) avancer
ou se dérouler
progress chaser res-
ponsable (mf) de suivi
progress payments
acomptes (mpl)
échelonnés

progress report rapport (m) d'avancement (du travail)
progressive (adj) progressif (-ive)
progressive taxation imposition (f) progressive
prohibitive (adj) exorbitant(e) *ou* inabordable
project (n) [plan] projet (m) *ou* plan (m)
project analysis analyse (f) de projet
project manager chef (m) de projet
projected (adj) prévu(e)
projected sales ventes (fpl) prévues
promise (n) promesse (f)
promise (v) promettre
promissory note billet (m) à ordre
promote (v) [advertise] faire de la publicité

promote (v) [give better job] donner de l'avancement *ou* promouvoir
promote a corporate image promouvoir l'image d'une société
promote a new product lancer un nouveau produit
promotion (n) [publicity] promotion (f)
promotion (n) [to better job] promotion (f)
promotion budget budget (m) promotionnel
promotion of a product promotion (f) d'un produit
promotional (adj) promotionnel (-elle)
promotional budget budget (m) promotionnel
prompt (adj) prompt(e) *ou* rapide
prompt payment paiement (m) immédiat

prompt service
service (m) rapide
proof (n) preuve (f)
proportion (n) part
(f) *ou* partie (f)
proportional (adj)
proportionnel (-elle)
proposal (n)
proposition (f)
proposal (n) *[insur-*
ance] proposition
(f) d'assurance
propose (v) *[a*
motion] proposer
propose to (v)
[do something]
proposer de
proprietary company
[US] holding (m)
proprietor (n)
propriétaire (mf)
proprietress (nf)
propriétaire (f)
prosecute (v) pour-
suivre en justice
prosecution (n)
[legal action] pour-
suites (fpl) judiciaires
prosecution *[party*
in legal action] la
partie plaignante *ou*
l'accusation (f)

prosecution
counsel procureur
(m) général
prospective (adj)
probable *ou* possible
prospective buyer
acheteur (m) poten-
tiel *ou* prospect (m)
prospects (n)
perspectives (fpl)
prospectus (n)
prospectus (m)
protective (adj)
protecteur (-trice)
protective tariff tarif
(m) protectionniste
protest (n)
[against something]
protestation (f)
protest (n) *[official*
document] protêt (m)
(pour non-paiement)
protest (v) *[against*
something]
protester contre
quelque chose
protest a bill
dresser un protêt
protest strike grève
(f) de protestation
provide (v) con-
stituer une provision

provide for (v)
tenir compte
de *ou* prévoir
provided that *or*
providing à condi-
tion (que *ou* de) *ou*
pourvu que
provision (n) *[con-*
dition] stipulation
(f) *ou* clause (f)
provision *[money*
put aside] provision
(f) *ou* réserve (f)
provisional (adj)
provisoire
provisional budget
budget (m)
provisoire
provisional forecast
of sales chiffres
(mpl) provisoires
des ventes
proviso (n)
condition (f)
proxy (n) *[deed]*
procuration (f)
proxy (n) *[person]*
fondé (m) de pouvoir
proxy vote vote
(m) par procuration
public (adj) public
(publique)

public finance
finances (fpl)
publiques
public funds fonds
(mpl) publics
public holiday jour
(m) férié
public image image
(m) de marque
Public Limited
Company (Plc)
société (f) anonyme
(S.A.) *[cotée en*
Bourse]
public opinion
opinion (f) publique
public relations
(PR) relations (fpl)
publiques
public relations
department service
(m) des relations
publiques
public relations
officer chargé(e)
des relations
publiques
public sector
secteur (m) public
public transport
transports (mpl)
en commun

publicity (n)
publicité (f)
publicity budget
budget (m)
publicitaire
publicity campaign
campagne (f)
publicitaire
publicity depart-
ment service (m)
de publicité
publicity expendi-
ture dépenses (fpl)
de publicité
publicity manager
chef (m) *ou* respon-
sable (mf) (du serv-
ice) de la publicité
publicize (v)
faire de la
publicité (pour)
punt *[Irish cur-*
rency] livre (f)
(irlandaise)
purchase (n) achat
(m) *ou* acquisition (f)
purchase (v)
acheter *ou* acquérir
purchase ledger
grand livre (m)
des achats

purchase order
commande (f) *ou*
ordre (m) d'achat
purchase price prix
(m) coûtant
purchase tax taxe
(f) à l'achat
purchaser (n)
acheteur (m) *ou*
acquéreur (m)
purchasing (n)
achat (m)
purchasing depart-
ment service (m)
des achats
purchasing manager
directeur (-trice) du
service des achats
purchasing power
pouvoir (m) d'achat
put (v) *[in a place]*
mettre *ou* fixer
put back (v) *[later]*
reporter *ou* remettre
(à plus tard)
put in writing mettre
par écrit *ou* rédiger
put money down
verser un acompte
pyramid (n) selling
vente (f) pyramidale

Qq

qty (= quantity)
quantité (f)
qualified (adj)
[skilled] qualifié(e)
qualified *[with reser-*
vations] sous réserve
qualify (v) (as)
se spécialiser *ou*
faire des études
spécialisées
quality (n) qualité (f)
quality control con-
trôle (m) de qualité
quality controller
responsable (mf) du
contrôle de qualité
quality label label
(m) de qualité
quantity (n) (qty)
quantité (f)
quantity discount
remise (f) sur quantité
quarter (n) *[25%]*
quart (m)
quarter *[three*
months]
trimestre (m)

quarter day jour
(m) de règlement
trimestriel
quarterly (adj)
trimestriel (-elle)
quarterly (adv)
trimestriellement *ou*
tous les trois mois
quay (n) quai (m)
quorum (n)
quorum (m)
quorum: have a
quorum atteindre
le quorum
quota (n) quota (m)
ou contingent (m)
quotation (n)
[estimate of cost]
devis (m)
quote (n) *[estimate*
of cost] devis (m)
quote (v) *[a refer-*
ence number] rap-
peler une référence
quote (v) *[estimate*
costs] citer *ou*
donner un prix
quoted (adj)
[company, shares]
coté(e) en Bourse

Rr

R&D (research and development) R et D (Recherche et développement)
racketeer (n) racketteur (m)
racketeering (n) racket (m)
rail (n) chemin (m) de fer
rail transport transport (m) par chemin de fer
railway *[GB]* **or railroad** *[US]* chemin (m) de fer
railway station gare (f) (de chemin de fer)
raise (v) *[increase]* augmenter
raise (v) *[obtain money]* se procurer des fonds *ou* des capitaux
raise an invoice rédiger une facture

raise (v) (a question) soulever (une question)
rally (n) reprise (f)
rally (v) remonter *ou* se redresser
random (adj) aléatoire
random check contrôle (m) aléatoire
random error erreur (f) aléatoire
random sample échantillon (m) aléatoire
random sampling échantillonnage (m) aléatoire
range (n) *[series of items]* gamme (f) *ou* variété (f)
range (n) *[variation]* éventail (m)
range (v) from ... to ... aller de ... à ... *ou* s'étendre de ... à ...
rate (n) *[amount]* taux (m)
rate (n) *[price]* tarif (m) *ou* prix (m)

rate of exchange
taux (m) de change
rate of inflation
taux (m) d'inflation
rate of
production taux
(m) de production
rate of return taux
(m) de rendement
ratification (n)
ratification (f)
ratify (v) ratifier
rating (n) *[credit]*
notation (f) *ou* note
(f) financière (d'une
société)
ratio (n) ratio (m) *ou*
rapport (m); taux (m)
rationalization (n)
rationalisation (f)
rationalize (v)
rationaliser
raw materials
matières (fpl)
premières
reach (v) *[arrive]*
atteindre
reach *[come to]*
arriver à
reach a decision
prendre une décision

reach an agreement
arriver à un accord
readjust (v)
rajuster *ou* réajuster
readjustment (n)
rajustement (m) *ou*
réajustement (m)
ready (adj) prêt(e)
ready cash argent
(m) comptant; cash
ready-to-wear
clothes confection (f)
ou prêt-à-porter (m)
real (adj) vrai(e)
ou véritable
real estate biens
(mpl) immobiliers
real estate agent
[US] agent (m)
immobilier
real income *or* real
wages revenu (m)
net *ou* salaire (m) net
real-time system
[computer] système
(m) en temps réel
realizable assets
actif (m) réalisable
realization of
assets réalisation
(f) d'actif

realize (v) [sell for money] réaliser [des biens, etc.]
realize (v) [understand] comprendre ou se rendre compte de
realize (v) a project or a plan réaliser un projet ou un plan
realize property or assets réaliser une propriété ou des biens
reapply (v) poser sa candidature une deuxième fois
reappoint (v) désigner de nouveau
reappointment (n) renouvellement (m) de mandat
reassess (v) réévaluer
reassessment (n) réévaluation (f)
rebate (n) [money back] remboursement (m) [d'un trop-perçu]
rebate [price reduction] remise (f) ou ristourne (f)

receipt (n) [paper] reçu (m) ou quittance (f)
receipt [receiving] réception (f)
receipt book carnet (m) de quittances
receipts (n) and expenditure recettes (fpl) et dépenses
receivable (adj) à recevoir
receivables (n) comptes (mpl) clients ou créances (fpl)
receive (v) recevoir; réceptionner [marchandises]
receiver (n) destinataire (mf)
receiver [liquidator] administrateur (m) judiciaire
receiving (n) réception (f)
reception (n) réception (f)
reception clerk réceptionniste (mf) ou préposé(e) à la réception

reception desk
bureau (m) de la
réception; bureau
d'accueil
receptionist (n)
réceptionniste (mf)
ou préposé(e) à la
réception
recession (n)
récession (f)
reciprocal (adj)
réciproque;
bilatéral(e)
reciprocal agree-
ment accord (m)
réciproque
reciprocal trade
commerce (m)
bilatéral
reciprocity (n)
réciprocité (f)
recognition (n)
reconnaissance (f)
recognize (v) a
union reconnaître
officiellement un
syndicat
recommend (v)
[say something is
good] recommander
[un produit, etc.]

recommend
[suggest action]
recommander *ou*
conseiller *[de faire*
quelque chose]
recommendation
(n) recommandation
(f) *ou* conseil (m)
reconcile (v)
rapprocher *ou* faire
concorder *[comptes]*
reconciliation (n)
réconciliation (f) *ou*
rapprochement (m)
reconciliation of
accounts rapproche-
ment (m) de comptes
reconciliation
statement état (m)
de rapprochement
(bancaire)
record (n)
[better than before]
record (m)
record (n) *[for*
personnel] état (m)
de service (d'un
employé)
record (n) *[of what*
has happened] rap-
port (m); registre (m)

record (v) noter
ou consigner *ou*
enregistrer
record sales *or*
record losses *or*
record profits
ventes record *ou*
pertes record *ou*
profits record
record: for the
record pour mémoire
record: off the
record en privé *ou*
officieusement
record: on record
publiquement *ou*
officiellement
record-breaking
record *ou* qui bat
tous les records
recorded delivery
envoi (m)
recommandé
records (n)
archives (fpl);
dossiers (mpl)
recoup (v) one's
losses récupérer
son argent *ou* se
dédommager de
ses pertes

recover (v) *[get*
better] se remettre;
se reprendre
recover *[get*
something back]
récupérer *ou* recou-
vrer *ou* retrouver
recoverable (adj)
récupérable *ou*
recouvrable
recovery (n) *[get-*
ting better] reprise
(f) *ou* relance (f)
[de l'économie]
recovery (n) *[get-*
ting something back]
recouvrement (m)
ou récupération (f)
rectification (n)
rectification (f)
rectify (v) rectifier
recurrent (adj) qui
revient; périodique
recycle (v)
recycler; se recycler
[personne]
recycled paper
papier (m) recyclé
red: in the red
dans le rouge;
(compte) débiteur

red tape
paperasserie (f)
administrative
redeem (v) rembourser *ou* amortir
redeem a bond
demander le
remboursement
d'une obligation
redeem a debt
rembourser
une dette
redeem a pledge
retirer un gage
redeemable (adj)
remboursable
redemption (n) *[of a loan]* remboursement (m) *ou*
amortissement (m)
[d'une dette]
redemption date
date (f) d'échéance
du remboursement
redevelop (v)
réaménager
redevelopment (n)
réaménagement (m)
[d'une zone]
redistribute (v)
redistribuer

reduce (v) réduire
ou diminuer
reduce a price
baisser un prix
reduce expenditure
réduire les dépenses
reduced (adj) *[on sale]* en solde
reduced (adj) rate
tarif (m) réduit
reduction (n)
réduction (f)
redundancy (n)
licenciement (m)
(économique)
redundant (adj)
(employé(e))
licencié(e)
re-elect (v) réélire
re-election (n)
réélection (f)
re-employ (v)
réembaucher *ou*
réemployer *ou*
réengager
re-employment (n)
réemploi (m)
re-export (n)
réexportation (f)
re-export (v)
réexporter

refer (v) *[pass to someone]* soumet-tre *ou* transmettre
refer to (v) *[go to]* se reporter à *ou* se référer à
refer to (v) *[mention]* mentionner
reference (n) *[dealing with]* référence (f)
reference *[person who reports]* répondant (m)
reference *[report on person]* référence (f) *ou* recommandation (f)
reference number numéro (m) de référence (f)
refinancing (n) of a loan refinancement (m) d'un prêt
refitting (n) *[of shop]* rénovation (f) *ou* réaménagement (m)
refresher course cours (m) *ou* stage (m) de recyclage
refund (n) remboursement (m)

refund (v) rembourser
refundable (adj) remboursable
refundable deposit avance (f) remboursable
refunding of a loan remboursement (m) d'un prêt
refusal (n) refus (m)
refuse (v) refuser
regarding concernant
regardless of malgré *ou* sans considération de
regional (adj) régional(e)
register (n) *[large book]* registre (m)
register (n) *[official list]* registre (m) *ou* état (m) *ou* liste (f)
register (v) *[at hotel]* se faire enreg-istrer *ou* s'inscrire
register (v) *[in official list]* enregistrer *ou* inscrire *ou* immatriculer

register (v) *[letter]*
recommander (une
lettre)
**register (v) a com-
pany** immatriculer
une société
register a property
inscrire une pro-
priété au cadastre
**register a trade-
mark** déposer une
marque de commerce
**register (n) of
directors** register
(m) des administra-
teurs d'une société
**register of share-
holders** registre
(m) des actionnaires
registered (adj)
enregistré(e)
registered design
modèle déposé
registered letter
lettre (f)
recommandée
registered office
siège (m) social
**registered trade-
mark** marque (f)
déposée

registrar (n) officier
(m) de l'état civil
**Registrar of
Companies** greffier
(m) du tribunal de
commerce
registration (n)
enregistrement (m)
registration fee
droit (m) d'enreg-
istrement *ou* droit
d'inscription
registration form
formulaire (m)
d'inscription
**registration num-
ber** numéro (m)
d'enregistrement *ou*
d'immatriculation
registry (n)
bureau (m)
d'enregistrement
registry office
*[births, marriages,
deaths]* bureau (m)
de l'état civil
regular (adj)
*[always at same
time]*
régulier (-ière) *ou*
habituel (-elle)

regular [ordinary]
ordinaire *ou*
normal(e)
regular customer
client(e) fidèle
regular income
salaire régulier
regular size taille
normale
regular staff
personnel régulier
regulate (v)
[adjust] régler *ou*
ajuster
**regulate (v) [by
law]** réglementer
regulation (n)
réglementation (f)
regulations (n)
règlements (mpl)
reimbursement (n)
remboursement (m)
**reimbursement of
expenses** rembourse-
ment (m) des frais
reimport (n)
[action]
réimportation (f)
reimport (n)
[goods] marchan-
dise (f) réimportée

reimport (v)
réimporter
reimportation (n)
réimportation (f)
reinsurance (n)
réassurance (f)
reinsure (v)
réassurer
reinsurer (n)
compagnie (f) de
réassurance
reinvest (v)
réinvestir
reinvestment (n)
réinvestissement (m)
reject (n) article
imparfait; article
(m) de rebut
reject (v) rejeter
ou refuser
rejection (n)
refus (m)
**relating to *or* in rela-
tion to** se rapportant
à *ou* relatif (-ive) à
relations (n)
relations (fpl)
release (v) [free]
libérer
**release (v) [make
public]** publier

release (v) *[put on the market]* mettre en vente

release dues liquider les commandes en attente

relevant (adj) approprié(e)

reliability (n) fiabilité (f)

reliable (adj) honnête *ou* fiable *ou* sûr(e)

remain (v) *[be left]* rester

remain *[stay]* demeurer

remainder (n) *[things left]* reste (m) *ou* reliquat (m)

remind (v) rappeler à

reminder (n) lettre (f) de rappel

remit (n) compétence (f)

remit (v) régler

remit by cheque régler par chèque

remittance (n) règlement (m)

remote control télécommande (f)

removal (n) *[sacking someone]* renvoi (m)

removal *[to new house]* déménagement (m)

remove (v) enlever *ou* supprimer

remunerate (v) rémunérer *ou* rétribuer

remuneration (n) rémunération (f)

render (v) an account présenter un compte *ou* facturer

renew (v) renouveler

renew a bill of exchange prolonger une traite

renew a lease renouveler un bail

renew a subscription renouveler un abonnement

renewal (n) renouvellement (m)

renewal notice avis (m) de renouvellement

renewal of a bill
prolongation (f)
d'une traite
renewal of a lease
renouvellement
d'un bail
**renewal of a
subscription**
renouvellement
d'un abonnement
renewal premium
prime (f) de
renouvellement
rent (n) loyer (m)
rent (v) *[pay money
for]* louer *[prendre
en location]*
rent collector
receveur (m) des
loyers
rent control
contrôle (m) des
loyers
rent tribunal
commission (f)
du logement
rent-free sans
payer de loyer
rental (n) loyer
(m) *ou* prix (m) de
location

rental income
revenu (m) locatif
renunciation (n)
abandon (m)
(d'actions)
reorder (n)
commande (f) de
réapprovisionnement
reorder (v) renou-
veler une commande
ou se réapprovisionner
reorder level
niveau (m) de réap-
provisionnement
reorganization
réorganisation (f)
reorganize (v)
réorganiser
**rep (representa-
tive)** délégué(e)
commercial(e) *ou*
représentant(e) *ou*
VRP (mf)
repair (n)
réparation (f)
repair (v) réparer
ou remettre en état
repay (v)
rembourser
repayable (adj)
remboursable

repayment (n)
remboursement (m)
repeat (v) répéter
repeat an order
renouveler une
commande
repeat order nou-
velle commande (f)
ou commande de
réapprovisionnement
replace (v) remplacer
replacement (n)
[item]
remplacement (m)
replacement [per-
son] remplaçant(e)
replacement value
valeur (f) de
remplacement
reply (n) réponse (f)
reply (v) répondre
reply coupon
coupon-réponse (m)
report (n)
rapport (m)
report (v) signaler;
faire un rapport
report (v) *[go to a*
place] se présenter
report a loss
annoncer un déficit

report for an inter-
view se présenter
à un entretien
report on (v) the
progress of the work
rendre compte de l'a-
vancement du travail
report to someone
relever (directe-
ment) de quelqu'un
repossess (v)
saisir *[un article*
non payé]
repossession (n)
saisie (f)
represent (v)
représenter; faire de
la représentation
representative
(adj) représentatif
(-tive)
representative (n)
[company]
représentant (m)
representative (n)
[person]
délégué(e) commer-
cial(e) *ou* représen-
tant(e) *ou* VRP (mf)
repudiate (v)
rejeter *ou* refuser

repudiate an agreement refuser d'honorer un accord
request (n) demande (f) *ou* requéte (f)
request (v) demander *ou* solliciter
request: on request sur demande
require (v) [demand] demander *ou* réclamer *ou* exiger
require (v) [need] nécessiter
requirements (n) besoins (mpl)
resale (n) revente (f)
resale price prix (m) de revente
resale price maintenance régime (m) *ou* politique (f) des prix imposés
rescind (v) annuler *ou* résilier *[un contrat]*
research (n) recherche (f) *ou* étude (f)

research (v) faire une étude *ou* faire des recherches (sur)
research and development (R & D) Recherche et développement (R et D)
research programme programme (m) de recherche
researcher (n) chercheur (-euse)
reservation (n) réservation (f)
reserve (n) [money] réserve (f)
reserve (n) [supplies] réserves (fpl) *ou* provisions (fpl)
reserve (v) [book] réserver *ou* retenir
reserve a room *or* a table *or* a seat retenir une chambre *ou* réserver une table *ou* réserver une place
reserve currency monnaie (f) de réserve

reserve price prix
(m) minimum fixé;
mise (f) à prix
reserves (n) *[kept
in case of need]*
réserves (fpl)
residence (n)
[staying] résidence
(f) *ou* séjour (m)
residence permit
carte (f) de séjour
resident (adj)
résident(e)
resident (n)
résident(e)
resign (v)
démissionner
resignation (n)
démission (f)
resolution (n)
résolution (f)
resolve (v) décider
resources (n)
ressources (fpl)
respect (v) respecter
response (n)
réaction (f)
responsibilities (n)
responsabilités (fpl)
responsibility (n)
responsabilité (f)

**responsible (for)
(adj)** responsable de
**responsible to
someone** relever
(directement) de
quelqu'un
restock (v) se
réapprovisionner
restocking (n)
réapprovision-
nement (m)
restraint (n)
contrôle (m) *ou*
restriction (f)
restraint of trade
limitation (f) à la
liberté du commerce
restrict (v) limiter
restrict credit
limiter le crédit
restriction (n)
restriction (f) *ou*
limitation (f)
restrictive (adj)
restrictif (-ive)
**restrictive
practices** pratiques
(fpl) restrictives
restructure (v)
restructurer *ou*
réorganiser

restructuring (n)
restructuration (f)
ou réorganisation (f)
**restructuring of a
loan** reconfigura-
tion (f) d'un
emprunt
**restructuring of
the company**
restructuration (f)
d'une société
result (n) *[general]*
résultat (m)
result from (v)
découler de *ou*
provenir de
result in (v) avoir
pour résultat de *ou*
aboutir à
results (n)
***[company's
profit or loss]***
résultats (mpl)
resume (v) recom-
mencer *ou* reprendre
**resume negotia-
tions** reprendre les
négociations
retail (n) détail
(m) *ou* vente (f) au
détail

retail (v) *[goods]*
vendre des marchan-
dises au détail
**retail (v) *[sell for a
price]*** se vendre à
retail dealer
détaillant(e);
revendeur (m)
retail (v) goods
vendre des
marchandises
au détail
retail (n) outlets
magasins (mpl)
(de détail)
retail price prix
(m) de détail
retail price index
indice (m) des prix
à la consommation
retailer (n)
détaillant(e)
retailing (n) détail
(m) *ou* vente (f) au
détail
**retire (v) *[from
one's job]*** prendre
sa retraite *ou* partir
à la retraite
retirement (n)
retraite (f)

retirement age âge
(m) de la retraite
retiring (adj) *[at
end of elected term]*
sortant(e)
retrain (v) recycler
quelqu'un; se
recycler
retraining (n)
recyclage (m)
retrenchment (n)
compression (f)
des dépenses
retrieval (n)
recherche (f)
retrieval system
système (m) de
recherche (de
données)
retrieve (v)
retrouver; extraire
(des données)
retroactive (adj)
rétroactif (-ive)
**retroactive pay
rise** rappel (m)
(de salaire)
return (n) *[declara-
tion]* déclaration (f)
return (n) *[going
back]* retour (m)

return (n) *[profit]*
revenu (m) *ou*
rendement (m)
return (n) *[sending
back]* retour (m)
return (v) *[declare]*
déclarer
return (v) *[send
back]* renvoyer *ou*
retourner
**return a letter to
sender** renvoyer
une lettre à
l'expéditeur;
retour à l'envoyeur
return address
adresse (f) de
retour *ou* de
l'expéditeur
**return on
investment (ROI)**
rentabilité (f) d'un
investissement
returnable (adj)
consigné(e)
returned empties
bouteilles (fpl)
consignées
returns (n) *[prof-
its]* recettes (fpl)
ou rentrées (fpl)

returns (n)
[unsold goods]
invendus (mpl)
revaluation (n)
réévaluation (f)
revalue (v)
réévaluer
revenue (n)
recette (f) *ou* ren-
trée (f); revenu (m)
revenue accounts
compte (m) de
produits
revenue from
advertising recettes
(fpl) publicitaires
reversal (n)
revers (m)
reverse (adj)
inverse
reverse (v)
inverser *ou* faire
marche arrière
reverse charge call
[phone] appel (m)
en PCV
reverse takeover
contre-OPA (f)
reverse (v) the
charges appeler
en PCV

revise (v) réviser
revoke (v)
révoquer *ou* annuler
revolving credit
crédit (m)
permanent *ou*
renouvelable
rider clause (f)
supplémentaire
ou avenant (m)
right (adj) *[not*
left] droit(e); de
droite
right (adj) *[not*
wrong] correct(e);
exact(e) *ou* juste
right (n) *[legal*
title] droit (m)
right of veto droit
(m) de veto
right of way *[on*
land] servitude (f)
rightful (adj)
légal(e) *ou* légitime
rightful claimant
ayant droit (m)
rightful owner
propriétaire (mf)
légitime
right-hand man
bras (m) droit

rights issue
[shares] émission
(f) prioritaire
rise (n) [increase]
augmentation (f)
rise (n) [salary]
augmentation (f)
(de salaire)
rise (v) augmenter
risk (n) risque (m)
risk (v) [money]
risquer
risk capital
capital-risque (m)
risk premium
prime (f) de risques
risk-free investment
placement (m) sûr
risky (adj)
risqué(e) *ou*
hasardeux (-euse)
rival company
société (f)
concurrente
road (n) route (f)
road haulage
transports (mpl)
routiers
road haulier
entreprise (f) de
transports routiers

road tax taxe (f)
différentielle sur les
véhicules (à moteur)
road transport
transports (mpl)
routiers
rock-bottom prices
prix (mpl) les
plus bas
**ROI (return on
investment)**
rentabilité (f) d'un
investissement
**roll on/roll off
ferry** ferry (m) *ou*
car-ferry (m)
**rollout (n) [of
product]**
lancement (m)
**roll over (v) credit
or a debt**
reconduire un crédit
ou une dette
rolling plan plan
(m) continu
room (n) [general]
pièce (f) *ou* salle (f)
room [hotel]
chambre (f) d'hôtel
room [space]
place (f)

room reservations
bureau (m) de
réservation des
chambres
room service service
(m) des chambres
rough (adj)
approximatif (-ive)
ou sommaire
rough calculation
calcul (m)
approximatif
rough draft
brouillon (m)
rough estimate
estimation (f)
approximative
round down (v)
arrondir au chiffre
inférieur
round up (v)
arrondir au chiffre
supérieur
routine (adj) de
routine *ou* routinier
(-ière)
routine (n) routine
(f); de routine
royalty (n) royalties
(fpl) *ou* redevances
(fpl) *[d'auteur, etc.]*

rubber check *[US]*
chèque (m) en bois
ou sans provision
rule (n) règle (f)
rule (v) *[be in force]*
être en vigueur
**rule (v) *[give deci-
sion]*** déclarer *ou*
statuer
ruling (adj) actuel
(-elle) *ou* courant(e)
ou en vigueur
ruling (n) décision
(f) *ou* jugement (m)
**run (n) *[regular
route]*** parcours (m)
**run (n) [work rou-
tine]*** exécution (f);
série (f) *ou*
séquence (f)
run (v) *[be in force]*
être valable *ou*
durer
**run (v) *[buses,
trains]*** fonctionner
ou être en service
run (v) *[manage]*
diriger *ou* gérer
**run (v) *[work
machine]*** faire
fonctionner

run a risk courir un risque

run into debt s'endetter

run out of manquer de

run to monter *ou* s'élever à

running (n) *[of machine]* marche (f) *ou* fonctionnement (m)

running costs *or* running expenses coûts opérationnels *ou* coûts d'exploitation

running total total (m) reporté

rush (n) ruée (f)

rush (v) accélérer *ou* activer

rush hour heures (fpl) de pointe

rush job travail (m) urgent *ou* travail d'urgence

rush order commande (f) urgente

Ss

sack someone renvoyer *ou* licencier quelqu'un

safe (adj) sûr(e); en sûreté

safe (n) coffre-fort (m)

safe deposit dépôt (m) en coffre-fort

safe investment placement (m) sûr

safeguard (v) sauvegarder *ou* protéger

safety (n) sécurité (f)

safety measures *or* safety precautions mesures (fpl) de sécurité

safety regulations consignes (fpl) de sécurité

salaried (adj) salarié(e)

salary (n) salaire (m)

salary cheque
chèque (m) de
salaire
salary review révi-
sion (f) de salaire
**sale (n) [at a low
price]** solde (m)
sale (n) [selling]
vente (f)
sale: on sale en
vente
sale by auction vente
(f) aux enchères
sale or return
vente (f) à condition
ou avec possibilité
de reprise des
invendus
saleability (n)
qualité (f)
marchande
saleable (adj)
vendable
**sales (n) [clearance
sale]** soldes
(mpl & fpl)
sales (n) [selling]
ventes (fpl)
sales analysis
analyse (f) des
ventes

sales book
[accounts] journal
(m) des ventes
sales budget budget
(m) commercial
sales campaign
campagne
commerciale
sales chart
diagramme (m) des
ventes ou courbe (f)
des ventes
sales clerk vendeur
(m) ou vendeuse (f)
sales conference
réunion (f) du
service commercial
sales curve courbe
(f) des ventes
sales department
service (m)
commercial
sales executive
directeur (-trice)
commercial(e)
sales figures chiffre
(m) des ventes;
chiffre d'affaires
sales force équipe
(f) de vente ou
force (f) de vente

sales forecast prévisions (fpl) des ventes
sales ledger grand livre (m) des ventes
sales ledger clerk employé(e) aux écritures (du grand livre des ventes)
sales literature brochures (fpl) *ou* prospectus (mpl)
sales manager directeur (-trice) commercial(e)
sales people commerciaux (mpl)
sales pitch baratin (m) (d'un vendeur)
sales promotion promotion (f) des ventes
sales receipt ticket (m) de caisse
sales representative représentant(e) *ou* délégué(e) commercial(e) *ou* VRP (mf)
sales revenue produit (m) des ventes; chiffre (m) d'affaires

sales target objectif (m) de vente
sales tax taxe (f) sur les ventes
sales team équipe (f) de vente; commerciaux (mpl)
sales volume volume (m) des ventes
salesman (n) *[in shop]* vendeur (m)
salesman *[representative]* représentant (m) *ou* délégué commercial
saleswoman (n) *[in shop]* vendeuse (f)
saleswoman *[representative]* représentante (f) *ou* déléguée commerciale
salvage (n) *[action]* sauvetage (m)
salvage (n) *[things saved]* matériel (m) sauvé *ou* récupéré
salvage (v) sauver *ou* effectuer un sauvetage

sample (n)
[group, part]
échantillon (m)
sample (v) *[ask questions]* faire un
sondage (d'opinion)
sample (v) *[test]*
essayer; *[tasting]*
goûter
sampling *[statistics, testing]*
échantillonnage (m)
satisfaction (n)
satisfaction (f)
satisfy (v) *[customer]* satisfaire
satisfy a demand
répondre à *ou* satisfaire à la demande
saturate (v) saturer
saturate the market
saturer le marché
saturation (n)
saturation (f)
save (v) *[money]*
économiser *ou* faire
des économies
save (v) *[not waste]* économiser
save (v) *[on computer]* sauvegarder

save on (v)
économiser
save up (v)
épargner *ou*
économiser
savings (n)
économies (fpl)
savings account
compte (m) d'épargne
savings bank
banque (f) d'épargne
scale (n) *[system]*
échelle (f) *ou*
barème (m)
scale down (v)
réduire suivant un
barème
scale (n) of charges
tarif (m) *ou* barème
(m) des prix
scale up (v)
augmenter suivant
un barème
scarcity value
valeur (f) de rareté
scheduled flight
vol (m) régulier
scheduling (n)
établissement (m)
d'un plan *ou* d'un
programme

scheduling of worktime aménagement (n) du temps de travail
screen (v) (candidates) sélectionner (des candidats)
scrip (n) [share, bond, etc.] titre (m)
scrip issue émission (f) d'actions gratuites
seal (n) sceau (m)
seal (v) [attach a seal] sceller
seal (v) [envelope] fermer *ou* cacheter (une enveloppe)
sealed envelope enveloppe (f) fermée *ou* cachetée
sealed tenders soumissions (fpl) cachetées
season (n) [time for something] saison (f)
season [time of year] saison (f)
season ticket carte (f) d'abonnement
seasonal (adj) saisonnier (-ière)

seasonal adjustments corrections (fpl) des variations saisonnières
seasonal demand demande saisonnière
seasonal variations variations (fpl) saisonnières
seasonally adjusted figures chiffres (mpl) désaisonnalisés *ou* chiffres corrigés des variations saisonnières
second (adj) deuxième *ou* second(e)
second (v) [member of staff] détacher
second quarter deuxième trimestre (m)
second-class de deuxième classe; de seconde [train]
secondary industry industrie (f) de transformation *ou* secteur (m) secondaire

secondhand (adj)
d'occasion
seconds (n) arti-
cles (mpl) déclassés
ou de second choix
secret (adj)
secret (-ète)
secret (n)
secret (m)
secretarial college
école (f) de
secrétariat
secretary (n)
secrétaire (mf)
**secretary [company
official]** secrétaire
général(e)
**secretary [govern-
ment minister]**
ministre (mf)
sector (n)
secteur (m)
secure (v) funds se
procurer des fonds
**secure (adj)
investment**
placement (m) sûr
secure (adj) job
emploi (m) sûr
secured creditor
créancier privilégié

secured debts
dettes (fpl)
garanties
secured loan
emprunt (m) garanti
securities (n)
titres (mpl) *ou*
valeurs (fpl)
**Securities and
Investment Board
(SIB)** Commission
(f) des opérations
de Bourse (COB)
**security (n) [being
safe]** sécurité (f)
**security (n) [guar-
antee]** garantie (f)
ou caution (f)
security guard
vigile (m) *ou* gardien
(m) de la sécurité
**security of employ-
ment** sécurité (f)
de l'emploi
**security of tenure
[job]** stabilité (f)
d'emploi
**security of tenure
[rented home]** droit
(m) d'occupation
d'un logement

see-safe (n) vente (f) avec possibilité de retour des invendus

seize (v) saisir *ou* confisquer

seizure (n) saisie (f) *ou* confiscation (f)

selection (n) sélection (f) *ou* choix (m)

selection procedure procédure (f) de sélection

self-employed (adj) indépendant(e) *ou* qui travaille à son compte

self-financed (adj) autofinancé(e)

self-financing (adj) qui peut s'autofinancer

self-financing (n) autofinancement (m)

self-regulation (n) autorégulation (f)

self-regulatory (adj) autorégula-teur (-trice)

sell (v) vendre

sell forward vendre à terme

sell off liquider *ou* écouler

sell out [all stock] vendre la totalité du stock

sell out [sell one's business] vendre son entreprise

sell-by date date (f) limite de vente

seller (n) vendeur (m)

seller's market marché (m) à la hausse

selling (n) vente (f)

selling price prix (m) de vente

semi-finished products produits (mpl) semi-finis

semi-skilled workers ouvriers (mpl) spécialisés

send (v) envoyer *ou* expédier

send a package by airmail expédier un paquet par avion

send a package by surface mail expédier un colis par courrier ordinaire

send a shipment by sea expédier des marchandises par mer *ou* par bateau

send an invoice by post envoyer une facture par la poste

sender (n) expéditeur (-trice)

senior (adj) plus âgé(e); plus important(e)

senior manager *or* senior executive cadre (m) supérieur

senior partner associé(e) principal(e)

separate (adj) séparé(e)

separate (v) diviser

separate: under separate cover sous pli séparé

sequester (v) *or* sequestrate (v) séquestrer *ou* mettre sous séquestre

sequestration (n) séquestration (f) *ou* mise (f) sous séquestre

sequestrator (n) administrateur (m) séquestre *ou* séquestre (m)

serial number numéro (m) de série

series (n) série (f)

serve (v) servir

serve a customer servir un client

service (n) *[company, bureau]* société (f) de services

service (n) *[dealing with customers]* service (m)

service (n) *[of machine]* entretien (m) *ou* maintenance (f)

service (n) *[train, bus]* service (m)

service (n) *[working for a company]* service (m)

service (v) *[a machine]* entretenir; réviser *[une machine]*
service a debt servir *ou* payer les intérêts d'une dette
service centre atelier (m) de réparations
service charge service (m)
service department service (m) d'entretien
service industry industrie (f) de services *[secteur tertiaire]*
service manual manuel (m) d'entretien
set (adj) fixé(e)
set (n) jeu (m) *ou* ensemble (m)
set (v) fixer
set against déduire
set (adj) price prix (m) imposé *ou* prix fixe
set (v) targets fixer des objectifs

set up (v) a company créer *ou* constituer *ou* fonder une société
set up in business monter *ou* démarrer une affaire; s'établir
setting up costs frais (mpl) de mise en route *ou* d'établissement
setback (n) revers (m) *ou* recul (m)
settle (v) *[an invoice]* payer *ou* régler (une facture)
settle *[arrange things]* (s')arranger
settle a claim payer des dommages-intérêts *ou* indemniser
settle an account régler un compte
settlement *[agreement]* accord (m)
settlement *[payment]* règlement (m) *ou* paiement (m)
setup (n) *[company]* boîte (f)

setup *[organization]*
organisation (f)
share (n) part (f)
**share (n) *[in a com-*
*pany]*** action (f)
**share (v) *[divide*
*among]*** partager
**share (v) *[use with*
*someone]*** partager
share an office
partager un bureau
share capital
capital-actions (m)
share certificate
certificat (m)
d'action(s)
share issue émis-
sion (f) d'actions
shareholder (n)
actionnaire (mf)
shareholding (n)
actions (f);
participation (f)
sharp practice
combine (f) *ou*
pratique (f)
malhonnête
sheet (n) of paper
feuille (f) de papier
shelf (n) étagère
(f) *ou* rayon (m)

shelf filler
employé(e) qui
réassortit les stocks
sur les rayons
shelf life of a
product durée (f)
de conservation
d'un produit
shell (n) company
société (f) prête-nom
shelter (n) abri (m)
shelve (v)
repousser *ou*
ajourner; abandon-
ner *[un projet]*
**shelving (n) *[post-*
*poning]*** ajournement
(m); abandon (n)
shelving *[shelves]*
rayonnage (m)
shift (n) *[change]*
mouvement (m) *ou*
changement (m)
**shift (n) *[team of*
*workers]*** équipe (f)
**shift key *[on key-*
*board]*** touche (f)
de majuscules
shift work travail
(m) posté *ou* travail
par équipe

ship (n) navire (m)
ship (v) expédier
ou envoyer
ship broker courtier
(m) maritime
shipment (n)
[goods] envoi (m)
ou chargement (m)
shipment (n) *[send-
ing]* envoi (m) *ou*
expédition (f)
shipper (n)
expéditeur (m)
shipping (n)
[sending] envoi (m)
ou expédition (f)
shipping agent
[maritime] agent
(m) maritime
shipping charges *or*
shipping costs frais
(mpl) de transport
shipping clerk
expéditionnaire (m)
shipping company
or shipping line
compagnie (f) de
navigation
shipping instructions
instructions (fpl)
pour l'expédition

shipping note note
(f) de chargement
ou billet (m) de bord
shop (n)
magasin (m)
shop around com-
parer les prix *[dans
différents magasins]*
shop assistant
vendeur (-euse)
shop window vitrine
(f) *[d'un magasin]*
shop-soiled (adj)
défraîchi(e)
shopkeeper (n)
commerçant(e)
shoplifter (n) voleur
(-euse) à l'étalage
shoplifting (n) vol
(m) à l'étalage *ou*
vol dans les rayons
shopper (n) acheteur
(-euse) *ou* client(e)
shopping (n)
[action]
courses (fpl)
shopping *[goods
bought]* achats (mpl)
shopping arcade
galerie (f)
marchande

shopping centre
centre (m)
commercial
shopping mall
galerie (f) marchande
shopping precinct
zone (f) piétonnière
**shopping: go
shopping** faire des
courses
short (adj) court(e)
**short credit [short-
term credit]** crédit
(m) à court terme
short: be short of
être à court de *ou* ne
pas avoir assez de
short-dated bills
effets (mpl) à
courte échéance
short-term (adj) à
court terme
**short-term contract
[work]** contrat (m)
à durée déterminée
short-term credit
crédit (m) à court
terme
short-term debts
dettes (fpl) à court
terme

short-term loan
emprunt (m) à court
terme; prêt (m)
à court terme
shortage (n) manque
(m) *ou* pénurie (f)
shortfall (n) déficit
(m) *ou* manqué (m)
shorthand (n)
sténo(graphie) (f)
**shorthand: take
shorthand** prendre
en sténo
shortlist (n) liste
(f) de sélection
shortlist (v)
sélectionner (des
candidats)
shorts (n)
obligations (fpl) à
court terme
**show (n) [exhibi-
tion]** salon (m) *ou*
exposition (f)
show (v) révéler
ou faire apparaître
show (v) a profit
révéler un bénéfice
**show (n) of hands
[vote]** vote (m) à
main levée

showcase (n) vitrine (f) *[armoire vitrée]*
showroom (n) salle (f) d'exposition
shrink-wrapped (adj) sous emballage pelliculé *ou* sous film
shrink-wrapping (n) emballage (m) pelliculé *ou* emballage sous film
shrink-wrapping *[action]* pelliculage (m)
shrinkage (n) rétrécissement (m); diminution (f)
shrinkage (n) *[losses of stock]* coulage (m)
shut (adj) fermé(e)
shut (v) fermer
SIB (Securities and Investment Board) COB (= Commission (f) des opérations de Bourse)
side (n) côté (m)
sideline (n) activité (f) secondaire

sight (n) vue (f)
sight draft traite (f) à vue
sign (n) panneau (m) publicitaire *ou* enseigne (f)
sign (v) (a cheque, a contract) signer (un chèque, un contrat)
signatory (n) signataire (mf)
signature (n) signature (f)
simple interest intérêts (mpl) simples
single (adj) simple *ou* unique
Single European Market Marché (m) unique
sister company société-soeur (f)
sister ship sistership (m)
sit-down protest *or* **sit-down strike** grève (f) sur le tas
site (n) site (m) *ou* emplacement (m)

site engineer
ingénieur (m) de
chantier
sitting tenant
locataire (mf)
occupant les lieux
situated (adj)
situé(e)
situation (n) [place]
emplacement (m) *ou*
situation (f)
**situation (n) [state
of affairs]** situation
(f) *ou* état (m)
**situations vacant
[jobs]** offres (fpl)
d'emploi; postes
(mpl) à pourvoir
size (n) taille (f)
skeleton staff per-
sonnel (m) réduit *ou*
personnel de base
skill (n) aptitude
(f) *ou* talent (m);
technique (f)
skilled (adj)
qualifié(e)
**skilled labour *or*
skilled workers**
ouvriers (mpl)
qualifiés

slack (adj)
peu actif (-ive)
slash (v) prices
casser les prix
**slash (v) credit
terms** réduire le
crédit
sleeping partner
associé commandi-
taire (m); bailleur
(m) de fonds
slip (n) [mistake]
erreur (f)
**slip (n) [piece of
paper]** fiche (f);
bordereau (m)
slow (adj) lent(e)
slow down (v)
ralentir
slow payer
mauvais payeur
slowdown (n)
ralentissement (m)
**slump (n) [depres-
sion]** crise (f)
économique *ou*
marasme (m)
**slump (n) [rapid
fall]** chute (f) *ou*
effondrement (m)
slump (v) s'effondrer

slump in sales
effondrement (m)
des ventes
small (adj) petit(e)
small ads petites
annonces
small businesses
petites entreprises;
petites et moyennes
entreprises (PME)
small businessman
petit patron
small change
petite monnaie
small-scale peu
important(e) *ou*
modeste
small-scale
enterprise petite
entreprise
SME (small and
medium-sized
businesses) PME
(petites et moyennes
entreprises)
soar (v) monter en
flèche
social (adj)
social(e)
social costs coûts
(mpl) sociaux

social security
sécurité (f) sociale
social security
contributions con-
tribution (f) sociale
généralisée (CSG)
society (n) *[club]*
club (m) *ou*
société (f)
society *[general]*
société (f)
socio-economic
groups groupes
(mpl) socio-
économiques
soft currency
devise (f) faible
soft loan prêt (m)
bonifié *ou* de faveur
soft sell vente (f)
non aggressive
software (n) *[com-*
puter] programme
(m) *ou* logiciel (m)
sole (adj) seul(e)
ou exclusif (-ive)
sole agency contrat
(m) d'exclusivité
sole agent agent
(m) exclusif *ou* con-
cessionnaire exclusif

sole owner seul propriétaire (m)
sole trader commerçant (m) indépendant *ou* seul propriétaire
solicitor (n) *[GB]* notaire (mf); avocat(e)
solution (n) solution (f)
solve (v) a problem résoudre un problème
solvency (n) solvabilité (f)
solvent (adj) solvable
source (n) of income source (f) de revenus
spare part pièce (f) détachée *ou* pièce de rechange
spare time temps (m) libre
special (adj) spécial(e)
special drawing rights (SDRs) droits (mpl) de tirage spéciaux (DTS)

special offer offre (f) spéciale *ou* promotion (f)
specialist (n) spécialiste (mf)
specialization spécialisation (f)
specialize se spécialiser
specifications (n) specifications (fpl); cahier (m) des charges *[d'un contrat]*
specify (v) spécifier *ou* indiquer
speech (n) of thanks discours (m) de remerciement
spend (v) *[money]* dépenser
spend *[time]* consacrer du temps à *ou* passer du temps à
spending money argent (m) pour les dépenses courantes
spending power pouvoir (m) d'achat
spinoff (n) produit (m) dérivé

spoil (n) abîmer *ou* endommager; gâcher
sponsor (n) sponsor (m) *ou* commanditaire (m)
sponsor (v) sponsoriser *ou* commanditer *ou* parrainer
sponsorship sponsorisation (f) *ou* parrainage (m)
spot (n) *[place]* endroit (m)
spot cash argent (m) comptant
spot price prix (m) au comptant *ou* prix spot
spot purchase achat (m) immédiat
spread (v) a risk répartir un risque
spreadsheet (n) *[computer printout]* tableau (m)
spreadsheet (n) *[program]* tableur (m)
stability (n) stabilité (f)

stabilization (n) stabilisation (f)
stabilize (v) stabiliser *ou* se stabiliser
stable (adj) stable
stable currency monnaie (f) stable
stable economy économie (f) stable
stable exchange rate taux (m) de change stable
stable prices prix stables
staff (n) personnel (m)
staff (v) employer du personnel
staff (n) appointment nomination (f) au niveau du personnel
staff meeting réunion (f) du personnel
stage (n) phase (f) *ou* stade (m) *ou* étape (f)
stage (v) *[organize]* mettre sur pied

stage a recovery
se remettre *ou* se
redresser
staged (adj)
payments
paiements (mpl)
échelonnés
stagger (v) étaler
ou échelonner
stagnant (adj)
stagnant(e)
stagnation (n)
stagnation (f)
stamp (n) [device]
tampon (m) *ou*
timbre (m)
stamp (n) [post]
timbre (m) *ou*
timbre-poste (m)
stamp (v) [letter]
affranchir *ou* timbrer
[coller un timbre]
stamp (v) [mark]
tamponner
stamp duty droit
(m) de timbre
stand (n) [at exhi-
bition] stand (m)
stand down (v) se
désister *ou* se
démettre

stand security for
[loan] avaliser *ou*
garantir *[un*
emprunt, un prêt]
stand surety for
(someone) se
porter garant de *ou*
se porter caution
pour (quelqu'un)
standard (adj) ordi-
naire *ou* standard
standard (n)
standard (m) *ou*
norme (f)
standard letter
lettre (f) standard
ou lettre type
standard rate (of
tax) taux (m)
d'imposition moyen
standardization (n)
standardisation (f)
ou normalisation (f)
standardize (v)
standardiser *ou*
normaliser
standby arrange-
ments [IMF] accord
(m) (de crédit) de
confirmation *ou*
accord stand-by

standby credit
crédit (m) d'appoint
ou de soutien *ou*
crédit stand-by
standby ticket
billet (m) (d'avion)
stand-by
standing (n)
standing (m) *ou*
réputation (f)
standing order
(ordre de)
prélèvement (m)
automatique
staple (n) agrafe (f)
staple (v) agrafer
**staple (adj) indus-
try** industrie (f)
principale *ou* de base
**staple (v) papers
together** attacher
des feuilles avec
une agrafe
staple (adj) product
produit (m) principal
stapler (n)
agrafeuse (f)
start (n)
commencement (m)
ou démarrage (m)
ou début (m)

start (v)
commencer *ou*
démarrer *ou* débuter
start-up (n)
démarrage (m)
(d'une affaire,
d'un produit)
start-up costs frais
(mpl) de démarrage
ou d'établissement
starting (adj)
de départ
starting date date
(f) d'ouverture; date
d'entrée en vigueur
starting point
point (m) de départ
starting salary
salaire (m) de départ
ou de débutant
**state (n) *[condi-
tion]*** état (m)
state (n) *[country]*
état (m)
state (v) déclarer
ou stipuler *ou*
préciser
**state-of-the-art
(adj)** de pointe
statement (n)
déclaration (f)

statement of account relevé (m) de compte

statement of expenses état (m) des dépenses

station (n) [train] gare (f) (ferroviaire)

statistical (adj) statistique

statistical analysis analyse (f) statistique

statistician (n) statisticien (-ienne)

statistics (n) statistiques (fpl) ou chiffres (mpl)

status (n) statut (m) ou position (f)

status inquiry enquête (f) sur la solvabilité d'un client

status symbol marque (f) de prestige

statute (n) of limitations loi (f) de prescription

statutory (adj) statutaire ou réglementaire

statutory holiday congé (m) légal ou fête (f) légale

stay (n) [time] séjour (m)

stay (v) séjourner ou demeurer

stay (n) of execution ordonnance (f) à surseoir ou sursis (m)

steadiness (n) régularité (f); stabilité (f) [du marché]

sterling livre (f) sterling

stevedore (n) débardeur (m) ou docker (m)

stiff (adj) competition concurrence (f) farouche

stimulate (v) the economy encourager ou stimuler l'économie

stimulus (n) stimulant (m)

stipulate (v) stipuler

stipulation (n) stipulation (f)

stock (adj)
[normal] courant(e)
ou normal(e)
stock (n) *[goods]*
stock (m)
stock (v) *[goods]*
stocker *ou*
entreposer
stock (n) code
numéro (m) de stock
stock control
contrôle (m) *ou* ges-
tion (f) des stocks
stock controller
contrôleur (m) *ou*
gestionnaire (m)
des stocks
Stock Exchange
Bourse (f)
stock level niveau
(m) de stocks
stock list
inventaire (m)
stock market marché
(m) *ou* Bourse (f)
(des valeurs)
stock market
valuation
capitalisation (f)
boursière *ou* valeur
(f) boursière

stock movements
mouvements (mpl)
de stocks
stock size taille (f)
courante
stock turn *or* stock
turnover *or* stock
turnround rotation
(f) des stocks
stock up (v) faire
des réserves *ou* des
provisions
stock (n) valuation
évaluation (f) des
stocks
stockbroker (n)
société (f) de Bourse
[agent de change]
stockbroking (n)
courtage (m)
stockist (n)
stockiste (mf) *ou*
dépositaire (mf)
stockpile (n)
réserves (fpl)
stockpile (v) faire
des réserves *ou*
stocker
stockroom (n)
réserve (f) *ou* entrepôt
(m) *ou* magasin (m)

stocktaking (n)
inventaire (m)
(des stocks)
stocktaking sale
solde (m) avant
inventaire
stop (n) stop (m) *ou*
arrêt (m) *ou* fin (f)
stop (v) *[doing*
something] arrêter
ou suspendre *ou*
cesser
stop a cheque
faire opposition
à un chèque
stop an account
bloquer un compte
stop payments
suspendre les
paiements
stoppage (n) *[act of*
stopping] arrêt (m)
ou suspension (f)
stoppage of
payments arrêt
(m) *ou* suspension
(f) des paiements
storage (n) *[com-*
puter] mémoire (f)
storage (n) *[cost]*
frais (mpl) d'entrepôt

storage (n)
[in warehouse]
entreposage (m)
storage capacity
capacité (f)
d'entreposage
storage facilities
entrepôt (m)
storage unit
[computer] unité
(f) de mémoire
store (n) *[items*
kept] réserve (f)
store (n) *[large*
shop] magasin (m);
grand magasin
store (n) *[place*
where goods are
kept] magasin (m)
ou dépôt (m) *ou*
entrepôt (m)
store (v) *[keep for*
future] mettre en
réserve
store (v) *[keep*
in warehouse]
entreposer
storeroom (n)
dépôt (m) *ou*
entrepôt (m) *ou*
magasin (m)

storm damage
dégâts (mpl) *ou*
dommages (mpl)
causés par une
tempête
straight line depre-
ciation amortisse-
ment (m) linéaire
strategic (adj)
stratégique
strategic planning
stratégie (f)
strategy (n)
stratégie (f)
street (n) rue (f)
street directory
répertoire (m) des
noms de rues *[sur*
un plan]
strike (n) grève (f)
strike (v) faire (la)
grève *ou* se mettre
en grève
striker (n)
gréviste (mf)
strong (adj) fort(e)
strong currency
devise (f) forte
structural (adj) de
structure *ou*
structurel (-elle)

structural adjust-
ment *or* **change**
changement (m)
structurel
structural unem-
ployment chômage
(m) structurel
structure (n)
structure (f)
structure (v)
[arrange] organiser
study (n) étude
(f); examen (m)
study (v) étudier;
examiner *ou*
analyser
sub judice (affaire)
qui passe devant les
tribunaux
subcontract (n)
contrat (m) de
sous-traitance
subcontract (v)
donner en sous-trai-
tance *ou* sous-traiter
subcontractor (n)
sous-traitant (m)
subject to sous
réserve de
sublease (n)
sous-location (f)

sublease (v)
sous-louer
sublessee (n)
sous-locataire (mf)
sublessor (n)
locataire (mf)
principal(e)
sublet (v)
sous-louer
subsidiary (adj)
secondaire
subsidiary (n)
filiale (f)
subsidiary
company filiale (f)
subsidize (v)
subventionner
subsidy (n)
subvention (f)
subtotal (n)
sous-total (m)
subvention (n)
subvention (f)
succeed (v) *[do as*
planned] réussir
succeed (v) *[do*
well] réussir
succeed (v) *[follow*
someone] succéder à
success (n)
succès (m)

successful (adj)
qui réussit *ou* qui
a du succès
successful
[candidate, bidder]
retenu(e)
sue (v) intenter un
procès à *ou* contre
quelqu'un; pour-
suivre quelqu'un
(en justice)
suffer (v) damage
subir des dégâts
sufficient (adj)
suffisant(e)
sum (n) *[of money]*
somme (f)
sum *[total]*
total (m)
summons (n)
convocation (f)
sundries (n) arti-
cles (mpl) divers
sundry items arti-
cles (mpl) divers
superior (adj)
[better quality]
supérieur(e) *ou*
meilleur(e)
superior (n) *[per-*
son] supérieur (m)

supermarket (n)
supermarché (m)
superstore (n)
hypermarché (m);
grande surface (f)
supervise super-
viser *ou* surveiller
supervision (n)
surveillance (f)
supervisor (n)
surveillant(e)
supervisory (adj)
de surveillance
supplement (n)
supplément (m)
supplementary (adj)
supplémentaire
supplier (n)
fournisseur (m)
supply (n) *[action]*
fourniture (f)
supply (n) *[stock of
goods]* stock (m)
ou provision (f)
supply (v)
approvisionner
ou fournir
supply and demand
l'offre et la demande
supply price
prix (m) livré

**supply side
economics**
économie (f)
de l'offre
support price prix
(m) de soutien
surcharge (n)
supplément (m);
surtaxe (f)
surety (n) *[person]*
garant *ou* caution (f)
surety (n) *[secu-
rity]* garantie (f) *ou*
nantissement (m)
surface mail cour-
rier (m) ordinaire
surface transport
transport (m) par
terre *ou* par mer
surplus (n)
surplus (m) *ou*
excédent (m)
surplus dividend
superdividende (m)
ou dividende (m)
complémentaire
surrender (n)
[insurance policy]
résiliation (f) (d'un
contrat) *ou* rachat
(m) (d'une police)

surrender (v)
[insurance] résilier
(un contrat) *ou*
racheter (une police)
surrender a policy
racheter une police
d'assurance
surrender value
valeur (f) de rachat
survey (n)
[examination:
building, damages]
expertise (f)
survey (n) *[general*
report] enquête (f)
ou sondage (m)
survey (v) *[inspect:*
building, damage]
expertiser
surveyor (n) expert
(m) (en bâtiments)
suspend (v)
suspendre
suspension (n) susp-
ension (f) *ou* interrup-
tion (f) *ou* arrêt (m)
suspension of
deliveries arrêt
(m) des livraisons
suspension of pay-
ments suspension *ou*
arrêt des paiements

swap (n) *or* **swop**
(n) échange (m)
swap (v) *or* **swop**
(v) échanger
swatch (n) (petit)
échantillon (m)
switch (v) *[change]*
changer *ou* remplacer
switch over to
passer à
switchboard (n)
standard (m)
(téléphonique)
sympathy strike
grève (f) de solidarité
syndicate (n) syn-
dicat (m) (financier)
synergy (n)
synergie (f)
system (n)
système (m)
systems analysis
analyse (f) de
systèmes
systems analyst
analyste (mf) de
systèmes *ou* infor-
maticien-analyste
(m), informatici-
enne-analyste (f)

Tt

tabulate (v)
disposer en tableau
ou en colonnes
tabulation (n)
disposition (f)
en tableau! en
colonnes
tabulator (n)
tabulateur (m)
tachograph (n)
tachygraphe (m)
tacit agreement *or*
tacit approval
accord (m) tacite
take (n) *[money*
received] rentrée
(f) *ou* recette (f)
take (v) *[need]*
prendre; falloir *ou*
nécessiter
take (v) *[receive*
money] gagner
take a call *[phone]*
répondre au
téléphone *ou*
prendre un appel
take a risk
prendre un risque

take action agir *ou*
intervenir *ou* pren-
dre des mesures
take industrial
action faire (la)
grève
take legal action
intenter un proces à
take legal advice
consulter un avocat
take note prendre
note (de)
take off (v)
[deduct] enlever *ou*
déduire *ou* rabattre
take off *[plane]*
décoller
take off *[rise fast]*
s'envoler
take on (v) freight
charger des marchan-
dises *ou* du fret
take on staff
embaucher du
personnel
take out (v) a policy
souscrire *ou* con-
tracter une assurance
take over (v) *[from*
someone else]
prendre la succes-
sion *ou* succéder

take place avoir lieu *ou* arriver

take someone to court poursuivre quelqu'un en justice

take stock faire l'inventaire

take the soft option choisir la solution de facilité

take time off work prendre un congé

take up an option lever une option

takeover (n) rachat (m); prise (f) de contrôle

takeover bid offre (f) publique d'achat (OPA)

takeover target société (f) opéable

takings (n) recettes (fpl)

tangible (adj) tangible

tangible assets biens (mpl) matériels *ou* actif (m) corporel

tanker (n) pétrolier (m) *ou* navire-citerne (m)

tare (n) tare (f)

target (n) objectif (m) *ou* but (m); cible (f)

target (v) avoir pour but; cibler

target market marché (m) ciblé

tariff (n) *[price]* tarif (m)

tariff barriers barrières (fpl) douanières

tax (n) impôt (m); taxe (f)

tax (v) imposer *ou* prélever un impôt; taxer

tax adjustment redressement (m) d'impôt

tax allowance abattement (m) à la base *ou* fiscal

tax assessment détermination (f) de l'assiette fiscale

tax avoidance
évasion (f) fiscale
tax code catégorie
(f) d'impôt
tax collection
perception (f)
des impôts
tax collector
percepteur (m)
tax concession
dégrèvement (m)
fiscal *ou* d'impôt
tax consultant
conseiller (m) fiscal
tax credit avoir
(m) fiscal *ou* crédit
(m) d'impôt
**tax deducted at
source** impôt (m)
retenu à la source
tax deductions
[taken from salary]
retenues (fpl) fis-
cales *ou* prélève-
ment (m) fiscal
tax evasion fraude
(f) fiscale
tax exemption
exonération (f)
ou exemption (f)
d'impôt

tax form formu-
laire (m) de déclara-
tion de revenus
tax haven paradis
(m) fiscal
tax inspector
inspecteur (m)
des impôts
tax loophole
moyen (légal)
d'échapper au fisc
tax offence
infraction (f) fiscale
tax paid taxe (f)
payée
tax rate taux (m)
d'imposition
tax rebate
remboursement (m)
(d'un trop-perçu)
d'impôt
tax relief dégrève-
ment (m) d'impôt
ou allègement (m)
fiscal
**tax return *or* tax
declaration**
déclaration (f) de
revenus *ou* d'impôts
tax shelter abri
(m) fiscal

tax system régime (m) fiscal

tax year année (f) fiscale

tax-deductible (adj) déductible (des impôts)

tax-exempt exonéré(e) *ou* exempt(e) d'impôt

tax-free hors taxe

taxable (adj) imposable *ou* taxable

taxable income revenu (m) imposable

taxation (n) imposition (f)

taxpayer (n) contribuable (mf)

telephone (n) téléphone (m)

telephone (v) téléphoner *ou* appeler (au téléphone)

telephone book annuaire (m) des téléphones

telephone call appel (m) (téléphonique)

telephone directory annuaire (m) des téléphones

telephone exchange central (m) téléphonique

telephone line ligne (f) téléphonique

telephone number numéro (m) de téléphone

telephone subscriber abonné(e) du téléphone

telephone switchboard standard (m) téléphonique

telephonist standardiste (mf) *ou* téléphoniste (mf)

telesales (n) *[telephone sales]* vente(s) (fpl) par téléphone

television (TV) (n) télévision (f)

teleworking (n) télétravail (m)

telex (n) télex (m)

telex (v) télexer *ou* envoyer un télex

teller (n) *[bank]*
préposé(e) à la
caisse *ou* caissier
(-ière)
temp (n) secrétaire
(f) intérimaire
temp (v) faire de
l'intérim
temp agency
agence (f) d'intérim
**temporary employ-
ment *or* work**
emploi (m) *ou* tra-
vail (m) temporaire
temporary staff
personnel (m)
temporaire
tenancy (n)
[agreement] bail
(m) de location
tenancy *[period]*
durée (f) du bail
tenant (n)
locataire (mf)
tender (n) *[offer to
work]* soumission (f)
**tender for a con-
tract** faire une
soumission pour un
travail *ou* soumis-
sionner un travail

tenderer (n)
soumissionnaire (mf)
tendering (n)
soumission (f)
tenure (n) *[right]*
jouissance (f) d'un
droit (à une propriété
ou à une fonction)
tenure *[time]*
période (f)
d'exercice d'une
fonction
term (n) *[part of
academic year]*
trimestre (m)
(juridique *ou*
universitaire)
term *[time of
validity]* terme (m)
ou durée (f)
term insurance
assurance (f) à
terme
term loan prêt (m)
à terme
terminal (adj) *[at
the end]* terminal(e)
terminal (n) *[air-
port]* terminal (m)
terminal (n) *[com-
puter]* terminal (m)

terminal (adj)
bonus prime (f) de
fin de contrat
terminate (v)
terminer *ou* résilier;
se terminer *ou*
prendre fin
terminate a contract
résilier un contrat
termination (n)
terminaison (f) *ou*
fin (f); résiliation
(f) (d'un contrat)
termination clause
clause (f)
résolutoire
terms (n) conditions
(fpl) *ou* termes (mpl)
**terms of employ-
ment** conditions
(fpl) d'emploi
terms of payment
modalités (fpl) de
paiement
terms of reference
[of committee, etc.]
attributions (fpl) *ou*
pouvoirs (mpl)
terms of sale
conditions (fpl)
de vente

territory (n)
[of salesman]
secteur (m)
**tertiary industry or
tertiary sector**
industrie (f) de
services *ou* secteur
(m) tertiaire
test (n) test (m)
ou contrôle (m)
test (v) tester *ou*
contrôler
theft (n) vol (m)
third party tiers (m);
tierce personne (f)
third quarter
troisième
trimestre (m)
third-party insurance
assurance (f) au tiers
threshold (n)
seuil (m)
**threshold
agreement** accord
(m) d'indexation
des salaires sur le
coût de la vie
threshold price
prix (m) de seuil
throughput (n)
rendement (m)

ticket (n) billet (m) *ou* ticket (m)

tie-up (n) *[link]* association (f)

tight money argent (m) cher *ou* rare

tighten up (v) (on) resserrer (le contrôle)

till (n) tiroir-caisse (m)

time and motion study étude (f) des temps et des mouvements *ou* de l'organisation scien-tifique du travail

time deposit dépôt (m) à terme

time limit délai (m)

time limitation lim-itation (f) de temps

time rate tarif (m) horaire

time scale délai (m) *[d'exécution]*

time: on time à l'heure; à temps

timetable (n) *[appointments]* emploi (m) du temps *ou* calendrier (m)

timetable (n) *[trains, etc.]* horaire (m) *ou* indicateur (m)

timetable (v) établir un calendrier

timing (n) choix (m) d'une date *ou* d'une heure

tip (n) *[advice]* tuyau (m)

tip (n) *[money]* pourboire (m)

tip (v) *[give money]* donner un pourboire

tip (v) *[say what might happen]* pronostiquer

TIR (Transports Internationaux Routiers) Transports Internationaux Routiers

token (n) symbole (m)

token charge participation (f) symbolique

token payment paiement (m) symbolique

toll (n) péage (m)
toll free *[US]*
gratuitement
toll free number *[US]*
numéro (m) vert
ton (n) tonne (f)
tonnage (n) tonnage (m) *ou* jauge (f)
tonne (n) tonne (f)
(métrique)
tool up (v)
équiper *ou* outiller
(une usine)
top (adj)
supérieur(e) *ou* extra
top (n) *[highest point]* sommet (m)
top (n) *[upper surface]* dessus (m)
top (v) *[go higher than]* dépasser
top-flight *or*
top-ranking (adj)
de haut niveau *ou*
très important(e)
top management
direction (f)
générale *ou* cadres
(mpl) supérieurs
top quality qualité
(f) supérieure

top-selling (adj)
qui se vend le mieux
total (adj) total(e)
total (n) total (m)
total (v) s'élever à
total amount total
(m) *ou* montant (m)
total
total assets actif
(m) total
total cost coût (m)
total
total expenditure
dépense (f) totale
total income
revenu (m) total
total invoice value
montant (m) total
de la facture
total output
production (f) totale
total revenue
revenu (m) total
track record expérience (f) professionnelle; dossier (m)
trade (n) *[business]*
commerce (m)
trade (v) faire
des opérations
commerciales

trade agreement
accord (m) de
commerce
international
trade association
association (f)
professionnelle
trade cycle cycle
(m) économique
trade deficit *or*
trade gap déficit
(m) commercial
trade description
designation (f) de
marchandises
trade directory
répertoire (m)
d'entreprises
trade discount
remise (f) commer-
ciale *ou* remise pro-
fessionnelle
trade fair foire (f)
commerciale
trade in (v) *[buy*
and sell] faire le
commerce (de) *ou*
être négociant (en)
trade in *[give in old*
item for new]
donner en reprise

trade-in (n) *[old*
item in exchange]
reprise (f)
trade-in price
valeur (f) de reprise
trade journal *or*
trade magazine
revue (m)
professionnelle *ou*
spécialisée
trademark (n) *or*
trade name marque
(f) de fabrique *ou*
de commerce
trade mission
mission (f)
commerciale
trade price prix
(m) de gros
trade terms remise
(f) professionnelle
trade union
syndicat (m) *ou*
Trade-union (f)
trade unionist
syndicaliste (mf) *ou*
trade-unioniste (mf)
trader (n)
commerçant(e) *ou*
négociant(e) *ou*
marchand(e)

trading (n)
affaires (fpl)
trading company
société (f) *ou* entre-
prise (f) commerciale
trading loss perte
(f) d'exploitation
trading partner
partenaire (m)
commercial
trading profit
bénéfice (m)
d'exploitation
train (n) train (m)
train (v) *[learn]*
suivre une formation
train (v) *[teach]*
former quelqu'un
trainee (n)
stagiaire (mf);
apprenti(e)
traineeship (n)
stage (m) de
formation
training (n)
formation (f)
training levy taxe
(f) d'apprentissage
training officer
responsable (mf)
de la formation

**transact (v) busi-
ness** traiter une
affaire *ou* effectuer
une transaction
transaction (n)
transaction (f)
transfer (n)
transfert (m)
transfer (v) *[move
to new place]*
transférer
transfer of funds
virement (m) de crédit
**transferable
(adj)** cessible *ou*
transmissible
transit (n)
transit (m)
transit lounge
salle (f) de transit
transit visa visa
(m) de transit
transit: in transit
en transit
translate (v)
traduire
translation (n)
traduction (f)
translation bureau
bureau (m) de
traduction

translator (n)
traducteur (-trice)
transport (n)
transport (m)
transport (v)
transporter
transport facilities
moyens (mpl)
de transport
travel agency
agence (f) de
voyages
travel agent agent
(m) de voyages
travelling expenses
frais (mpl) de
déplacement
Treasury (n)
Ministère (m) des
Finances
treble (v) tripler
trend (n)
tendance (f)
trial (n) *[court*
case] procès (m)
trial (n) *[test of*
product] essai (m)
trial and error
(apprentissage par)
essais (mpl) et
erreurs

trial balance bilan
(m) de vérification
trial period période
(f) d'essai
trial sample échan-
tillon (m) d'essai
triple (adj) triple
triple (v) tripler
triplicate: in
triplicate en trios
exemplaires
troubleshooter (n)
expert (m) en
problèmes de
gestion d'entreprise
truck (n) *[lorry]*
camion (m)
trucker (n)
camionneur (m)
trucking (n)
camionnage (m)
ou transport (m)
routier
true copy copie (f)
conforme
trust company
société (f) fiduciaire
tune (v) *[machine,*
etc.] ajuster
turn down (v)
refuser

turn over (v) *[make sales]* faire un chiffre d'affaires (de ...)
turnkey operation opération (f) clés en main
turnkey operator constructeur (m) clés en main
turnover (n) *[of staff]* rotation (f) (du personnel)
turnover (n) *[of stock]* rotation (f) (des stocks)
turnover (n) *[sales]* chiffre (m) d'affaires
turnover tax impôt (m) sur le chiffre d'affaires
turnround (n) *[goods sold]* rotation (f) (des stocks)
turnround *[making profitable]* redressement (m)
turnround *[of plane]* rotation (f); chargement, déchargement et entretien

Uu

unaccounted for (adj) inexpliqué(e)
unaudited (adj) non vérifié(e)
unaudited accounts comptes (mpl) non vérifiés
unauthorized expenditure dépenses (f) non autorisées
unavailability (n) indisponibilité (f)
unavailable (adj) non disponible
unchanged (adj) inchangé(e)
unchecked figures chiffres (mpl) non vérifiés
unclaimed baggage bagages (mpl) non réclamés
unconditional (adj) inconditionnel (-elle) *ou* sans réserve

unconfirmed (adj)
non confirmé(e)
undated (adj) non
daté(e) *ou* sans date
undelivered (adj)
non livré(e)
under *[according
to]* selon *ou* aux
termes de
under *[less than]*
moins de *ou*
inférieur(e) à
under construction
en construction
under contract
lié(e) par contrat
under control
sous contrôle
ou en main(s)
**under new
management**
changement (m) de
propriétaire *ou* de
direction
undercharge (v)
ne pas (faire)
payer assez
**undercut (v) a
rival** vendre
moins cher
qu'un concurrent

**underdeveloped
countries** pays
(mpl) en développe-
ment (PED)
underequipped (adj)
sous-équipé(e)
underpaid (adj)
sous-payé(e)
undersell (v) ven-
dre moins cher que
undersigned (adj)
soussigné(e)
underspend (v)
dépenser moins
(que prévu)
understand (v)
comprendre
understanding (n)
entente (f);
arrangement (m)
undertake (v)
[something]
entreprendre
[quelque chose]
undertake *[to do
something]*
s'engager à *[faire
quelque chose]*
undertaking (n)
[company]
entreprise (f)

**undertaking (n)
[promise]**
engagement (m)
**underwrite (v)
[guarantee]** garantir
**underwrite (v) [pay
costs]** prendre les
dépens en charge
**underwriting
syndicate** syndicat
(m) de garantie
**undischarged
bankrupt** failli (m)
non réhabilité
uneconomic rent
loyer (m) non rentable
unemployed (adj)
sans emploi; en *ou*
au chômage
unemployment (n)
chômage (m)
unemployment pay
allocation (f) de
chômage
unfair (adj) injuste
unfair competition
concurrence (f)
déloyale
unfair dismissal
licenciement (m)
abusif *ou* injuste

unfavourable (adj)
défavorable
**unfavourable
exchange rate**
taux (m) de change
défavorable
unfulfilled order
commande (f) non
exécutée
unilateral (adj)
unilatéral(e)
union (n) syndicat
(m) *[de travailleurs]*
union recognition
reconnaissance (f)
officielle d'un syndicat
(dans une entreprise)
**unique selling
point *or* proposition
(USP)** avantage
(m) spécifique d'un
produit
**unit (n) [in unit
trust]** action (f)
unit (n) [item]
unité (f)
unit cost coût (m)
unitaire
unit price prix (m)
unitaire *ou* prix de
l'unité

unit trust société (f) d'investissement à capital variable (SICAV)

unlimited liability responsabilité (f) illimitée

unload (v) *[goods]* décharger

unobtainable (adj) qu'on ne peut se procurer

unofficial (adj) officieux (-euse)

unpaid (adj) non payé(e) *ou* impayé(e)

unpaid invoices factures (fpl) impayées *ou* les impayés (mpl)

unsealed envelope enveloppe (f) non cachetée

unsecured creditor créancier (m) sans garantie

unskilled (adj) non qualifié(e)

unsold (adj) non vendu(e); invendu(e)

unsubsidized (adj) non subventionné(e)

unsuccessful (adj) qui ne réussit pas *ou* sans succès

up front à l'avance *ou* d'avance

up to jusqu'à *ou* jusqu'à concurrence de *ou* à hauteur de

up to date *[complete]* à jour

up to date *[modern]* moderne *ou* de pointe

up-market de luxe *ou* haut de gamme

update (n) mise (f) à jour

update (v) mettre à jour *ou* réviser

upset price *[reserve price]* prix (m) minimum fixé; mise (f) à prix

upturn (n) reprise (f)

upward trend tendance (f) à la hausse

urgent (adj)
urgent(e)
use (n) emploi (m)
ou utilisation (f)
use (v) utiliser *ou*
se servir de
use up spare
capacity utiliser la
capacité disponible
useful (adj) utile
user (n) utilisateur
(-trice)
user-friendly (adj)
convivial(e)
USP (unique selling
point *or* proposi-
tion) avantage (m)
spécifique d'un
produit
usual (adj)
habituel (-elle) *ou*
normal(e)
utilization (n)
utilisation (f)

Vv

vacancy (n) *[for
job]* poste (m)
vacant *ou* poste à
pourvoir
vacant (adj) vide *ou*
libre *ou* inoccupé(e)
vacate (v) quitter
[les lieux]
valid (adj) valide
ou valable
validity (n)
validité (f)
valuation (n)
évaluation (f) *ou*
expertise (f)
value (n) valeur (f)
value (v) évaluer
ou estimer
value added tax
(VAT) taxe (f)
sur la valeur
ajoutée (TVA)
valuer (n) expert
(m) (en évaluation)
van (n) *[for deli-
very]* camionnette
(f) (de livraison)

variable costs coûts (mpl) variables
variance (n) variation (f) *ou* écart (m)
variation (n) variation (f)
VAT (value added tax) TVA (taxe sur la valeur ajoutée)
VAT declaration déclaration (f) de TVA
VAT inspector inspecteur (m) de la TVA
VAT invoice facture (f) avec TVA
vehicle (n) véhicule (m)
vendor (n) vendeur (m), vendeuse (f)
venture (n) *[business]* affaire (f) *ou* entreprise (f)
venture (v) *[risk]* risquer
venture capital capital-risque (m)
venue (n) lieu (m) (de réunion)
verbal (adj) verbal(e)

verbal agreement entente (f) verbale *ou* accord (m) verbal
verification (f) vérification (f)
verify (v) vérifier
vertical communication communication (f) verticale
vertical integration intégration (f) verticale
vested interest droits (mpl) acquis *ou* intérêts (mpl)
veto (n) *[right]* (droit de) veto (m)
veto (v) a decision s'opposer à une décision *ou* mettre son veto à une décision
via via *ou* par
viable (adj) viable
videoconference (n) vidéoconférence (f)
VIP lounge salon (m) réservé aux personnages de marque

visa (n) visa (m)
visible imports
importations visibles
visible trade
commerce (m)
visible
voicemail (n)
messagerie (f)
vocale
void (adj) *[not
valid]* nul (nulle)
void (v) annuler
volume (n)
volume (m)
volume discount
ristourne (f) *ou*
remise (f) sur
quantité
volume of sales
volume (m) de
ventes
volume of trade *or*
volume of business
volume (m) d'affaires
voluntary liquida-
tion liquidation (f)
volontaire
voluntary redun-
dancy départ (m)
volontaire
vote (n) vote (n)

vote (v) voter
vote (n) of thanks
remerciements
(mpl) *[votés par
une assemblée]*
voucher (n)
*[document from an
auditor]* justificatif
(m) comptable
**voucher (n) *[paper
given instead of
money]*** bon (m)
(d'échange)

Ww

wage (n) paie (f)
ou salaire (m)
wage claim
revendication (f)
salariale
wage freeze
blocage (m) *ou* gel
(m) de salaires
wage levels niveau
(m) des salaires

wage negotiations
négociations (f)
salariales
wage scale
échelle (f) des
salaires *ou* grille (f)
des salaires
waive (v)
renoncer à
waive a payment
refuser tout
paiement
waiver (n) [of
right] renoncement
(m) *ou* abandon (m)
waiver clause
clause (f) d'abandon
warehouse (n)
entrepôt (m)
warehouse (v)
entreposer
warehouseman (n)
magasinier (m) *ou*
responsable (m)
d'un entrepôt
warehousing (n)
entreposage (m)
warrant (n) [docu-
ment] warrant (m)
warrant (v) [guar-
antee] garantir

warrant (v) [jus-
tify] justifier
warranty (n)
garantie (f)
wastage (n)
pertes (fpl) *ou*
gaspillage (m)
waste (n) déchets
(mpl); gaspillage (m)
waste (v) [use too
much] gaspiller
waybill (n) lettre
(f) de voiture
weak market
marché (m) faible
wear and tear
usure (f) normale
web (n): the web
le web
website (n) site
(m) web
week (n) semaine (f)
weekly (adj & adv)
hebdomadaire;
par semaine
weigh (v) peser
weighbridge (n)
pont (m) bascule
weight (n) poids (m)
weight limit poids
(m) maximum

weighted average
moyenne pondérée
weighted index
indice pondéré
weighting (n)
[added to salary]
indemnité (f)
de résidence
well-paid job travail
(m) rémunérateur
wharf (n) quai (m)
white knight
chevalier (m) blanc
whole-life insurance
assurance vie entière
wholesale (adv)
en gros
wholesale (selling)
vente (f) en gros;
commerce (m) de gros
wholesale dealer
grossiste (mf)
wholesale discount
remise (f) de gros
wholesale price
index indice (m)
des prix de gros
wholesaler (n)
grossiste (mf)
wildcat strike
grève (f) sauvage

win (v) a contract
remporter un contrat
wind up (v) *[a
company]* liquider
une société
wind up *[a meeting]*
lever la séance
winding up (n)
liquidation (f)
d'une société
window (n) *[of**
shop]* vitrine (f)
window display
étalage (m)
withdraw (v) *[an
offer]* retirer
withdraw *[money]*
retirer (de l'argent)
withdraw a
takeover bid retirer
une OPA
withdrawal (n) *[of
money]* retrait (m)
withholding tax
retenue (f) à la
source *[impôt]*
witness (n)
témoin (m)
witness (v) *[a docu-
ment]* signer en
qualité de témoin

witness (v) an agreement être témoin à la signature d'un contrat; signer en qualité de témoin

word-processing (n) traitement (m) de texte

wording (n) formulation (f) *ou* termes (mpl)

work (n) travail (m)

work (v) travailler

work in progress travail en cours

work permit carte (f) *ou* permis (m) de travail

work-to-rule (n) grève (f) du zèle

worker (n) travailleur (-euse); employé(e)

worker director délégué(e) du personnel

workforce (n) main-d'oeuvre (f) *ou* personnel (m)

working (adj) qui travaille

working capital fonds (m) de roulement

working conditions conditions (fpl) de travail

working party groupe (m) de travail

workplace (n) lieu (m) de travail

workshop (n) atelier (m)

workstation (n) *[at computer]* poste (m) de travail

world (n) monde (m)

World Bank Banque (f) mondiale

world market marché (m) mondial

worldwide (adj) mondial(e)

worldwide (adv) partout dans le monde

World Wide Web toile (f) mondiale

worth (n) *[value]* valeur (f)

worth: be worth valoir

worthless (n)
sans valeur
wrap up (v)
[discussion]
terminer *ou*
mettre fin à
wrap up (v) *[goods]*
emballer
wrapper (n) *or*
wrapping (n)
(papier d')
emballage (m)
wrapping paper
papier (m) d'embal-
lage; papier cadeau
wreck (n) *[com-*
pany] entreprise
qui a fait naufrage
wreck (n) *[ship]*
épave (f)
wreck (v) *[ruin]*
détruire; ruiner
writ (n)
injonction (f)
write (v) écrire
write down (v)
[assets] réduire la
valeur; amortir

writedown (n) *[of*
asset] amortisse-
ment (m)
write off (v) *[debt]*
passer par profits et
pertes
write-off (n) *[loss]*
perte (f) sèche
write out (v)
rédiger
write out a cheque
libeller un chèque
ou faire un chèque
writing (n) écrit
(m); écriture (f)
written agreement
convention écrite *ou*
contrat écrit
wrong (adj)
faux (fausse)
ou inexact
wrongful dismissal
renvoi (m) injustifié

Xx Yy   Zz

year (n) année (f)
year end fin (f)
d'exercice (financier)
yearly (adj) annuel
(-elle)
yearly (adv)
annuellement *ou*
chaque année
yearly payment
paiement annuel *ou*
versement annuel
yellow pages
pages (f) jaunes
(de l'annuaire des
téléphones)
yield (n) *[on
investment]*
rendement (m)
yield (v) *[interest]*
rapporter

zero (n) zéro (m)
zero-rated (adj)
assujetti(e) à un
taux zéro (de TVA)
zip code *[US]* code
(m) postal
zone (n) zone (f)
**zoning
regulations** plan
(m) d'occupation
des sols

Français-Anglais
French-English

Aa

**abandon (m)
d'actions** renunciation
(n) of shares
abandon d'un projet
shelving (n) of a plan
abandonner [renoncer]
renounce (v) [shares]
abandonner un projet
abandon (v) or shelve
(v) a plan
**abattement (m)
à la base [impôt]**
personal allowance
(n) or tax allowance
**abattement (m) fis-
cal** tax abatement (n)
abîmer [endommager]
damage (v) or cause
(v) damage; spoil (v)
**abonné(e)
[téléphone, revue,
etc.]** subscriber (n)
abonnement (m)
subscription (n)
**abonner:
s'abonner (à)**
subscribe (v) (to)

abri (m) fiscal tax
shelter (n)
absence (f)
absence (n)
absent(e) (adj) absent
(adj); off or away
**absorber [frais,
entreprise]**
absorb (v)
absorption (f) [fusion]
absorption (n)
**accaparer le
marché** corner (v)
the market
accélérer speed up (v)
acceptable
acceptable (adj)
**acceptation (f)
(d'une offre)**
acceptance (n)
(of an offer)
**acceptation
irrévocable**
irrevocable acceptance
**accepté(e)
[convenu]**
agreed (adj)
accepter accept (v)
or agree (v) (to)
accepter [approuver]
approve (v)

accepter de faire
quelque chose agree
to do something
accepter la respon-
sabilité (de) accept
liability (for)
accepter les prix
agree the prices
accepter une traite
accept a bill
accessoire (m)
[équipement]
fitting (n)
accessoires (mpl)
en option optional
(adj) extras
accident (m)
accident (n);
crash (n)
[car, plane]
accident du travail
industrial accident
or injuries (n)
accommodement (m)
composition (n) [with
creditors]
accompagnateur
(-trice) (n) courier
(n) or guide (n)
accompagner
accompany (v)

accord (m) [entre
deux parties]
settlement (n)
accord (m)
[convention,
contrat] agreement (n)
or contract (n)
accord (m) [marché,
entente] deal (n) or
arrangement (n)
accord à l'amiable
out-of-court
settlement
accord de commerce
trade agreement
accord de commer-
cialisation marketing
agreement
Accord de
libre-échange
nord-américain
(Aléna) North
American Free Trade
Agreement (NAFTA)
accord de longue
date long-standing
agreement
accord d'indexation
des salaires
threshold
agreement

accord flexible
ou non limité
open-ended
agreement
accord multilatéral
multilateral
agreement
accord réciproque
reciprocal agreement
accord tacite tacit
agreement
accord-type (m)
model agreement
accord unilatéral
one-sided agreement
accord verbal verbal
agreement
accord: être d'accord
agree (v) (with)
**accord: se mettre
d'accord sur** to come
to an agreement on
accorder give (v)
or grant (v)
accroissement (m)
gain (n)
accumulation (f)
accumulation (n)
**accumulation de
provisions** hoarding
(n) of goods

accumuler:
s'accumuler
accumulate (v);
accrue (v) [interest]
accusation (f)
[inculpation] charge
(n) [in court]
**accusation (f) [la
partie plaignante]**
(the) prosecution (n)
**accusé (m) de
réception**
acknowledgement (n)
accuser quelqu'un
[inculper] charge (v)
someone
**accuser réception
d'une lettre**
acknowledge
receipt of a lettre
achat (m)
[opération] buying
(n) or purchasing (n)
**achat (m) [article
acheté]** purchase (n)
or acquisition (n)
**achat à
tempérament** hire
purchase (HP)
achat à terme
forward buying

achat (au) comptant
cash purchase
achat en gros bulk
buying
achat impulsif *ou*
d'impulsion impulse
purchase
achats (mpl) central-
isés central purchasing
acheminement (m)
[expédition]
forwarding (n)
acheter (v) buy (v)
or purchase (v)
acheter à terme
buy forward
acheter au comptant
buy for cash
acheter une société
acquire (v) a company
acheteur (-euse)
buyer (n) *or*
purchaser (n)
acheteur impulsif
impulse buyer
acheteur potentiel
prospective buyer
acheteur sérieux
genuine buyer
achèvement (m) (de
travaux) completion (n)

acompte (m) down
payment (n) *or*
advance (n)
acompte (m) *[divi-*
dende intérimaire]
interim payment
acompte: en acompte
on account
acquéreur (m)
[acheteur]
purchaser (n) or
buyer (n)
acquérir *[acheter]*
purchase (v) *or* buy (n)
acquérir *[obtenir]*
gain (v) *or* get (v)
acquisition (f)
acquisition (n)
acquisition (f)
[achat] purchase (n)
or acquisition (n)
acquisition
d'immobilisations
capital expenditure (n)
[accounts]
acquisition: faire
l'acquisition
(de) acquire (v)
(something)
acquit: pour acquit
paid in full

acquitté(e) paid (adj)
acquittement (m)
d'une dette paying
(n) *or* clearing (n)
of a debt
acquitter une dette
[régler] pay (v) a
debt *or* clear off (v)
a debt
acquitter une traite
[honorer] honour (v)
a bill
acquitter: s'acquitter
d'une dette pay (v)
a debt *or* clear off (v)
a debt
acte (m) *[document]*
deed (n)
acte de cession deed
of transfer
acte de cession
[de créance] deed
of assignment
acte de propriété
title deeds
acte de vente bill
of sale
Acte unique Single
European Act
actif (m) *[avoir]*
assets (n)

actif circulant current
assets
actif corporel tangible
assets
actif et passif
assets and liabilities
actif immobilisé
fixed assets *or*
capital assets
actif net net assets
or net worth
actif réalisable
realizable assets
action (f) *[acte]*
action (n)
action (f) *[juridique]*
action (n)
action (f) *[valeur*
mobilière] share (n)
or stock (n)
action gratuite
bonus share
actions (fpl)
[portefeuille]
shareholding (n)
actions cotées
en Bourse
listed shares
actions ordinaires
ordinary shares;
common stock *[US]*

actions privilégiées
preference shares;
preferred stock *[US]*
actionnaire (mf)
shareholder (n) *or*
stockholder (n)
actionnaire
important major
shareholder
actionnaire
majoritaire majority
shareholder
actionnaire
minoritaire
minority shareholder
actionnaire: petit
actionnaire minor
shareholder
activer *[accélérer]*
speed up (v) *or* rush (v)
activer une commande
chase (v) an order
activité (f) sec-
ondaire sideline (n)
actuaire (mf)
actuary (n)
actuel (-elle)
present (adj) *or*
current (adj)
actuellement
currently (adv)

ad valorem ad
valorem
addition (f) *[facture*
au restaurant] bill (n)
addition (f)
[somme] addition (n)
[calculation]
additionner *[ajouter]*
add (v)
additionner (une
colonne de chiffres)
add up (v) (a column
of figures)
adéquat *[suffisant]*
adequate (adj)
adhésion (f)
membership *[being*
a member]
adjoint(e) (n & adj)
assistant (n) *or*
deputy (n)
adjuger un contrat
à quelqu'un award
(v) a contract to
someone
admettre (quelqu'un)
[laisser entrer] admit
(v) *or* let in (v)
(someone)
administrateur (-trice)
administrator (n)

**administrateur
(-trice)** (company)
director (n)
**administrateur
dirigeant** executive
director
**administrateur
judiciaire** official
receiver (n)
**administrateur
non dirigeant**
non-executive
director
**administrateur
séquestre**
sequestrator (n)
**administratif
(-ive) (adj)**
administrative (adj)
**administratifs
(mpl)** admin
people; admin (n)
administration (f)
administration (n)
**Administration
des douanes**
Customs and
Excise
admission (f)
[entrée] admission
(n) *or* entry (n)

**adopter (une réso-
lution)** carry (v) *or*
adopt (v) (a motion)
adoption (f)
adoption (n)
(of a proposal)
adresse (f) address (n)
**adresse de l'expédi-
teur** return address
**adresse de
réexpédition**
forwarding address
**adresse du bureau
ou du lieu de travail**
business address
adresse personnelle
home address
**adresse postale
*[boîte à lettres]***
accommodation
address
adresser address (v)
**adresser une lettre
ou un colis** address
a letter *or* a parcel
**adresser:
s'adresser à
quelqu'un** speak
(v) to someone
aérogare (f) air
terminal (n)

aérogramme (m)
air letter
aéroport (m)
airport (n)
affacturage (m)
[factoring]
factoring (n)
affaire (f)
[entreprise] business
(n) or venture (n)
affaire (f) [marché]
bargain (n) or deal (n)
affaire: faire
affaire (avec)
deal (v) or do
business (with)
affaires (fpl)
business (n)
affaires: pour
affaires on business
affecter [destiner]
allocate (v) or
earmark (v) [funds]
affecter des
fonds à un projet
earmark funds
for a project
affilié(e)
affiliated (adj)
affirmatif (-ive) (adj)
affirmative (adj)

afflux (m) (de
capitaux) influx
(n) (of capital)
affranchir [avec
machine] frank (v)
(a letter)
affranchir [coller un
timbre] stamp (v)
or put a stamp on
(a letter)
affranchir: machine
à affranchir franking
machine
affrètement (m)
[nolisage] charter (n)
or chartering (n)
affréter [noliser]
charter (v)
affréter un avion
charter (v) an aircraft
affréteur (m)
charterer (n)
âge (m) age (n)
âge de la retraite
retirement age
âge limite age limit
agence (f) agency (n)
or bureau (n)
agence (f) [d'une
banque] branch (n)
[of a bank]

agence de location
letting agency
agence de notation
financière credit
agency; credit
bureau *[US]*
agence de placement
employment agency
or bureau
agence de presse
news agency
agence de publicité
advertising agency
agence de
recouvrement (de
dettes) debt
collection agency
agence de
renseignements
commerciaux
trade bureau
agence de voyages
travel agency
agence d'intérim
temp agency
agence immobilière
(real) estate agency
agenda (m)
diary (n)
agenda de bureau
desk diary

agenda de poche
pocket diary
agent (m)
[intermédiaire]
agent (n); dealer (n);
broker (n)
agent agréé
authorized dealer
agent commercial
[représentant]
representative (n)
agent d'assurances
insurance agent *or*
broker
agent de change
stockbroker (n) *or*
broker (n)
agent de
recouvrement (de
dettes) debt
collector (n)
agent de voyages
travel agent
agent en brevets
patent agent
agent en douane
customs broker
agent exclusif
sole agent
agent immobilier
estate agent

agent maritime
shipping agent
**agios (mpl) *[frais
bancaires]*** bank
charges (n)
**agir *[prendre des
mesures]*** take
action *or* act (v)
agrafe (f) staple (n)
agrafer staple (v)
agrafeuse (f)
stapler (n)
agricole
agricultural (adj)
agriculture (f)
agriculture (n);
farming (n)
agroalimentaire (m)
food and agriculture
industry
agro-industrie (f)
agribusiness (n)
aide (f) *[assistance]*
assistance (n)
aider assist (v)
or help (v)
**aire (f) de charge-
ment** loading bay (n)
ajournement (m)
postponing (n)
or deferment (n)

**ajournement (m)
d'une réunion** post-
poning (n) *or* ajourning
(n) of a meeting
**ajourner (une
réunion)** postpone (v)
or adjourn (v)
(a meeting)
**ajourner la
réalisation d'un
projet** postpone (v)
or shelve (v) a plan
ajouter add (on) (v)
**ajouter 10% pour le
service** add on 10%
for service
**ajouter 10% pour le
transport** allow
10% for carriage
**ajustement (m)
*[de comptes]***
reconciliation (n)
**ajusteur (m)
(d'assurances)**
average adjuster (n)
aléatoire random (adj)
**Aléna (Accord de
libre-échange nord-
américain)** (NAFTA)
North-American Free
Trade Agreement

allègement (m)
fiscal tax relief (n)
aller go (v)
aller chercher
collect (v) *or*
fetch (v)
aller en augmentant
be on the increase
aller de ... à ...
[s'étendre] range
(v) from ... to ...
allocation (f)
[somme allouée]
allowance (n)
allocation (f) *[presta-*
tion] benefit (n)
allocation de
chômage
unemployment
benefit *or* pay
allouer allocate (v)
alternative (f)
alternative (n)
amélioration (f)
improvement (n)
améliorer *ou*
s'améliorer
improve (v)
aménagement (m)
[emploi du temps]
scheduling (n)

aménagement (m)
[magasin] fitting
out (n)
aménagement (m)
[région] (planning
and) development (n)
aménagement
du territoire
national planning
and development
aménagement
urbain town
planning (n)
aménager *[emploi du*
temps] schedule (v)
aménager *[magasin,*
etc.] fit out (v)
aménager *[région]*
develop (v)
amende (f) fine (n)
or penalty (n)
amendement (m)
amendment (n)
amener *[apporter]*
bring (v)
Américain (-aine)
American (n)
américain (-aine)
(adj) American (adj)
amortir depreciate
(v) *or* write down (v)

amortir [rembourser]
amortize (v) *or*
redeem (v)
amortissement (m)
[dépréciation]
depreciation (n) *or*
writedown (n)
amortissement (m)
[remboursement]
amortization (n)
or redemption (n)
amortissement
linéaire straight
line depreciation
amortissement
accéléré accelerated
depreciation
analyse (f)
analysis (n)
analyse de projet
project analysis
analyse de systèmes
systems analysis
analyse des coûts
cost analysis
analyse des tâches
job analysis
analyse des ventes
sales analysis
analyse du marché
market analysis

analyser analyse (v) *or*
analyze (v); study (v)
analyste (mf)
analyst (n)
analyste de
systèmes
[informatique]
systems analyst
anglais (-aise)
[britannique]
british (adj)
année (f) year
année budgétaire
financial year
année civile
calendar year
année de référence
base year
année fiscale tax
year *or* fiscal year
année: l'année
dernière last year
année: par année
per year *or* per
annum *or* yearly
années d'ancienneté
years of service
annexe (f) [document]
attached document
annexe: en annexe
attached

**annonce (f)
[déclaration]**
announcement (n);
news (n)
**annonce (f) [public-
ité]** advertisement
(n) *or* ad (n)
**annonce: mettre une
annonce** advertise (v);
put (v) an ad
annoncer announce
(v) *or* report (v)
**annoncer [faire
de la publicité]**
advertise (v)
annoncer un déficit
report a loss
**annoncer un poste
(dans un journal)**
advertise (v) a
vacancy
annonces classées
classified ads (n)
annonceur (m)
advertiser (n)
**annuaire (m)
des téléphones**
telephone
directory *or* book
annuel (-elle)
annual (adj)

**annuellement
[chaque année]**
annually (adv)
**annulation (f) d'un
contrat** annulment (n)
of a contract
**annulation d'un
rendez-vous**
cancellation (n) of
an appointment
annulé(e) cancelled
(adj) *or* off (adv)
annuler annul (v);
cancel (v)
annuler un chèque
cancel a cheque
**annuler une
commande** cancel
an order
annuler un contrat
annul (v) *or* rescind (v)
a contract
annuler une facture
void (v) an invoice
**annuler un
rendez-vous** cancel
an appointment
**antérieur(e)
[préalable]** prior (adj)
**antérieur(e) [précé-
dent]** previous (adj)

anticipé(e) advance (adj) (payment, etc.)

antidater antedate (v) *or* backdate (v)

anti-inflationniste anti-inflationary (adj)

appareil (m) machine (n); device (n)

appareil de démonstration demonstration model

appartement (m) flat (n) *or* apartment (n)

appartenir à belong to (v)

appel (m) *[d'un jugement]* appeal (n) *[against a decision]*

appel (m) *[téléphonique]* (telephone *or* phone) call (n)

appel de personne *[bip]* (radio-) paging (n)

appel d'offres *[pour un contrat]* invitation (n) to tender

appel en PCV reverse charge call; collect call *[US]*

appel international international call

appel venant de l'extérieur incoming call

appeler *[téléphoner]* phone (v) *or* call (v)

appeler d'un jugement appeal (v) against a decision

appeler en direct dial (v) direct

appeler en PCV reverse (v) the charges *or* call (v) collect

application (f) *[mise en pratique]* implementation (n)

appliquer *[mettre en pratique]* implement (v)

appréciation (f) *[augmentation en valeur]* appreciation (n) *[in value]*

apprécier: s'apprécier *[augmenter de valeur]* appreciate (v) *or* increase (v) in value

approbation (f) approval (n)

approbation: donner son approbation give (v) one's approval

approprié(e) relevant (adj)

approuver [accepter] approve (v) *or* agree (v)

approuver [sanctionner] approve *or* pass (v) *or* sanction (v)

approuver les comptes agree the accounts

approuver les termes d'un contrat approve the terms of a contract

approvisionnement (m) supply (n)

approvisionner [fournir] supply (v)

approvisionner: s'approvisionner shop at (v); obtain (v) supplies from

approximatif (-ive) approximate (adj) *or* rough (adj)

approximativement [environ] approximately (adv)

appui (m) (financier) backing (n)

appuyer (financièrement) back up (v)

apurer les comptes audit (v) the accounts

arbitrage (m) [médiation] arbitration (n)

arbitre (m) [juge] arbitrator (n) *or* adjudicator (n)

arbitrer un conflit arbitrate (v) in a dispute

archives (fpl) records (n) *or* archives (n)

argent (m) money (n)

argent (m) [fonds] funds (n)

argent (m) [métal] silver (n)

argent au jour le jour money at call *or* call money

argent bon marché cheap money

argent cher dear money
argent comptant [espèces] cash (n)
argent frais new money *or* fresh money
argent pour les dépenses courantes spending money
arranger [organiser] arrange (v) (a meeting, etc.)
arranger: s'arranger à l'amiable settle (v) out of court
arranger: s'arranger avec ses créanciers compound (v) with creditors
arrérages (mpl) arrears (n) (of payment)
arrêt (m) stop (n)
arrêt (m) [action] stoppage (n) *or* suspension (n)
arrêt (m) [panne] failure (n)
arrêt (m) [pause] break (n)

arrêt des livraisons stoppage *or* suspension of deliveries
arrêt des paiements stoppage of payments
arrêt: sans arrêt non-stop
arrêter stop (v) *[doing something]*
arrêter les comptes close (v) *or* balance (v) the accounts
arrêter les négociations break off (v) negotiations
arrêter le travail [débrayer] stop work *or* knock off
arrêter un plan d'action [décider] decide (v) on a course of action
arrhes (fpl) [acompte] deposit (n) *[paid in advance]*
arrhes non remboursables non-refundable deposit

arriéré (m) arrears (n)
or back payment (n)
arriéré de loyer
back rent (n)
arrivage (m)
consignment (n)
arriver *[avoir lieu]*
take (v) place
arriver à *[atteindre]*
reach (v) *or*
come to (v)
arriver à *[réussir à]*
manage to (v)
arriver à échéance
mature (v)
arriver à un accord
reach an agreement
arriver à une impasse
deadlock (v)
**arrondir au chiffre
inférieur** round
down (v)
**arrondir au chiffre
supérieur**
round up (v)
article (m) article (n)
or item (n)
article (m) *[d'un
contrat]* clause (n)
article unique *ou* **non
suivi** one-off item

article imparfait
reject (n)
article-réclame (m)
[produit d'appel]
loss-leader (n)
**articles (mpl) de
luxe** luxury goods
articles déclassés
ou **de second choix**
seconds (n)
articles divers
sundry items *or*
sundries (n)
articles manufacturés
manufactured goods
**articles qui se
vendent rapidement**
fast-selling items
ascenseur (m) lift
(n); elevator (n) *[US]*
assemblage (m)
[montage]
assembly (n)
assemblée (f)
assembly (n) *or*
meeting (n)
**assemblée d'ac-
tionnaires** share-
holders' meeting
assemblée générale
general meeting

assemblée générale annuelle annual general meeting (AGM)

assistance (f) judiciaire legal aid (n)

assistance sociale welfare (n)

assistant(e) assistant (n)

assistante de direction *[secrétaire]* personal assistant (PA)

assister à (une réunion) attend (v) (a meeting)

association (f) *[groupement]* association (n) *or* council (n)

association (f) *[société]* partnership (n)

association de consommateurs consumer council

Association européenne de libre-échange (AELE) European Free Trade Association (EFTA)

association professionnelle trade association

associé(e) (n) partner (n)

associé(e) *[collègue]* associate (n)

associé(e) principal(e) senior partner

associer: s'associer go into partnership with someone

assujetti(e) liable to (adj) *or* subject to (adj)

assujetti à un taux zéro (de TVA) zero-rated (adj)

assurable insurable (adj)

assurance (f) insurance (n)

assurance au tiers third-party insurance

assurance-automobile motor insurance

assurance-habitation house insurance

assurance-incendie *ou* contre l'incendie fire insurance

assurance maladie
medical insurance
assurance
multirisque
general insurance
assurance tous
risques comprehen-
sive insurance
assurance-vie
life assurance *or*
life insurance
assurance vie entière
whole-life insurance
assurer insure (v)
assurer quelqu'un
sur la vie assure (v)
someone's life
assurer une perma-
nence *[à un stand,*
etc.] man (v) (a stand,
etc.) 24 hours a day
assurer: s'assurer
take out (v) an
insurance
assureur (m) *[com-*
pagnie d'assurances]
insurer (n)
assureur maritime
marine underwriter
atelier (m)
workshop (n)

atelier de réparations
repair shop
attaché(e)
commercial(e)
commercial
attaché (n)
atteindre reach (v)
or arrive (v)
atteindre un objectif
meet a target
atteindre une
moyenne average (v)
atteindre: ne pas
atteindre son
objectif miss (v)
one's target
attendu(e) due
(adj); expected (adj)
attente: en attente
pending (adj)
attention (f)
attention (n)
attention: à l'atten-
tion de for the
attention of (FAO)
atterrir *[avion]*
land (v)
attestation (f)
provisoire
d'assurance
cover note

attirer attract (v)
attractif (-ive)
attractive (adj)
attribution (f)
d'actions share
allocation (n) *or*
allotment (n)
aubaine (f) good
value (for money)
audit (m) *[commis-*
saire aux comptes]
auditor (n)
audit (m)
[vérification
comptable] audit (n)
audit externe
external audit
audit interne
internal audit
auditeur (m) *[com-*
missaire aux
comptes] auditor (n)
auditeur *ou* audit
externe external
auditor
auditeur *ou* audit
interne internal
auditor
augmentation (f)
rise (n) *or* increase
(n); raise (n) *[US]*

augmentation (f)
[valeur] appreciation
(n) *or* increase in
value
augmentation de
salaire salary
increase *or* pay rise
augmentation
indexée sur le coût
de la vie cost-of-
living increase
augmentation
annuelle moyenne
mean annual increase
augmentation: en
augmentation
increasing (adj)
augmenter increase
(v) *or* rise (v)
augmenter *[majorer]*
mark up (v) (an item)
augmenter de prix
increase (v) in price
augmenter en
valeur *[s'apprécier]*
appreciate (v) *or*
increase (v) in value
augmenter le
prix d'un article
increase (v) the
price of an item

**augmenter suivant
un barème** scale up
austérité (f)
austerity (n)
authentifier
authenticate (v)
**authentique [vérita-
ble]** genuine (adj)
**autocopiant(e)
[sans carbone]**
carbonless (adj
autofinancé(e)
self-financed (adj)
autofinancement (m)
self-financing (n)
autogéré(e)
self-managed (adj)
autogestion (f)
self-management (n)
autorisation (f)
authorization (n)
**autorisation (f)
[permis]**
licence (n)
or permit (n)
**autorisation
d'absence** leave (n)
of absence
**autorisation
de découvert**
overdraft facility

autorisé authorized
(adj); entitled (adj)
autoriser authorize
(v); entitle (v)
autoriser le paiement
authorize payment
autorité (f)
authority (n)
**autorités (fpl)
portuaires** port
authority
avaliser back (v) or
guarantee (v)
**avaliseur (m) ou
avaliste (mf) [garant]**
guarantor (n)
avance (f) [acompte]
advance (n) on
account
**avance (f)
[paiement d'avance]**
money up front
avance (f) [prêt]
advance (n) or loan (n)
avance bancaire
bank advance
avance de caisse
cash advance
**avance sur
salaire** advance
against salary

avance: à l'avance *ou*
d'avance in advance
avancement (m)
[progrès]
progress (n)
avancement (m)
[promotion]
promotion (n)
avancement: avoir
de l'avancement
earn (v) promotion
avancer (de l'argent)
advance (v) *or* lend (v)
(money)
avancer *[progresser]*
progress (v)
avant-projet (m)
draft project (n)
avantage (m)
advantage (n)
avantage (m)
spécifique d'un
produit unique
selling point (USP)
avantages
sociaux fringe
benefits *or*
perks (n)
avantageux (-euse)
favourable (adj);
economical (adj)

avarie (f) *[assur-*
ance] average (n)
avarie commune
general average
avenant (m) *[à un*
contrat] rider (n)
avenant (m)
[à une police
d'assurance]
endorsement (n)
[on insurance]
avenir (m) future (n)
avenir: à l'avenir
in future
avertissement (m)
notice (n) *or*
warning (n)
avion (m) aircraft (n)
or plane (n)
avion-cargo (m)
freight plane *or*
freighter (n)
avion charter *ou*
avion nolisé char-
ter plane
avis (m) note (n)
or notification (n)
avis d'exécution
contract note
avis d'expédition
advice note

Bb

avis de renouvelle-
ment renewal notice
aviser *[informer]*
notify (v)
avocat(e) lawyer
(n); barrister (n) *[GB]*
avocat-conseil (m)
counsel (n)
avocat de la défense
defence counsel
avocat représen-
tant la partie
plaignante prose-
cution counsel
avoir (m) *[actif]*
assets (n)
avoir (m) fiscal
[crédit d'impôt]
tax credit (n)
avoir (v) de
l'importance
[importer] matter (v)
avoir (v) en stock
carry (v) *or* have (v)
in stock
avoir (v) lieu *[se
tenir]* take (v)
place *or* be held
ayant droit (m)
beneficiary (n) *or*
rightful claimant (n)

bagages (mpl)
luggage (n) *or*
baggage (n)
bagages à main
hand luggage
bagages non
réclamés unclaimed
baggage
bail (m) *[loyer]*
lease (n)
bail à céder lease
for sale
bail de courte
durée short lease
bail de longue
durée long lease
bailleur (m), bailler-
esse (f) *[qui donne
à bail]* lessor (n)
bailleur (m) de fonds
[commanditaire]
backer (n)
baisse (f) *[chute]*
drop (n) *or* fall (n)
baisse (f)
[diminution]
decrease (n)

baisse (f) *[ralentisse-ment]* decline (n)

baisse (f) *[recul, repli]* downturn (n)

baisse des prix drop in prices *or* price cut

baisse: en baisse *[marché, franc]* falling (adj)

baisser *[chuter]* drop (v) *or* fall (v) *or* go down (v)

baisser *[réduire]* lower (v) *or* cut (v) *or* reduce (v)

baisser les prix lower prices

baisser un prix reduce a price

baisser: faire baisser les prix bring down (v) *or* force down (v) prices

baisser: faire baisser les stocks run down (v) stocks

baissier (m) *[spéculateur à la baisse]* bear (n) *[Stock Exchange]*

balance (f) *[appareil]* weighing machine (n); (pair of) scales (n)

balance (f) *[bilan]* balance (n)

balance commerciale balance of trade

balance commerciale bénéficiaire favourable balance of trade

balance commerciale en déficit unfavourable balance of trade

balance commerciale en dollars dollar balance

balance des comptes trial balance

balance des paiements balance of payments

balancer balance (v)

bancable *[effet]* bankable (paper)

bande (f) magnétique magnetic tape *or* mag tape (n)

banque (f) bank (n)
banque (f) *[activité bancaire]* banking (n)
banque centrale central bank
banque d'affaires merchant bank
banque de compensation clearing bank
banque de crédit credit bank
banque de données *[informatique]* data bank
banque d'épargne savings bank
banque d'escompte discount house *or* bank
banque émettrice *ou* **banque d'émission** issuing bank
Banque Européenne d'Investissement (BEI) European Investment Bank (EIB)
Banque mondiale World Bank
banqueroute (f) *[faillite]* bankruptcy (n) *or* commercial failure (n)

banqueroute: faire banqueroute go (v) bankrupt
banquier (m) banker (n)
baratin (m) (d'un vendeur) sales pitch (n)
barème (m) scale (n)
barème des prix scale of charges
barème fixe fixed scale (of charges)
barème d'imposition tax schedules
barrer *[rayer ou radier]* cross out (v)
barrer un chèque cross (v) a cheque
barrière (f) *[obstacle]* barrier (n)
barrières (fpl) douanières customs barriers *or* tariff barriers
bas (m) bottom (n)
bas (basse) (adj) low (adj)
bas de gamme down-market (adj)
bas: au bas de (la facture, etc.) at the bottom of (the invoice, etc.)

base (f) *[fonde-ment]* basis (n) *or* base (n)

base de données *[informatique]* database

baser: se baser (sur) base (v) (on)

bassin (m) dock (n)

bâtiment (m) building (n)

bâtiment principal main building

battre un record break (v) a record

bénéfice (m) profit (n); earnings (n)

bénéfice avant impôts pretax profit *or* profit before tax

bénéfice brut gross profit

bénéfice commercial operating profit

bénéfice d'exploitation trading profit

bénéfice imposable taxable profit

bénéfice net clear profit *or* net profit

bénéfice net *[après impôts]* after-tax profit *or* profit after tax

bénéfice net (d'un bilan) bottom line (n)

bénéfice théorique paper profit

bénéfice: faire un bénéfice make (v) a profit

bénéfices (mpl) d'une société corporate profits

bénéfices (mpl) exceptionnels excess profits

bénéfices (mpl) non distribués retained earnings

bénéficiaire (mf) beneficiary (n); payee (n) *or* recipient (n)

bénéficiaire (adj) profitable (adj) *or* profit-making (adj)

bénéficier de benefit from (v)

besoins (mpl) requirements (n) *or* needs (n)

besoins en main-d'oeuvre man-power requirements

bien (n) property (n); goods (n); asset (n)

bien masqué hidden asset

biens (mpl) de consommation consumer goods *or* consumable goods

biens de consom-mation durables consumer durables *or* durable goods

biens d'équipement capital goods *or* capital equipment

biens immobiliers real estate

biens incorporels intangible assets

biens matériels [actif corporel] tangible assets

biens meubles moveable property

biens personnels personal property

biens sociaux company assets *or* company property

bilan (m) balance sheet (n)

bilan de fin d'exercice closing balance (n)

bilan de vérification trial balance

bilan initial opening balance

bilatéral(e) bilateral (adj)

billet (m) [voyage, théâtre, etc.] ticket (n)

billet à ordre [banque] promissory note *or* note of hand

billet de banque (bank) note (n); (bank) bill [US]

billet gratuit *ou* **billet de faveur** complimentary ticket

billet open [voyage] open ticket

billet stand-by standby ticket

billet vert [dollar américain] green-back (n) *or* (ameri-can) dollar (n)

billetterie (f)
cash dispenser (n)
or cashpoint (n)
bimensuel (-elle)
[deux fois par mois]
twice a month *or*
fortnightly (adv)
blanc (m) *[case]*
blank (n)
blanchiment (m)
(de capitaux)
laundering (n)
(of money)
blanchir (des
capitaux) launder (v)
(money)
blister (m) blister
pack *or* bubble pack (n)
bloc (m) (d'actions)
block (n) *[of shares]*
bloc d'immeubles
block (n) *[building]*
blocage (m) *[gel]*
freeze (n)
bloquer block (v)
or freeze (v)
bloquer des capi-
taux *[immobiliser]*
lock up (v) capital
bloquer les prix *[à*
un niveau déterminé]
peg (v) prices

bloquer les salaires
et les prix freeze (v)
wages and prices
bloquer un compte
stop (v) an account
boîte (f) box (n)
boîte (f) *[petite*
compagnie] setup
(n) *or* small
company (n)
boîte à *ou* **aux**
lettres letter box
boîte en carton
[carton] cardboard
box (n) *or*
carton (n)
boîte postale
PO Box
bon (m)
coupon (n)
bon (m) *[d'échange]*
voucher (n)
bon (bonne) (adj)
good (adj)
bon-cadeau (m)
gift voucher (n)
bon d'achat
gift coupon
bon de caisse
[certificat de
dépôt] certificate
(n) of deposit

**bon du Trésor
*[obligation]***
(government) bond (n)
**bon marché
(adj & adv)**
cheap (adj & adv)
bonne affaire good
buy
bonne gestion good
management
bonne qualité good
quality
bonus (m) bonus (n)
**bonus (m) *[assur-
ance]*** no-claims bonus
boom (m) *[expansion]*
boom (n)
**bord: à bord *[navire,
etc.]*** on board
bordereau (m)
note (n) *or* slip (n)
[piece of paper]
**bordereau d'expédi-
tion** dispatch note
or consignment note
**bordereau de
versement *[banque]***
deposit slip *or*
paying-in slip
Bourse (f) Stock
Exchange (n)

Bourse (f) *[marché]*
stock market (n)
**bourse de commerce
*[matières premières]***
commodity
exchange (n)
Bourse de Paris
Paris Stock Exchange
bouteille (f) bottle (n)
**bouteilles (fpl)
consignées**
returned empties
boutique (f) shop (n)
or boutique (n)
boutique hors taxe
duty-free shop
boycottage (m)
boycott (n)
boycotter boycott (v)
**bras droit (m)
*[personne]***
right-hand man
**brevet (m) d'inven-
tion** patent (n) *or*
letters patent
breveté(e)
patented (adj)
**breveter: faire
breveter (une inven-
tion)** patent (v) *or*
take out (v) a patent

britannique *[anglais, -aise]* British (adj)
brochure (f)
brochure (n)
brouillon (m)
rough draft (n)
brouillon: faire un brouillon de lettre
draft (v) a letter
brut(e) gross (adj)
budget (m) *[gouvernement, société]* budget (n)
budget de publicité
publicity budget *or* advertising budget
budget des frais généraux overhead budget
budget des ventes
sales budget
budget opérationnel
operational budget *or* operating budget
budget promotionnel
promotion *or* promotional budget
budget provisoire
provisional budget
budgétaire budget *or* budgetary (adj)

budgéter *ou* **budgétiser** budget (v)
budgétisation (f)
budgeting (n)
bulletin (m) *[formulaire]* form (n)
bulletin (m) *[revue, journal, etc.]* news-letter (n); journal (n)
bulletin de commande
order form (n)
bulletin de livraison
delivery note (n)
bulletin de paie
pay slip (n)
bulletin de vote
ballot paper (n)
bureau (m) *[meuble]* desk (n)
bureau (m) *[pièce]*
office (n)
bureau (m) *[service]* department (n) *or* office (n)
bureau à modules *ou* **bureau paysager**
open-plan office
bureau central *ou* **principal** *[siege]*
head office *or* main office

Bureau d'assurance crédit à l'exportation Export Credit Guarantee Department (ECGD)
bureau de change bureau de change
bureau de la réception *ou* d'accueil reception desk
bureau de l'état civil registry office
bureau de location *[places de théâtre]* booking office *or* ticket office
bureau de placement employment agency *or* bureau
bureau de poste post office
bureau de renseignements inquiry office; information bureau
bureau de tourisme tourist information office
bureau de traduction translation bureau
bureau d'études design department *or* design studio
bus (m) *[autobus]* bus (n)
but (m) *[objectif]* aim (n); target

Cc

cabinet-conseil (m) consultancy firm (n)
cachet (m) de la poste date stamp (n)
cacheter *[une enveloppe]* seal (v)
cadastre (m) land register (n)
caddie (m) *[de supermarché]* trolley (n); cart (n) *[US]*
cadeau (m) gift (n) *or* present (n)
cadeau d'affaires business gift

**cadre (m)
débutant** *ou* **jeune
cadre** junior
manager (n) *or* junior
executive
cadre supérieur
senior manager (n)
or senior executive
cadre moyen
middle manager
**cadres (mpl)
[direction]**
management (n) *or*
managerial staff (n)
cadres supérieurs
top management
**CAF (coût, assurance,
fret)** c.i.f. (cost,
insurance and freight)
**cahier (m) des
charges** (contract)
specification (n)
caisse (f) [argent]
(cash) float (n)
or petty cash
**caisse (f) [boîte
d'emballage]** packing
case (n) *or* crate (n)
**caisse (f) [dans un
magasin]** cash desk (n)
or pay desk

**caisse (f) [dans un
supermarché]**
checkout (n)
**caisse (f)
[pour monnaie]**
(petty) cash box (n)
caisse de retraite
pension fund (n)
caisse enregistreuse
cash register (n)
or till (n)
**caisse noire
[réserves occultes]**
hidden reserves (n)
caissier (-ière)
cashier (n)
or pay desk
attendant (n)
calcul (m)
calculation (n)
calcul approximatif
rough calculation
**calcul du prix de
revient**
costing (n)
(of a product)
calculatrice (f)
calculator (n)
calculatrice de poche
ou **calculette (n)**
pocket calculator

calculer calculate
(v) *or* work out (v)
(figures)
calendrier (m)
calendar (n);
diary (n)
calendrier (m)
[emploi du temps]
timetable (n)
or schedule (n)
cambiste (mf)
foreign exchange
dealer *or* broker (n)
camion (m) lorry
(n) *or* truck (n)
camion (n) *[contenu]*
lorry-load (n) *or*
truck-load (n)
camionnage (m)
[transport]
road haulage (n)
or trucking (n)
**camionnette (f) de
livraison**
delivery van
camionneur (m)
lorry driver (n)
or trucker (n)
**campagne (f) *[pro-
motion]*** compaign
(n) *or* drive (n)

campagne (f)
[province]
country (n) *[not
town]*
**campagne commer-
ciale** sales campaign
**campagne
publicitaire**
publicity *or* adver-
tising campaign
**canal (m)
(de distribution)**
(distribution)
channel (n)
candidat(e) candidate
(n) *or* applicant (n)
**candidature (f)
(à un emploi)**
application (n)
(for a job)
**capacité (f) *[rende-
ment, volume]***
capacity (n)
capacité d'emprunt
borrowing power
**capacité d'entre-
posage** storage
capacity
**capacité de produc-
tion** manufacturing
capacity

capacité industrielle industrial capacity
capital (m) principal (n) *[money]*
capital (m) *ou* **capitaux (mpl)** capital (n)
capital actions share capital
capital à risque *ou* capital-risque risk capital *or* venture capital
capital disponible available capital
capital initial *ou* d'investissement initial capital
capital nominal nominal capital
capital obligations debenture capital *or* debenture stock
capital roulant *ou* capital circulant circulating capital
capital social equity capital
capitalisation (f) capitalization (n)

capitalisation boursière market valuation *or* capitalization
capitaliser capitalize (v)
capitaliser les intérêts add (v) interest to the capital
capitaux (mpl) capital (n)
capitaux propres equity (n) *or* shareholders' equity
carat (m) carat (n)
carbone (m) carbon paper (n)
carbone: sans carbone *[autocopiant]* carbonless
cargaison (f) cargo (n)
cargo (m) cargo ship *or* cargo boat
carnet (m) (de banque, de chèques, de quittances) (bank, cheque, receipt) book (n)

carnet de comman-des order book

carte accréditive *[d'un magasin]* charge card (n)

carte à puce *ou* à mémoire smart card

carte bancaire cheque (guarantee) card

carte d'abonnement *[concert, etc.]* season ticket (n)

carte de crédit credit card

carte de débarque-ment landing card

carte d'embarque-ment boarding card *or* boarding pass

carte de membre (membership) card

carte de retrait cash card

carte de séjour residence permit

carte de travail work permit

carte professionnelle (business) card

cartel (m) cartel (n)

carton (m) *[matériau]* carton (n) *or* cardboard (n) *[material]*

carton (m) *[boîte en carton]* cardboard box (n) *or* carton (n) *[box]*

cash (m) *[argent comptant]* cash (n) *or* ready cash

cash (adv) cash (adv)

cash-flow (m) cash flow (n)

cash-flow (m) négatif negative cash flow

cash-flow positif positive cash flow

cash-flow actualisé discounted cash flow (DCF)

casse (f) breakages (n)

casser les prix slash (v) prices

catalogue (m) cata-logue (n); list (n)

**catalogue de vente
par correspondance**
mail-order catalogue
**catastrophe (f)
naturelle**
act (n) of God
catégorie (f) cate-
gory (n) *or* class (n)
**catégorie: de pre-
mière catégorie**
high-quality (adj)
**caution (f)
*[garantie]***
guarantee (n)
**caution (f) *[per-
sonne]*** surety (n) *or*
guarantee (n)
**caution: se porter
caution (pour
quelqu'un)**
stand (v) security *or*
go guarantee (for)
**cautionner
quelqu'un** bail (v)
someone out
**central (m)
téléphonique**
telephone
exchange (n)
central(e) central
(adj)

centralisation (f)
centralization (n)
centraliser
centralize (v)
centre (m)
centre (n) *[impor-
tant town]*
centre commercial
shopping centre *or*
shopping precinct
**centre de coût
*[comptabilité]*** cost
centre
**centre de
production *[unité]***
production unit (n)
**centre de profit
*[comptabilité]***
profit centre
centre des affaires
business centre
**centre
industriel**
industrial centre
centre(-)ville (m)
downtown (n)
certificat (m)
certificate (n)
**certificat d'ac-
tion(s)** share
certificate

certificat de douanes customs clearance certificate
certificat de garantie certificate of guarantee
certificat d'homologation certificate of approval
certificat d'immatriculation [société] certificate of incorporation
certificat d'origine certificate of origin
certificat médical doctor's certificate
certifier certify (v)
cesser stop (v); discontinue (v) [doing something]
cessible [transmissible] transferable (adj)
cession (f) [transfert] cession (n) or assignment (n) or assignation (n)
cession-bail (m) lease-back (n) (arrangement)

cessionnaire (mf) assignee (n)
chaîne (f) de magasins chain (n) [of stores]
chaîne (f) de montage assembly line (n)
chaîne (f) de production production line
chambre (f) d'hôtel hotel room (n) or hotel accommodation (n)
Chambre de commerce et d'industrie Chamber (n) of Commerce
chambre (f) froide cold store (n)
change (m) (foreign) exchange (n) [currency]
changement (m) [modification] change (n) or alteration (n)

changement de propriétaire *ou* **de direction**
under new management [shop]
changer [modifier]
change (v)
or alter (v)
changer de l'argent
change (v) some money
changer de propriétaire change hands (n) [shop]
chapardage (m)
pilferage (n) *or* pilfering (n)
charge (f) [chargement] load (n)
charge (complète) d'un camion
lorry-load (n) *or* truck-load (n)
charge en lourd
deadweight (n)
charge utile payload (n) *or* commercial load
charge: (frais) à la charge de (costs) payable by

chargé(e) (n) (de)
manager (n) *or* officer (n)
chargé(e) des relations publiques
public relations officer
chargement (m)
load (n); loading (n) [action]
charger des marchandises *ou* **du fret** take on (v) freight *or* cargo
charger un camion *ou* **un navire** load (v) a lorry *or* a ship
charger un programme [informatique] load (v) a (computer) program
charges (fpl) costs (n) *or* charges (n)
charges constatées d'avance [comptabilité]
accruals (n)
charges d'exploitation
running costs

charges sociales
social benefit
contributions (n)
**chariot (m) éléva-
teur** fork-lift truck
chef (m) [directeur]
chief (n) or head (n)
or manager (n)
chef comptable
chief accountant;
controller [US]
chef de bureau chief
clerk or head clerk
**chef de la
fabrication**
production manager
chef d'entreprise
company head
chef de projet
project manager
**chef de rayon [d'un
magasin]** depart-
ment manager
chef de service
head of department
or manager
chef du personnel
personnel manager
**chef du service des
réclamations**
claims manager

**chef du service
export**
export manager
**chemin (m)
de fer** rail (n) or
railway (n);
railroad [US]
chèque (m) cheque
(n); check [US]
chèque au porteur
cheque to bearer
chèque barré
crossed cheque
chèque-cadeau (m)
gift voucher (n)
chèque certifié
certified cheque
chèque de caisse
cheque to self
**chèque de
dividende** dividend
warrant (n)
**chèque de
salaire**
salary cheque
or pay cheque
chèque en blanc
blank cheque
chèque-livre (m)
book
token (n)

chèque non barré ou chèque négociable open cheque *or* uncrossed cheque

chèque postal Post Office cheque

chèques personnalisés personalized cheques

chèque-repas (m) luncheon voucher (n)

chèque sans provision *ou* chèque en bois dud cheque; rubber check *[US]*

chéquier (m) *[carnet de chèques]* cheque book (n)

cher (chère) (adj) *[coûteux]* dear (adj) *or* expensive (adj)

cher (chère) (adj) *[début de lettre]* dear [Sir, Madam, etc.]

cher: coûter *ou* être plus cher be more expensive *or* cost (v) more

chercheur (-euse) researcher (n) *or* research worker (n)

chevalier (m) blanc white knight (n)

chez *[aux bons soins de]* care of (c/o) *[on letter]*

chiffre (m) figure (n) *or* digit (n)

chiffre d'affaires turnover (n)

chiffre de vente(s) sales figures

chiffres (mpl) figures (n)

chiffres d'origine historical figures

chiffres réels actuals (n)

choisir choose (v)

choisir *[élire]* elect (v)

choisir la solution de facilité take (v) the soft option

choix (m) choice (n)

choix (m) *[sélection]* choice *or* selection (n)

choix: de choix choice (adj)

chômage (m) unemployment (n)

**chômage: au *ou* en
chômage** out of
work (adj) *or*
unemployed (adj)
chômeur (-euse)
unemployed person
**chômeur (-euse):
les chômeurs** the
unemployed (n)
chute (f) *[baisse]*
drop (n) *or* fall (n)
or slump (n)
chuter *[baisser]*
drop (v) *or* fall (v)
or slump (v)
**chuter *[baisser
rapidement]***
plummet (v)
cible (f) target (n)
**cibler *[avoir pour
but]*** target (v)
circulaire (f)
circular (n) *or*
circular letter (n)
**circulation (f)
*[distribution,
argent, voitures]***
circulation (n)
citer *[un prix]*
quote (v)
(a price)

clair(e) clear
(adj) *or* easy to
understand
**classe (f) *[caté-
gorie]*** class (n)
**classe affaires *[voy-
age]*** business class
**classe touriste
*[voyage]*** economy
class *or* tourist class
**classement (m)
*[de documents]***
filing (n) *[action]*
classer classify (v)
or order (v)
**classer (des
documents, dans
un classeur)** file
(v) (documents)
classeur (m)
filing cabinet (n)
classification (f)
classification (n)
clause (f) clause
(n) *or* provision (n)
clause d'exclusion
exclusion clause
**clause d'indexation
ou de rèvision
des coûts** escalator
clause

clause échappatoire
escape clause
clause pénale
penalty clause
clause résolutoire
termination clause
clause
supplémentaire
[avenant] rider (n)
clavier (m)
keyboard (n)
clavier numérique
[pavé] numeric
keypad (n)
claviste (m)
keyboarder (n)
clé (f) *ou* clef (f)
key *[to door;*
important]
client fidèle
regular customer
client(e) customer
(n) *or* client (n)
client(e) *[acheteur]*
shopper (n)
client potentiel
prospect (n) *or*
potential customer
clientèle (f)
custom (n) *or*
clientele (n)

clôture (f) close
(n) *or* end (n) *or*
finish (n)
clôture: après
clôture *[Bourse]*
after hours
clôturer un compte
[fermer] close (v)
an account
club (m) *[société]*
club (n) *or*
society (n)
coassocié(e) (n)
copartner (n)
coassurance (f)
co-insurance (n)
COB (Commission
des opérations de
Bourse) SIB
(Securities and
Investments Board)
cocréancier (-ière)
(n) co-creditor (n)
code (m) code (n)
code (à) barres
bar code
code civil *[droit*
civil] (French) code
of civil law
code postal postcode
(n); zip code *[US]*

codirecteur (-trice)
co-director (n)
codirection (f) *ou*
cogestion (f) joint
management (n)
coefficient (m)
de remplissage
[avion] load
factor (n) *[of plane]*
coefficient de
rentabilité
profitability (n)
coentreprise (f)
joint venture (n)
coffre-fort (m)
safe (n)
coffret (m)
[jeu d'outils, etc.]
boxed set (n)
colis (m)
parcel (n)
collaborateur
(-trice)
contributor (n)
collaborateur
(-trice) indépen-
dant(e)
freelancer (n) *or*
freelance (worker)
collaboration (f)
collaboration (n)

collaborer
collaborate (v) *or*
co-operate (v)
collectif (-ive)
collective (adj) *or*
joint (adj)
collectivités (fpl)
locales local
authorities (n)
collègue (mf)
[associé]
associate (n)
colonne (f)
column (n)
colonne des crédits
credit column
or credit side
colonne des débits
debit column *or*
debit side
combine (n) *[pra-*
tique malhonnête]
fiddle (n); sharp
practice (n)
comité (m)
committee (n) *or*
board (n) *or*
council (n)
comité de
consommateurs
consumer council

comité consultatif
advisory board
comité d'entreprise
[travailleurs]
works committee *or*
works council
commande (f)
order (n)
[for goods]
commande de
réapprovision-
nement repeat
order *or* reorder (n)
commande par
téléphone
telephone order
commande urgente
rush order
commandes en
attente
outstanding orders
or back orders
commandes en
attente
[anticipées]
dues (n) *[items not*
yet on the market]
commandé(e)
(adj) on order
commander
order (v) (goods)

commanditaire (m)
sleeping partner (n)
commencement (m)
start (n)
commencer start
(v) *or* begin (v);
initiate (v)
commerçant(e)
shopkeeper (n) *or*
trader (n)
commerçant
indépendent
independant trader
commerce (m)
commerce (n)
or trade (n)
commerce *[entre-*
prise] business (n)
commerce bilatéral
reciprocal trade
commerce d'expor-
tation export trade
commerce
éléctronique
e-commerce (n)
commerce en ligne
e-commerce (n)
commerce
extérieur
overseas trade *or*
foreign trade

commerce intérieur
domestic trade
commerce
international inter-
national trade
commerce invisible
invisible trade
commerce
multilatéral
multilateral trade
commerce unilatéral
one-way trade
commerce visible
visible trade
commercial(e)
commercial (adj)
commercialisation
(f) commercializa-
tion (n);
marketing (n)
commercialiser
[rendre commercial]
commercialize (v)
commercialiser
[vendre]
market (v) or put
(v) on the market
commerciaux
(mpl)
sales people or
sales team

commissaire (m)
aux comptes
[audit] auditor (n)
commission (f)
[comité]
commission (n) or
committee (n)
commission (f)
[d'agent] commis-
sion (n) [money]
commission (f)
[d'agent de change
ou courtage]
brokerage (n) or
broker's commission
commission
d'enquête commis-
sion of inquiry
Commission des
opérations de
Bourse (COB)
Securities and
Investments Board
(SIB)
commission du
logement rent
tribunal
commission: faire
partie d'une com-
mission sit (v) on a
committee

commun(e)
[conjoint] common
or joint (adj)
commun(e)
[courant] common
(adj) *or* frequent
(adj)
communauté (f)
community (n)
communication (f)
communication (n)
communication (f)
[message]
communication *or*
message (n)
communication (f)
(téléphonique)
(phone *or*
telephone) call (n)
communication avec
pré-avis
[téléphone]
person-to-person call
communication
interurbaine
[téléphone] trunk
call *or* long
distance call
communication
urbaine *[téléphone]*
local call

communications
(fpl) communica-
tions (n)
communiqué (m)
de presse press
release (n)
communiquer com-
municate (v)
compagnie (f)
[société] company
(n) *or* firm (n) *or*
house (n)
compagnie
aérienne airline
(n); air carrier (n)
compagnie
d'assurances
insurance company
compagnie
d'assurance-vie
assurance company
compagnie de
navigation
shipping company *or*
shipping line
comparabilité (f)
comparability (n)
comparable
comparable (adj)
comparaison (f)
comparison (n)

comparaître (en justice) appear (v) before a court

comparer compare (v)

comparer les prix [de différents magasins] shop around (v)

compensation (f) [dédommagement] compensation (n)

compensation (f) [d'un chèque] clearance (n) of a cheque

compenser [dédommager] make up (v) (a loss)

compenser un chèque clear (v) a cheque

compétence (f) [autorité] jurisdiction (n) or authority (n)

compétence (f) [habileté, savoir-faire] expertise (n) or know-how (n)

compétent(e) (adj) [habile] competent (adj); skilled (adj)

compétent(e) [expérimenté] experienced (adj)

compétitif (-ive) competitive (adj)

compétition (f) [concurrence] competition (n)

compétitivité (f) competitiveness (n)

complémentaire complementary (adj)

complet [annonce devant un hôtel, etc] no vacancy

complet (-ète) [achevé] complete (adj)

complet (-ète) [entier] clear (adj) [day]

complet (-ète) [hôtel, vol] fully booked or booked up (adj)

complexe (m) industriel industrial complex (n)

**composer un
numéro** *[téléphone]*
dial (v) a number
comprendre
understand (v)
comprendre
[consister en]
consist of (v)
comprendre
[inclure] include (v)
comprendre
[se rendre compte]
realize (v) *or*
understand (v)
compression (f)
[des dépenses, etc.]
retrenchment (n)
compris(e) *[inclus]*
inclusive of (adj)
**compris(e): non
compris** exclusive
of (adj)
compromis (m)
compromise (n);
arrangement (n)
comptabiliser
enter (v) in an
account
comptabilité (f)
[comptes]
accounts (n)

comptabilité (f)
[système]
accounting (n)
comptabilité (f)
[tenue de livres]
bookkeeping (n)
**comptabilité
analytique** cost
accounting
**comptabilité de
gestion**
management
bookkeeping
**comptabilité en
partie double**
double-entry
bookkeeping
**comptabilité en
partie simple**
single-entry
bookkeeping
**comptabilité
générale** *ou*
financière financial
accounting
**comptabilité: tenir
la comptabilité**
keep (v) the
accounts
comptable (mf)
accountant (n)

comptant *ou* **au comptant** cash (adv)

compte (m) account (n)

compte à découvert overdrawn account

compte bancaire bank account

compte bloqué account on stop

compte-chèque postal (CCP) Post Office account

compte clients *[créances]* accounts receivable *or* receivables (n)

compte courant current account *or* drawing account

compte crédit *[à la banque]* budget account

compte créditeur account in credit

compte d'achat *ou* **compte permanent** credit account *or* charge account

compte d'affectation appropriation account

compte de caisse cash account

compte de capital capital account

compte de chèques cheque account

compte de contrepartie contra account

compte de dépôt *ou* **compte sur livret** deposit account

compte d'épargne savings account

compte d'épargne en actions (CEA) Personal Equity Plan (PEP)

compte de non-résident external account

compte de régularisation *[société]* accruals

compte de résultat *ou* **de pertes et profits** profit and loss account

compte détaillé
detailed account *or*
itemized account
**compte
d'exploitation**
trading account
**compte
fournisseurs
[dettes]** accounts
payable *or*
payables (n)
compte joint joint
account
**compte
numéroté**
numbered account
**compte oisif *ou*
compte qui dort**
dormant account *or*
dead account
compte ouvert
open account
**compte: avoir un
compte** have (v) an
account
**compte: suivant
compte remis** for
account rendered
**comptes (mpl)
(de la société)**
company's accounts

comptes consolidés
consolidated
accounts
**comptes de fin de
mois** month-end
accounts
comptes de gestion
management
accounts
**comptes de
l'exercice** annual
accounts
**comptes de
quinzaine**
mid-month accounts
**comptes
semestriels**
half-yearly accounts
compter count (v)
or add (v)
**compter sur
(quelqu'un,
quelque chose)**
count on (v) *or*
depend on (v) *or*
rely on (v)
comptoir (m)
counter
**conception (f) (de
produit) [design]**
(product) design (n)

concerner concern (v); affect (v)

concession (f) *[droit exclusif de vente]* concession (n) *or* distributorship (n)

concessionnaire (mf) concessionaire (n) *or* distributor (n)

concevoir *[dessiner]* design (v)

conciliation (f) conciliation (n)

conclure un accord conclude (v) an agreement

conclure une affaire, un marché clinch (v) a deal *or* make (v) a deal

concorder (avec) *[correspondre]* agree with (v) *or* be the same as

concorder: faire concorder *[comptes, états]* reconcile (v)

concurrence (f) competition (n)

concurrence déloyale unfair competition

concurrence farouche stiff *or* cut-throat *or* keen competition

concurrence: faire concurrence à quelqu'un compete (v) with someone

concurrencer compete (v)

concurrent(e) (n) competitor (n) *or* rival (n)

concurrent(e) (adj) competing (adj) *or* rival (adj)

concurrentiel (-elle) *[en concurrence]* competing (adj) *or* competitive (adj)

condamner (quelqu'un) à une amende fine (v) (someone)

condition (f) condition (n)

condition (f) *[état]* condition *or* state (n)

condition:
(acheter) à
condition (buy) on
approval *or* on appro
condition: à (la)
condition que on
condition that *or*
provided that
condition: (vente)
sous condition
conditional (adj)
(sale)
conditions (fpl)
[modalités, état]
terms (n) *or*
conditions (n)
conditions
avantageuses
favourable terms
conditions d'emploi
terms of
employment *or* of
service
conditions de
travail working
conditions
conditions de vente
conditions *or* terms
of sale
conditionnel (-elle)
conditional (adj)

conditionnement
(m) [emballage]
packaging *[action,*
material]
conditionnement
(m) [présentation]
display pack *or*
display box (n)
conditionner
[emballer]
package (v)
conducteur (-trice)
[voiture] driver (n)
conduire (une
voiture) drive (v)
(a car)
confection (f)
ready-to-wear (adj)
(clothing)
conférence (f)
conference (n)
conférence de
presse press
conference
conférence: en
conférence in a
meeting
confiance (f)
confidence (n)
confidentialité (f)
confidentiality (n)

confidentiel (-elle)
confidential (adj)
confidentiellement
confidentially (adv)
or in confidence
confier entrust (v)
confirmation (f)
confirmation (n)
confirmer
confirm (v)
**confirmer une
embauche** confirm
someone in a job
**confirmer une
réservation**
confirm a booking
confiscation (f)
seizure (n) *or*
forfeiture (n)
confisquer seize
(v) *or* declare (v)
forfeit
conflit (n) conflict
(n); dispute (n)
conflit d'intérêts
conflict of interest
conflits du travail
industrial disputes
or labour disputes
conformément à
(l'échantillon, la

facture) as per
(sample,
invoice, etc.)
**conformément à un
contrat**
contractually (adv)
**conformer: se
conformer à**
comply with (v)
**congé (m)
[autorisation
d'absence]** leave
(n) *or* leave of
absence
**congé (m)
[vacances]**
holiday (n)
**congé de maladie
ou congé-maladie
(m)** sick leave
congé de maternité
maternity leave
**congé légal [fête
légale]** statutory
holiday
congé payé paid
leave *or* paid holiday
congé sans solde
unpaid leave
**congé: partir en
congé** go on holiday

congé: prendre un congé take time off ; take a short holiday
congédier dismiss (v) *or* pay off (v) *or* sack (v)
conglomérat (m) conglomerate
congrès (m) conference (n)
conjointement jointly (adv)
conjoncture (f) économique economic trends (n) *or* situation (n)
connaissement (m) bill of lading (n)
conseil (m) *[comité]* board (n) *or* council (n)
conseil (m) *[personne]* consultant (n)
conseil (m) *[recommandation]* (piece of) advice (n)
conseil d'adminis-tration board of directors

conseil d'arbitrage adjudication tribunal
conseil de prud'hommes industrial (arbitration) tribunal
conseil juridique *[recommandation]* legal advice
conseil municipal town council
conseillé(e) recommended (adj)
conseiller (v) advise (v); recommend (v)
conseiller (-ère) (n) adviser (n) *or* advisor (n); consultant (n)
conseiller en gestion d'entreprise management consultant (n)
conseiller fiscal tax consultant *or* tax adviser
conseiller juridique legal adviser

**conserver
[maintenir]**
maintain (v) or keep
(v) at same level
**considération: sans
considération de**
regardless of
**consignataire (mf)
[destinataire]**
consignee (n)
consigne (f) left
luggage office
consigné(e)
returnable (adj)
**consigné(e): non
consigné(e)**
non-returnable (adj)
(packing, etc.)
**consigner [donner
en dépôt]**
consign (v)
**consigner
[enregistrer]** record
(v); minute (v) [at a
meeting]
**consignes (fpl) de
sécurité** safety
regulations (n)
**consignes (fpl) en
cas d'l'incendie**
fire regulations

consister en
consist of (v)
**consolidation (f)
(d'une dette)**
funding (n) (of
debt)
**consolidé(e)
[compte]**
consolidated (adj)
**consolidé(e)
[dette]** funded (adj)
consolider
consolidate (v)
**consommateur
(-trice)**
consumer (n)
**consommateur (m)
final** end user (n)
consommation (f)
consumption (n)
**consommation des
ménages** house-
hold consumption
**consommation
domestique ou
nationale** domestic
or home consumption
consortium (m)
consortium (n)
constant(e)
constant (adj)

constituer *[créer]*
form (v) *or* set up
(v) (a company)
constitution (f)
*[statuts d'une
société]*
constitution (n)
constructeur (m)
constructor (n) *or*
builder (n)
constructeur (m)
[fabricant]
manufacturer (n) *or*
maker (n)
**constructeur clés
en main** turnkey
operator
construction (f)
construction (n) *or*
building (n)
**construction: en
construction** under
construction
consultant (m)
consultant (n)
consulter
consult (v)
consulter un avocat
take legal advice
contact (m) con-
tact (n) *[general]*

contact (m)
[relation] contact
(n) *[person]*
contacter *[joindre]*
contact (v)
contenant (m)
[récipient]
container (n)
conteneur (m)
container (n)
**conteneurisation
(m)** *ou* mise (f) en
conteneur(s)
containerization (n)
conteneuriser *ou*
**mettre en
conteneurs**
containerize
(v) *or* put into
containers
contenir contain
(v) *or* hold (v)
**contentieux
(m)** legal
department (n) *[of
company]*
contenu (m)
[physique]
contents (n)
contenu (m)
[teneur] content (n)

**contingent (m) *ou*
contingentement
(m)** quota (n)
**contingentement
d'importation**
import quota
**contingenté(e)
(adj) *[produit]***
subject to a quota
continu(e)
continuous (adj)
continuel (-elle)
continual (adj)
**continuellement
*[sans cesse]***
continually (adv)
continuer continue
(v) *or* carry on (v)
or go on (v)
**contourner (une dif-
ficulté)** get round
(v) (a problem)
contracter
contract (v)
**contracter des
dettes** incur (v)
debts
**contracter une
assurance** take out
(v) an insurance
policy

contractuel (-elle)
contractual (adj)
contraire
contrary (adj)
contraste (m)
contrast (n)
contrat (m)
contract (n) *or*
agreement (n)
**contrat à durée
déterminée**
fixed-term contract
**contrat à durée
indéterminée**
permanent contract
**contrat d'associa-
tion *ou*** de société
deed of partnership
contrat d'assurance
insurance contract
**contrat d'exclu
sivité** exclusive
agreement
**contrat de produc-
tivité** productivity
agreement
contrat de service
service contract
**contrat de
sous-traitance**
subcontract (n)

contrat de travail
contract of
employment
**contrat de travail à
durée déterminée
(CDD)** fixed-term
contract
**contrat de vente
*[acte de vente]*** bill
(n) of sale
**contrat forfaitaire
ou contrat à prix
ferme** fixed-price
agreement
contrat global
blanket agreement;
package deal
**contrat sous seing
privé** private
contract
**contrefaçon (f)
*[copie]*** imitation
(n) *or* copy (n) *or*
forgery (n)
**contrefaçon (f)
*[délit]***
infringement (n) (of
patent, etc.)
contrefaire
counterfeit (v);
pirate (v)

**contrefaire un
produit protégé par
un brevet** infringe
(v) a patent
contre-OPA (f)
reverse takeover (n)
contrepassation (f)
rectifying (n) (an
entry)
**contrepasser une
écriture** rectify (v)
an entry
**contre-proposition
(f)** counter-offer (n)
contresigner
countersign (v)
contribuable (mf)
taxpayer (n)
**contribuer (une
somme)**
contribute (v)
contribution (f)
contribution (n)
**contributions
directes** direct
taxes *or* direct
taxation
**contributions
indirectes** indirect
taxes *or* indirect
taxation

**contrôle (m)
[administration]**
control (n)
**contrôle (m)
[essai]** control *or*
test (n)
**contrôle (m)
[maîtrise]**
control (n)
**contrôle (m)
[restriction]** control
or limitation (n) *or*
restriction (n)
**contrôle (m)
[vérification]**
control *or* check (n)
or examination (n)
contrôle budgétaire
budgetary control
contrôle de qualité
quality control
**contrôle des
changes** exchange
control
contrôle des loyers
rent control
contrôle des prix
price control
contrôle des stocks
stock control; inven-
tory control *[US]*

contrôle douanier
customs examina-
tion; baggage check
**contrôlé(e) par
l'Etat** government-
controlled (adj)
contrôler control (v)
**contrôler [faire
l'essai]** test (v) *or*
control (v)
contrôler [vérifier]
inspect (v) *or* moni-
tor (v) *or* control (v)
contrôleur (m)
controller (n)
**contrôleur des
stocks** stock
controller
**convenir [être d'ac-
cord]** agree with
(v) *[of same
opinion]*
**convenir [faire
l'affaire]** fit (v) *or*
be suitable
convention (f)
agreement (n)
**convention
collective sur les
salaires** collective
wage agreement

convention écrite
ou contrat écrit
written agreement
convenu(e)
[accepté]
agreed (adj)
conversion (f)
conversion (n)
convertibilité (f)
convertibility (n)
convertible
convertible (adj)
convivial(e)
user-friendly (adj)
convocation (f)
summons (n)
convoquer (une
assemblée) call (v)
or convene (v) (a
meeting)
coopératif (-ive)
(adj) co-operative
(adj)
coopération (f)
co-operation (n)
coopérative (f)
[société]
co-operative (n) *or*
co-operative society
coopérer
co-operate (v)

coopter quelqu'un
co-opt (v) someone
coordonnées (fpl)
[détails]
particulars (n)
coordonnées
bancaires bank
details (n)
coparticipation (f)
copartnership (n)
copie (f) *[d'un*
document] copy (n)
or duplicate (n)
copie carbone
carbon copy
copie certifiée
conforme certified
copy
copie conforme
true copy
copie (sur) papier)
[d'imprimante]
hard copy
copropriétaire (mf)
joint owner (n) *or*
part owner
copropriété (f) joint
ownership (n) *or*
part-ownership (n)
copyright (m)
copyright (n)

corbeille *[Bourse]*
trading floor (n)
corporation (f)
[guilde] guild (n)
correction (f)
correction (n)
correspondance (f)
[courrier]
correspondence (n)
correspondance (f)
[transport] con-
necting flight, etc.
**correspondance
commerciale** busi-
ness correspondance
correspondant(e)
[courrier, journaliste]
correspondent (n)
**correspondre (à
quelque chose)**
correspond (v) (with
something)
**correspondre avec
quelqu'un** corre-
spond with someone
**corrigé(e) des
variations saison-
nières** seasonally
adjusted (figures)
corriger correct
(v); adjust (v)

**corrompre
(quelqu'un)** bribe
(v) (someone)
cosignataire (mf)
joint signatory (n)
cote (f) *[Bourse]*
quotation (n)
cote (de crédit)
(financial) rating (n)
**coté(e) (adj) en
Bourse** quoted
(adj) *or* listed (adj)
on the Stock
Exchange
côté (m) side (n)
coter (en Bourse)
quote (v) (on the
Stock Exchange)
**cotisation (f) *[à un
club, à une revue,
etc.]*** subscription (n)
cotisation (f)
[contribution]
contribution (n)
**cotiser *[à un club, à
une revue, etc.]***
subscribe (v)
cotiser *[contribuer]*
contribute (v)
coulage (m) *[perte]*
leakage (n)

coulage (m) *[vol]*
shrinkage (n)
coupon (m)
coupon (n)
coupon attaché
cum coupon
coupon détaché ex
coupon
coupon-prime (m)
gift voucher (n)
coupon-réponse
(m) reply coupon
coupure (f) *[billets*
de banque]
denomination (n)
cour (f) *[tribunal]*
court (n)
cour de justice law
courts
courant *[de ce*
mois] instant
(adj) *or* inst.
courant(e) current
(adj)
courant(e) *[actuel]*
current (adj) *or*
going (adj) *[price]*
courant(e)
[commun] common
(adj) *or*
frequent (adj)

courant(e) *[de*
base] stock (adj)
[normal]
courant(e)
[quotidien] day-to-
day *[expenses]*
courbe (f) curve (n)
courbe des ventes
sales curve
courir *[s'accumuler]*
accrue (v)
courir un risque
run (v) a risk
couronne (f) *[unité*
monétaire:
Danemark, Norvège]
krone (n)
couronne (f) *[unité*
monétaire: Suède,
Islande] krona (n)
courrier (m) post
(n) *or* mail (n)
courrier à l'arrivée
incoming mail
courrier au départ
outgoing mail
courrier
électronique email
(n) *[system]*
courrier ordinaire
surface mail

cours (m) [études]
course (n)
cours (m) [taux]
rate (n); price (n)
cours à terme
forward rate
cours de clôture
[Bourse] closing
price
cours de commerce
commercial course
cours de gestion
d'entreprise
[management]
management course
cours demandé
asking price
cours de recyclage
refresher course
cours d'ouverture
[Bourse] opening
price
cours du change
rate of exchange
cours du jour
today's rate
cours du marché
market rate
cours par corre-
spondence corre-
spondence course

cours: au cours de
during (adv) or in
the course of
cours: en cours in
progress
cours: (monnaie)
qui a cours legal
tender
courses (fpl)
shopping (n)
[action]
courses: faire des
ou ses courses go
shopping or do
some shopping
coursier (m)
[commissionnaire]
(office)
messenger (n)
coursier (m) [en
vélo, moto, voiture]
courier (n)
court(e) short (adj)
court(e): à court
de short of
court(e): à court
terme short-term
(adj)
courtage (m)
[profession]
stockbroking (n)

courtage (m)
[commission
d'agent] brokerage
(n) *or* broker's
commission (n)
courtier (m)
broker (n)
courtier
d'assurances
insurance broker
courtier en devises
foreign exchange
broker *or* dealer (n)
courtier en valeurs
mobilières stockbro-
ker (n) *or* broker (n)
courtier maritime
ship broker
couru(e) (adj)
[intérêt] accrued
(adj)
coût (m) cost (n)
coût, assurance,
fret (CAF) cost,
insurance and
freight (c.i.f.)
coût courant
current cost
coût d'acquisition
d'immobilisations
capital expenditure

coût de fabrication
ou **de production**
production cost;
manufacturing cost
coût de la
main-d'oeuvre
labour cost(s)
coût de lancement
launching cost
coût de la vie cost
of living
coût de revient (de
marchandise ven-
due) cost of sales
coût d'exploitation
ou **coût opéra-**
tionnel operating
cost *or* running cost
coût fixe fixed cost
coût historique *ou*
coût d'acquisition
historical cost
coût majoré
cost plus
coût marginal
marginal cost
coût unitaire
unit cost
coût proportionnel
ou **coût variable**
variable cost

coûter cost (v)
coûteux (-euse)
[cher] dear (adj) *or*
expensive (adj) *or*
costly (adj)
couvert (m) *[au
restaurant]* cover
charge (n)
couverture (f)
[garantie] cover (n)
couverture contre
l'inflation hedge
(n) against inflation
couverture
d'assurance
insurance cover
couverture des
dividendes
dividend cover
couverture (f)
médiatique media
coverage
couvrir *[dépenses]*
cover (v) *[expenses,
a position]*
couvrir les coûts de
production cover
costs
créance (f) debt (n)
créance douteuse
bad debt

créance exigible
debt due
créances (fpl)
outstanding debts
or monies owing
créances (fpl)
[comptes clients]
accounts receivable
or receivables (n)
créancier (m)
creditor (n)
créancier
chirographaire
unsecured creditor
créancier
prioritaire
preferential *or*
preferred creditor
créancier privilégié
secured creditor
créancier sans
garantie unsecured
creditor
crédit (m) credit (n)
crédit à court
terme short
credit *or* short-term
credit
crédit à découvert
[découvert autorisé]
open credit

crédit à long terme
long credit *or*
extended credit
crédit-bail (m)
[leasing] leasing
(n) (with option to
purchase)
crédit bancaire
bank credit
crédit d'appoint *ou*
crédit stand-by
standby credit
crédit d'impôt *[avoir*
fiscal] tax credit
crédit gratuit
interest-free credit
crédit immédiat
instant credit
crédit permanent
ou **renouvelable**
revolving credit
crédit-relais (m)
bridging loan (n)
crédit: à crédit on
credit
crédit: faire crédit
give credit
créditer un compte
(d'une somme)
credit (a sum) to an
account

créditeur (-trice)
(adj) in credit
créditrentier
(-ière) annuitant (n)
crédits (mpl) à la
consommation
consumer credit
crédits gelés
frozen credits
créer (une société)
set up (v)
(a company)
créneau (m) sur le
marché gap (n) *or*
niche (n) in the
market
crise (f) crisis (n)
crise du dollar
dollar crisis
crise économique
slump (n) *or*
recession (n)
crise financière
crash (n) *or*
financial crisis
croissance (f)
growth (n) *or*
expansion (n)
croissance
économique
economic growth

croissance externe
external growth
culminer [atteindre
un niveau élevé]
peak (v)
cumulatif (-ive)
cumulative (adj)
cumulé(e) accrued
(adj)
curriculum (m)
vitae (CV)
curriculum
vitae (CV)
cycle (m) cycle (n)
cycle économique
economic cycle *or*
trade cycle
cyclique cyclical
(adj)

Dd

date (f) date (n)
date d'achèvement
(de travaux)
completion date

date d'échéance
maturity date
date de livraison
delivery date
date d'entrée en
vigueur effective
date; starting date
date d'ouverture
opening date
date de réception
date of receipt
date d'expiration
expiry date
date limite closing
date *or* deadline (n)
date limite de
vente sell-by date
date: de longue
date long-standing
(adj)
date: en date de
dated (adj)
date: sans date
undated
daté(e) dated (adj)
daté(e): non
daté(e) undated
dater date (v)
débardeur (m)
[docker]
stevedore (n)

débarquer land (v)
[passengers, cargo]
débarquer des
marchandises land
goods (at a port)
débarrasser: se
débarrasser de get
rid of (something)
débit (m) debit (n)
débit et crédit
[passif et actif]
debits and credits
débiter un compte
debit (v) an account
débiteur (m)
debtor (n)
débiteur (-trice)
(adj) *[compte]*
showing a debit; in
the red
débours (mpl)
out-of-pocket
expenses (n)
débourser
disburse (v)
débrayer *[arrêter le*
travail] knock off
(v) *or* stop (v) work
débrouiller: se
débrouiller cope
(v) *or* get along (v)

début (n)
beginning (n)
débutant(e) (n)
beginner (n)
débuter begin (v)
or start (v)
décentralisation (f)
decentralization (n)
décentraliser
decentralize (v)
déchargement (m)
unloading (n)
décharger
[marchandises]
unload (v) (goods)
déchets (mpl)
(industriels)
(industrial) waste (n)
déchiqueteur (m)
ou **déchiqueteuse**
(f) shredder (n)
décider *ou* prendre
une décision
decide (v) *or* come
(v) to a decision *or*
reach a decision
décider : se décider
make up (v)
one's mind
décideur (m)
decision maker (n)

décimale (f)
decimal (n)
décisif (-ive)
deciding (adj)
décision (f)
decision (n)
déclaration (f)
declaration (n) *or*
statement (n)
déclaration (f)
[annonce]
announcement (n)
déclaration de
revenus
declaration of
income
déclaration de
sinistre insurance
claim
déclaration de TVA
VAT declaration
déclaration
d'impôts tax return
or tax declaration
déclaration en
douane customs
declaration
déclaration sous
serment affidavit
déclarer declare
(v) *or* state (v)

déclarer *[statuer]*
rule (v)
déclarer des
marchandises à la
douane declare
goods to customs
déclarer quelqu'un
en faillite declare
someone bankrupt
déclarer un
dividende declare a
dividend
déclarer: rien à
déclarer nothing to
declare
décoller *[avion]*
take off (v)
décommander *[un*
rendez-vous]
cancel (v)
découler de result
from (v)
découvert (m) *[à la*
banque]
overdraft (n)
découvert autorisé
[crédit] open credit
découvert:
(compte) à décou-
vert overdrawn
(adj) (account)

décroissant(e)
decreasing (adj) *or*
diminishing (adj)
**dédommagement
(m)** compensation
(n) (for damage) *or*
indemnification (n)
**dédommager
*[indemniser]***
compensate (v) *or*
indemnify (v)
**dédommager: se
dédommager** recoup
(v) (one's losses)
**dédouanage (m) *ou*
dédouanement (m)**
customs clearance
**dédouané(e)
*[marchandise]***
duty-paid *[goods]*
**dédouaner des
marchandises** clear
(v) goods through
customs
déductible
deductible (adj)
**déductible des
impôts**
tax-deductible (adj)
déduction (f)
deduction (n)

déduire
[retrancher] deduct
(v) *or* take off (v)
déduire des impôts
set (v) against tax
**défaillance (f)
*[d'un appareil]***
breakdown (n)
**défaillance (f)
*[d'une société]***
bankruptcy (n)
défaillant(e) *[témoin]*
defaulter (n)
défaut (m) defect
(n) *or* fault (n)
**défaut (m) de
paiement**
non-payment (n)
défavorable
adverse (adj) *or*
unfavourable (adj)
défectueux (-euse)
defective (adj) *or*
faulty (adj)
**défectuosité (f)
*[imperfection]***
imperfection (n) *or*
defect (n)
**défendeur (m),
défenderesse (f)**
defendant (n)

défendre *[en justice]* defend (v)

défendre *[interdire]* forbid (v)

défendre: se défendre en justice defend (v) a lawsuit

défense (f) *[interdiction]* interdiction (n)

défense (f) *[juridique, protection]* defence (n)

déficit (m) deficit (n) *or* loss (n)

déficit (m) *[manque]* shortfall (n)

déficit commercial trade deficit *or* trade gap

déficitaire showing a deficit *or* unfavourable (adj)

défiscaliser exempt (v) from tax

déflation (f) deflation (n)

déflationniste deflationary (adj)

défraîchi(e) (en magasin) shop-soiled (item)

défrayer defray (v) (costs)

dégâts (mpl) *[dommage]* damage (n)

dégâts causés par le feu fire damage

dégâts causés par la tempête storm damage

dégrèvement (m) fiscal *ou* d'impôt tax concession (n) *or* tax relief (n)

déjeuner (m) d'affaires business lunch

délai (m) time limit (n) *or* deadline (n)

délai de livraison delivery time

délai d'exécution *ou* de production lead time

délai de préavis *ou* délai-congé (m) period of notice

délai de réflexion
cooling off period
[after purchase]
délai de
remboursement *ou*
d'amortissement
payback period
délai: à bref délai
at short notice
délai: dans les délais
within the time limits
délai: dernier délai
final date
délégation (f)
delegation (n)
délégué(e) (n)
delegate (n)
délégué(e)
commercial(e)
(sales) representa-
tive (n) *or* rep (n)
délégué(e) du
personnel worker
director (n)
délégué(e)
syndical(e) *[à un*
congrès] trade
union delegate
délégué(e) syndi-
cal(e) *[dans l'usine]*
shop steward (n)

déléguer
delegate (v)
délit (m)
d'initié(s) insider
dealing (n)
délit (m) par
abstention
nonfeasance (n)
demande (f) *[des*
consommateurs]
demand (n)
demande (f) *[récla-*
mation] demand
(n) *or* claim (n)
demande (f)
[requête] request
(n) *or* requisition (n)
demande (f) *[de*
remboursement]
call (n) *[for money]*
demande de brevet
déposée patent (n)
applied for *or* patent
pending
demande d'emploi
job application *or*
application for a job
demande de
reseignement(s)
inquiry (n) *or*
enquiry (n)

**demande
reconventionnelle**
counter-claim (n)
**demande
saisonnière**
seasonal demand
**demande: faire une
demande par écrit**
apply (v) in writing
**demande: sur
demande** on demand
or on request
demander *[exiger]*
demand (v)
**demander *[faire
payer]*** charge (v)
**demander
*[réclamer]*** ask for
(v) *or* request (v)
[something]
**demander de faire
quelque chose** ask
(v) (someone) to do
something
**demander des
renseignements**
ask for details *or* for
particulars
**demander un
remboursement**
ask for a refund

**démarchage (m)
*[porte-à-porte]***
door-to-door selling
(n) *or*
canvassing (n)
démarcheur (m)
door-to-door
salesman (n) *or*
canvasser (n)
**démarquer *[réduire
le prix]*** mark down
(v) (an article)
démarrage (m)
start (n)
**démarrage à *ou* de
zéro** cold start
**démarrage (d'une
affaire *ou* d'un pro-
duit)** start-up (n)
démarrer start (v)
or begin (v);
open (v)
**démarrer une
affaire *[s'établir]***
set up in business
**démettre: se
démettre (de ses
fonctions)** stand
down (v)
demeurer *[habiter]*
live (v)

demeurer
[séjourner] stay (v)
demi(e) (adj) half
(adj)
demi-douzaine (f)
half a dozen *or* a
half-dozen (n)
demie (f) half (n)
démission (f)
resignation (n)
démissionner
resign (v) *or*
leave (v)
démodé(e) old-
fashioned (adj) *or*
out of date (adj)
démonstrateur
(-trice) (n)
demonstrator (n)
démonstration (f)
demonstration (n)
déni (m) de
responsabilité
disclaimer (n)
denrée (f)
commodity (n)
denrées alimen-
taires foodstuffs (n)
denrées périssables
perishable goods *or*
perishables (n)

dépareillé(e) odd
(adj) *[not a pair]*
départ (m)
departure (n)
départs naturels
[employés] natural
wastage (n)
départs volontaires
[employés] voluntary
redundancy (n)
départemental(e)
departmental (adj)
dépassé(e)
[démodé(e)]
old-fashioned (adj)
or out of date (adj)
dépasser go (v)
higher than
dépasser *[excéder]*
exceed (v)
dépasser son
budget overspend
one's budget
dépeçage (m)
[d'une société]
asset-stripping (n)
dépendre de *ou*
compter sur
depend on (v)
dépense (f) expense
(n) *or* expenditure (n)

**dépense exception-
nelle [hors bilan]**
below-the-line
expenditure
dépenses (fpl)
outgoings (n)
[money paid out]
**dépenses de
consommation**
consumer spending
dépenser spend (v)
[money]
dépenser trop
overspend (v)
dépenser trop peu
underspend (v)
déport (m)
backwardation (n)
déposant(e) (n)
depositor (n)
**déposer une
demande de brevet**
file (v) an application
for a patent
**déposer une marque
de commerce** register
(v) a trademark
déposer une motion
propose (v) a motion
déposer une requéte
file (v) a request

dépositaire (mf)
[stockiste] stockist (n)
dépôt (m)
[d'argent]
deposit (n) *[in bank]*
dépôt (m)
[entrepôt] depot (n)
dépôt (m)
[magasin] store (n)
or storeroom (n)
dépôt à terme time
deposit
dépôt à terme fixe
fixed deposit
dépôt à vue
demand deposit
dépôt bancaire
bank deposit
dépôt de nuit [coffre]
night safe (n)
dépôt en coffre-fort
safe deposit
dépôt en espèces
cash deposit
dépôt rémunéré
interest-bearing
deposit
dépréciation (f)
depreciation (n)
déprécier
depreciate (v)

déprécier: se dép-
récier depreciate (v)
dépression (f)
(economic)
depression (n)
déréglementation
(f) deregulation (n)
dernier (-ière) last
one (n)
dernier (-ière) *[final]*
last (adj) *or* closing
(adj) *or* final (adj)
dernier (-ière) *[plus*
récent] latest (adj)
dernier entré,
premier sorti
(DEPS) last in first
out (LIFO)
dernier rappel final
demand (n)
dernier trimestre
last quarter (n)
dernière enchère
closing bid (n)
dérouler: se
dérouler *[opération]*
progress (v)
description (f)
description (n)
description de la fon-
ction job description

description
mensongère false
description
déséconomies (fpl)
d'échelle disec-
onomies of scale
désencadrer
le crédit lift (v)
credit
restrictions
désendettement (n)
[d'une société]
degearing (n)
design (m) design (n)
désinflation (f)
disinflation (n)
désinvestir
disinvest (v)
désister: se désister
stand down (v)
dessin (m) industriel
industrial design (n)
dessiner *[concevoir]*
design (v)
destinataire (mf)
addressee (n)
destinataire (mf)
[consignataire]
consignee (n)
destination (f)
destination (n)

détacher second (v)
[member of staff]
détail (m)
[précision] detail (n)
détail (m)
[ventilation]
breakdown (n)
détail *ou* **vente au**
détail retail (n);
retailing (n)
détaillant(e) retailer
(n) *or* retail dealer (n)
détaillé(e) *[compte]*
detailed *or* itemized
(account)
détailler detail (v)
or itemize (v)
détailler: se détailler
retail (v) (at)
détails (mpl)
[coordonnées]
particulars (n)
or details (n)
détenir *[garder]*
hold (v) *or* keep (v)
détenir *[posséder]*
hold (v) *or* own (v)
détenteur (-trice)
holder (n) *[person]*
détermination (f)
[fixation] fixing (n)

détermination de
l'assiette fiscale
tax assessment (n)
déterminer *[fixer]*
determine (v)
déterminer un prix
fixe (v) a price
détournement (m)
de fonds
misappropriation (n)
or embezzlement (n)
détourner des fonds
misappropriate (v) *or*
embezzle (v) funds
dette (f) *[argent]*
debt (n) *or* liability (n)
dette irrécouvrable
irrecoverable debt
dettes (fpl) à court
terme short-term
liabilities
dettes à long terme
long-term liabilities
dettes garanties
secured debts
dettes privilégiées
senior debts
deuxième *[second]*
second (adj)
deuxième trimestre
second quarter (n)

dévalorisation (f)
fall (n) in value
dévaloriser: se
dévaloriser fall (v)
in value
dévaluation (f)
devaluation (n) *or*
depreciation (n)
dévaluer devalue (v)
développement (m)
development (n)
développement
(m) *[croissance]*
expansion (n)
développement
économique economic
development
développement
industriel industrial
expansion
développer
develop (v)
développer: se
développer *[grandir]*
expand (v) *or* grow (v)
devenir become (v)
devenir prospère
boom (v)
devis (m) estimate
(n) *or* quote (n) *or*
quotation (n)

devise (f)
(étrangère) (foreign)
currency (n); foreign
exchange (n)
devise convertible
convertible currency
devise faible soft
currency
devise forte hard
currency
devise non
convertible
blocked currency
devoir (de l'argent)
owe (v) (money)
diagramme (m)
diagram (n) *or*
chart (n)
diagramme circulaire
ou **en camembert**
pie chart
diagramme des
ventes sales chart
diagramme en
bâtons bar chart
Dictaphone (m) dic-
tating machine (n)
dictée (f) dictation (n)
dictée: prendre en
dicté take (v)
dictation

dicter dictate (v)

différé(e)
deferred (adj)

différence (f)
difference (n)

différence de prix
price difference *or*
difference in price

différent(e)
different (adj)

différentiel (-elle)
differential (adj)

différer *[être*
différent] differ (v)

différer *[remettre à*
plus tard] defer (v)

différer un
paiement defer
payment

diffuser *[distribuer]*
distribute (v)

diffusion (f)
[distribution]
distribution (n)

dilution (f) du
capital dilution (n)
of equity

dimensions (fpl)
measurements (n)

diminuer *[chuter]*
diminish (v) *or* fall
(v) *or* decrease (v)

diminuer *[supprimer]*
cut (v) *or* reduce (v)
or lower (v)

diminuer de valeur
[se déprécier]
depreciate (v) *or*
lose (v) value

diminution (f)
[chute] fall (n)
or decrease (n) *or*
reduction (n)

direct(e) direct (adj)

directement direct
(adv)

directeur (-trice) (n)
(company) director (n)
or manager (n)

directeur (-trice)
[chef de service]
(department) head
(n) *or* manager (n)

directeur (-trice)
adjoint(e) assistant
manager *or* deputy
manager

directeur (-trice)
commercial(e)
sales manager *or*
sales executive

directeur (-trice)
d'agence branch
manager

directeur (-trice)
d'agence *[banque]*
bank manager
directeur (-trice)
de la production
production manager
directeur (-trice)
de la publicité
publicity manager
directeur (-trice)
du marketing
marketing manager
directeur (-trice)
général(e) (DG) general manager *or* managing director (MD)
directeur (-trice)
général(e)
adjoint(e) deputy
managing director
directeur (-trice)
intérimaire acting
manager
direction (f)
direction (n)
direction (f) *[poste de directeur]* directorship (n) *or* managership (n)
direction (f) *[l'administration, les cadres]*
management (n) *or*
managerial staff

direction générale
[cadres supérieurs]
top management
directive (f)
directive (n) *or*
guideline (n)
dirigeant (m)
executive (n)
diriger *[gérer]*
manage (v) *or*
run (v)
diriger *[mener]*
lead (v) *or*
conduct (v) *or*
direct (v)
discours (m)
speech (n)
discrimination (f)
sexiste sexual
discrimination (n)
discussion (f)
discussion (n)
discuter discuss (v)
disponibilité (f)
availability (n)
disponibilités (fpl)
[liquidités] liquid
assets (n); cash
reserves (n)
disponible
available (adj);
obtainable (adj)

disponible: non disponible
unavailable (adj);
unobtainable (adj)
disposer en tableau ou en colonnes
tabulate (v)
dispositif (m) device
disposition (f) en tableau ou en colonnes
tabulation (n)
disque (m) disk (n)
disque CD ou disque compact compact
disc or CD
disque (m) dur
hard disk
disquette (f) diskette
(n) or floppy (disk)
disquette de sauvegarde backup copy (n)
dissimulation (f) d'actif concealment
of assets
dissoudre (une association) dissolve
(v) (a partnership)
distancer: se laisser distancer
fall behind (v)

distribuer [actions, marchandises)
distribute
[shares, goods]
distribuer [partager]
distribute (v);
allocate (v)
distributeur (m)
distributor (n)
distributeur automatique de billets (DAB)
cash dispenser (n);
cashpoint (n)
distribution (f) [diffusion]
distribution (n)
divers (mpl)
sundries (n)
divers(e) (adj)
miscellaneous (adj)
diversification (f)
diversification (n)
diversifier diversify (v)
dividende (m)
dividend (n)
dividende à recevoir ou dividende cumulé
accrued dividende
dividende complémentaire
surplus dividend

dividende intérimaire
interim dividend
dividende: avec
dividende cum
dividend
dividende: sans div-
idende ex dividend
division (f) *[secteur*
d'une société]
division (n)
docker (m)
stevedore (n)
document (m) docu-
ment (n) *or* paper (n)
document justificatif
documentary evidence
documentaire (adj)
documentary (adj)
documentation (f)
documentation (n);
literature (n)
dollar (m)
(américain) (US)
dollar (n) *or*
greenback (n)
domicile (m)
domicile (n)
domicilier
domicile (v)
dommage (m)
[dégâts] damage (n)

dommages-intérêts
ou **dommages et**
intérêts damages (n)
[insurance]
dommages matériels
damage to property
données (fpl) *[infor-*
matique] data (n)
données de sortie
output (n) *[computer]*
donner give (v)
donner de l'avance-
ment *[promouvoir]*
promote (v)
donner des
explications
inform (v); brief (v)
donner en reprise
trade in *[give in old*
item in part exchange]
donner en sous-trai-
tance *[sous-traiter]*
subcontract (v)
donner un pourboire
tip (v) *or* give (v) a tip
dos (m) back (n)
dossier (m) *[ensemble*
des documents] file
(n) *or* record (n)
dossier *[pochette avec*
documents] file (n)

**doter en capital
[capitaliser]**
capitalize (v)
douane (f) customs (n)
douanier (m) customs
official (n) *or* customs
officer (n)
double double (adj)
double (m) [copie]
copy (n) *or* duplicate
(n); carbon copy
double imposition
double taxation
doubler double (v)
douzaine (f) dozen (n)
**douze douzaines
[grosse]** gross (n)
(= 144)
**droit (m) [à quelque
chose]** right (n) *or*
entitlement (n)
droit (m) [science]
law (n) *[study]*
droit (m) [taxe]
duty (n) *or* tax (n)
or charge (n)
**droit(e) (adj)
[côté]** right (adj)
**droit (d'entrée) [rede-
vance]** (admission)
charge (n) *or* fee (n)

**droit civil, droit
commercial** civil
law, commercial law
droit d'auteur
copyright (n)
**droit d'enregistrement
ou d'inscription**
registration fee
droit de douane
customs duty
**droit de participa-
tion** equity (n)
droit de timbre
stamp duty
droit de veto right
of veto
**droit des contrats
et des obligations**
contract law
droit des sociétés
company law
droit international
international law
droit maritime
maritime law
**droits acquis
[intérêts]** vested
interest (n)
**droits (mpl)
de bassin** port
charges *or* port dues

droits de régie
excise duty
droits de tirage
spéciaux (DTS)
special drawing
rights (SDRs)
dû (due) due (adj)
or owing (adj)
ducroire del credere
dûment duly
dumping (m)
dumping (n)
duplicata (m)
[copie] duplicate (n)
or copy (n)
durée (f) *[période]*
period (n) *or* term (n)
durée de conservation
d'un produit shelf life
of a product
durée d'un bail
tenancy (n)
durer last (v)

Ee

écart (m)
discrepancy (n) *or*
differential (n)
écart de prix price
differential
écarts de salaires
wage differentials
échange (m) exchange
(n) *or* swap (n)
échange (m)
[troc] bartering (n)
échange: en échange
in exchange
échanges commer-
ciaux trade (n)
échangeable
exchangeable (adj)
échanger exchange (v)
or swap (v)
échanger *[un article*
acheté] exchange (v)
échantillon (m)
sample (n)
échantillon aléatoire
random sample
échantillon d'essai
trial sample

échantillon gratuit
free sample
**échantillon-témoin
(m)** check sample
échantillonnage (m)
sampling (n)
échec (m) failure (n);
flop (n) *[familiar]*
échelle (f) *[barème]*
scale (n)
échelle de prix fixe
fixed scale of charges
échelle des salaires
wage scale
échelle des tarifs
scale of charges
**échelle mobile des
salaries** incremental
scale
échelonner *[étaler]*
stagger (v)
échouer fail (v) *or*
not to succeed (v)
or flop (v)
**échouer
[négociations]**
break down (v)
échouer [projet]
fall through (v)
école (f) school (n);
college (n)

**école (f) de
secrétariat**
secretarial college
**école supérieure de
commerce** commercial
college
écologique (adj)
environmentally
friendly
économie (f) *[épargne]*
economy (n)
économie (f) *[système]*
economy (n)
**économie (f) de
l'offre** supply
side economics
**économie de
marché** *ou*
économie libérale
free market economy
économie dirigée
controlled economy
économie mixte
mixed economy
économie parallèle
ou **non officielle**
black economy
économie politique
economics (n)
économies (fpl)
savings

économies d'échelle
economies of scale
**économies: faire
des économies**
economize (v) *or*
save (up) (v)
économique
economic (adj)
**économique *[moins
cher]*** economical
économiquement
economically (adv)
économiser economize
(v) *or* save (up) (v)
économiser l'énergie
save energy
**économiser: qui
économise
l'énergie**
energy-saving (adj)
économiste (mf)
economist (n)
économiste financier
market economist
écouler *[liquider]*
sell off (v)
**écouler le surplus
de stock** dispose
(v) of excess stock
écouler: s'écouler
flow (v)

**écran (m) (d'ordina-
teur)** monitor (n) *or*
screen (n)
écrire write (v)
écrit (m) written
document (n)
écrit(e) written (adj)
**écrit(e) à la main
*[manuscrit]***
handwritten (adj)
écriture (f)
handwriting (n)
**écriture (f) *[compt-
abilité]*** entry (n)
écriture au crédit
credit entry
écriture au débit
debit entry
**écriture de
contrepartie**
contra entry (n)
**écrouler: s'écrouler
*[s'effondrer]*** collapse
(v) *or* slump (v)
**éditeur (-trice) *[qui
corrige]*** editor (n)
**éditeur (-trice) *[qui
publie]*** publisher (n)
**éditeur de texte
*[programme]***
(text) editor

édition (f) [d'un livre] edition (n)

effectif (m) labour force (n) *or* workforce (n)

effectuer carry out (v)

effet (m) [document] bill (n)

effet (m) [réaction] effect (n) *or* result (n)

effet à courte échéance short-dated bill

effet à longue échéance long-dated bill

effet bancaire bank bill (n)

effet de commerce negotiable instrument (n)

effet de levier [de la dette] gearing (n) *or* leverage (n)

effet escomptable *ou* bancable bankable paper (n)

effet négociable negotiable instrument

effet non négociable non-negotiable instrument

effets à payer bills payable *or* payables (n)

effets à recevoir bills receivable *or* receivables (n)

efficace efficient (adj *or* effective (adj)

efficacité (f) efficiency (n) *[ability to work well]*

efficacité (f) effectiveness (n) *[producing results]*

effondrement (m) collapse (n) *or* slump (n) *or* crash (n)

effondrement des ventes slump in sales

effondrer: s'effondrer slump (v) *or* collapse (v)

effondrer: s'effondrer [faire faillite] collapse (v) *or* go bankrupt *or* crash (v)

égal(e) equal (adj)

égaler equal (v)

égalisation (f) equalization (n)

égalité (f) equality (n)

élasticité (f)
elasticity (n)
élection (f) election (n)
élever: s'élever
[se monter à]
amount to (v)
or run to (v) *or*
total (v)
élire elect (v)
e-mail (m) email (n)
emballage (m)
[action] packing (n)
or packaging (n)
emballage (m)
[matériau] packing
material *or* packaging
material
emballage consigné
returnable packing
emballage de
présentation
display pack
emballage factice
dummy pack
emballage non
consigné *ou* perdu
non-returnable
packing
emballage
pelliculé
shrink-wrapping (n)

emballer pack (v)
or package (v) *or*
parcel up (v)
emballer
[envelopper] wrap
up (v)
emballer *[dans des*
cartons] pack (v)
goods *[into cartons]*
emballeur (-euse)
packer (n)
embargo (m)
embargo (n)
embargo: lever
l'embargo lift (an
embargo)
embargo: mettre
l'embargo (sur)
embargo (v) *or* put
an embargo (on)
embarquement (m)
embarkation (n)
embarquer
[des marchandises]
load (v)
embarquer
[monter à bord]
embark (v)
embaucher du
personnel hire (v)
or take on (v) staff

émettre (des actions, une lettre de crédit) issue (v) (shares, a letter of credit)

émission (f) d'actions share issue (n)

émission d'actions gratuites scrip issue *or* bonus issue

émission d'obligations debenture issue

émission prioritaire rights issue

empaqueter pack (v); parcel up (v)

emplacement (m) location (n) *or* site (n) *or* situation (n)

emploi (m) *[travail]* job (n) *or* employment (n) *or* post (n)

emploi (m) *[utilisation]* use (n)

emploi du temps schedule (n) *or* timetable (n)

emploi temporaire temporary employment

emploi: sans emploi *[au chômage]* unemployed (adj)

employé(e) (n) *[salarié]* employee (n)

employé(e) (adj) *[utilisé]* used (adj) *or* employed (adj)

employé(e) à temps partiel *ou* **à mi-temps** part-timer (n)

employé(e) aux écritures bookkeeper

employé(e) aux écritures (du grand livre des achats) bought ledger clerk

employé(e) aux écritures (du grand livre des ventes) sales ledger clerk

employé(e) de bureau office clerk (n) *or* office worker (n)

employé(e) qui réassortit les stocks sur les rayons shelf filler (n)

employé(e) subalterne junior clerk

employer use (v)
or employ (v)
employer [du person-
nel] employ (v) [staff]
employeur (-euse)
employer (n)
emprunt (m)
[somme reçue]
borrowing (n)
emprunt (m) [somme
prêtée] loan (n)
emprunt à court
terme short-term loan
emprunt à long
terme long-term loan
emprunt bancaire
bank borrowing
emprunt garanti
secured loan
emprunt obligataire
loan stock
emprunter borrow (v)
emprunteur (-euse)
borrower (n)
emprunteur sur
hypothèque
mortgager or mort-
gagor (n)
en dehors des
heures de bureau
outside office hours

en dehors des
heures de pointe
off-peak
en plus ou en sus
extra
encadrement (m)
du crédit credit
control (n) or credit
squeeze (n)
encadrer [limiter]
limit (v) or freeze (v)
or squeeze (v)
encaissable
cashable
encaisse (f) float (n)
encaissement (m)
cashing (n)
encaisser un chèque
cash (v) a cheque
encart (m) publici-
taire magazine
insert (n)
enchère (f) [offre]
bid (n) or bidding (n)
enchère (f) ou
vente aux
enchères auction (n)
enchérir sur
quelqu'un put (v)
a higher bid than
someone

enchérisseur (m)
bidder (n)
encombrer (le
marché) glut (v)
(the market)
endetté(e) (adj) in
debt; debtor (nation)
endettement (m)
indebtedness (n);
debt (n)
endettement:
société à fort coef-
ficient d'endette-
ment highly-geared
company
endetter get (v)
(someone) into debt
endetter: s'endetter
get (v) into debt *or*
run (v) into debt
endommagé(e)
damaged (adj)
endommager
[abîmer]
damage (v)
endossataire (mf)
endorsee (n)
endossement (m)
endorsement (n)
endosser un chèque
endorse (v) a cheque

endosseur (m)
endorser (n)
endroit (m) place (n)
énergie (f)
[électricité] energy
(n) *or* electricity (n)
enfreindre la loi
break (v) the law
engagement (m)
commitment (n) *or*
engagement (n)
engager *[entamer]*
enter (v) into
(negotiations)
engager (des
dépenses) incur (v)
(costs)
engager: s'engager
à agree (v) to (do
something)
enlèvement (m)
collection (n) *[of*
goods]
enlever *[déduire ou*
rabattre] take off (v)
or deduct (v)
enlever *[supprimer]*
remove (v)
énoncé (m)
[formulation] form (n)
of words

enquête (f)
investigation (n) *or*
survey (n)
enquêter investigate (v)
enregistré(e)
registered (adj)
enregistrement
(m) *[à l'aéroport]*
check-in (n) *[at*
airport]
enregistrement (m)
[immatriculation]
registration (n)
enregistrer *[imma-*
triculer ou inscrire]
register (v)
enregistrer *[noter]*
enter (v) *or* write
in (v)
enregistrer:
se faire enregistrer
[s'inscrire] register
(v) *[at hotel, etc.]*
enseigne (f)
sign (n)
entamer *[démarrer]*
open (v) *or* begin (v)
or enter into (v)
entamer des
négociations
open negotiations

entente (f)
[arrangement]
understanding (n)
or agreement (n)
entier (-ière)
complete (adj)
entrée (f)
admittance (n)
or admission (n)
entrée (f) *[prix]*
admission charge (n)
or entry (n)
entreposage (m)
storage (n) *or*
warehousing (n)
entreposer store (v)
or keep (v) in
warehouse
entrepôt (m)
[bâtiment] ware-
house (n) *or* depot (n)
entrepôt (m)
[magasin]
storeroom (n)
entrepôt (m) *[port]*
entrepot port
entrepôt de douanes
bonded warehouse
entrepôt
frigorifique
cold store

entreprendre
undertake (v) *or*
embark on (v)
entrepreneur (m)
[homme d'affaires]
entrepreneur (n)
entrepreneur (m)
[en construction, etc.]
contractor (n)
entrepreneur de
transports routiers
haulage contractor
entreprise (f) *[opéra-*
tion] undertaking (n)
or venture (n)
entreprise (f)
[organisation]
enterprise (n) *or*
business (n)
entreprise du
secteur public
state enterprise
entreprise privée
private enterprise
entreprise:
dans l'entreprise
in-house
entrer enter (v) *or*
go in (v)
entretenir *[faire*
durer] maintain (v)

entretien (m)
[d'une machine]
service (n) *or*
maintenance (n)
entretien (m) *[pour un*
poste] interview (n)
[for a job]
enveloppe (f)
envelope (n)
enveloppe à fenêtre
window envelope
enveloppe (f)
budgétaire
[montant] budget (n)
enveloppe longue
foolscap envelope
environ *[approxi-*
mativement]
approximately (adv)
or about (adv)
envoi (m) *[expédi-*
tion] dispatch (n)
or shipment (n);
delivery (n)
envoi (m)
[marchandises]
consignment (n)
or shipment (n)
envoi groupé
consolidated
shipment

envoi par la poste
[publipostage]
mailing (n)
envoler: s'envoler
[monter rapidement]
rise (v) fast
envoyer
[expédier] send
(v) *or* ship (v)
envoyer par
avion send by air;
airmail (v) *[post]*
envoyer par fax *ou*
par télécopie fax (v)
envoyer par la poste
send (v) by post *or*
mail (v) *or* post (v)
envoyeur (-euse)
sender (n)
épargne (f)
[économie] saving (n)
épargne (f)
[sommes] savings (n)
épargner save (v)
(money) *or* put (v)
(money) aside
épuisé(e) (adj)
[article] out of stock
équilibrer balance (v)
équilibrer un budget
balance (v) a budget

équipe (f) shift (n)
or team (n)
équipe de jour day
shift (n)
équipe de nuit
night shift
équipe de vente
[les commerciaux]
sales team *or* sales
force
équipe dirigeante
management team
équipement (m)
equipment (n)
équiper equip (v)
équiper *[outiller]*
tool up (v) *[a
factory]*
équitable
[raisonnable]
fair (adj)
erreur (f) error (n)
or mistake (n)
erreur (f) *[écart]*
discrepancy (n)
erreur aléatoire
random error
erreur de calcul
miscalculation (n)
erreur d'ordinateur
computer error

erreur: faire une erreur make (v) a mistake

erreur: faire une erreur de calcul miscalculate (v)

escomptable discountable (adj)

escompte (m) discount (n)

escompte de caisse cash discount

espace (m) publici-taire advertising space (n)

espèces (fpl): en espèces (in) cash

espérance (f) de vie life expectancy (n)

espionnage (m) industriel industrial espionage (n)

esquisse (f) (d'un plan) draft (n)

esquisser [ébaucher] draft (v)

essai (m) trial (n) or test (n)

essai (m) [machine, voiture] test run (n)

essai: (acheter) à l'essai (buy) on approval or on appro

essai: (prendre quelqu'un) à l'essai (take someone) on probation

essayer try (v) or test (v)

essayer [une voiture] test drive (a car)

essence (f) petrol (n)

essentiel (-elle) essential (adj) or basic (adj)

esthétique (f) industrielle industrial design (n)

estimatif (-ive) estimated (adj)

estimation (f) estimate (n)

estimation approximative rough estimate or (rough) guess (n)

estimation des ventes estimated sales

estimation prudente conservative estimate

estimé(e) (adj)
estimated (adj)
estimer [calculer]
estimate (v) or
calculate (v)
estimer [évaluer]
estimate (v) or assess
(v) or value (v)
estimer [juger]
estimate (v) or
judge (v)
établi(e) estab-
lished (adj)
or fixed (adj)
établi(e) depuis
longtemps [société]
old-established
(adj) (company)
établir [fonder]
establish (v)
établir les comptes
make up (v)
the accounts
établir un chèque,
une facture write
out a cheque, an
invoice
établir un devis
(pour un
travail) estimate (v)
for a job

établir un nouveau
record set (v) a
new record
établissement (m)
setting up (n)
établissement (m)
[bâtiment] building
(n) or premises (n)
établissement
d'un plan
ou d'un programme
scheduling (n)
étage (m) floor (n)
étagère (f) shelf (n)
étalage (m)
[en vitrine]
window display (n)
étalage (m) [présen-
tation] display (n)
étalage (m)
[présentoir] display
stand (n)
étaler [échelonner]
stagger (v)
état (m) [condition]
state (n) or
condition (n)
état (m) [division
d'un pays] state (n)
état (m) [document]
statement (n)

Etat (m)
[gouvernement]
government (n)
or State (n)
état (m) *[situation]*
situation (n) *or*
state of affairs
état civil (civil)
status (n)
état: en parfait
état de marche in
full working order
étendre: s'étendre
de ... à ... range (v)
from ... to ...
étiquetage (m)
labelling (n)
étiqueter label (v)
étiquette (f) label (n)
or tag (n)
étiquette-adresse (f)
address label
étiquette de prix
price tag *or* price label
étranger (-ère) (n)
foreigner (n)
étranger (-ère) (adj)
foreign (adj)
étranger: à l'étranger
overseas
être be (v)

étude (f) *[conception]*
design (n)
étude (f) *[recherche]*
study (n) *or* research
(n); analysis (n)
étude de marché
market research
étude des temps et
des mouvements
time and motion study
étude du rapport
coût-bénéfice cost-
benefit analysis
études (fpl) *[uni-*
versitaires, etc.]
studies (n)
étudier study (v)
or research (v);
analyze (v)
étudier le potentiel
du marché analyse
the market potential
euro (m) euro (n)
eurochèque (m)
Eurocheque (n)
eurodevise (f)
Eurocurrency (n)
eurodollar (m)
Eurodollar (n)
Euromarché (m)
Euromarket (n)

européen (-éenne) European (adj)

eurozone (f) eurozone (n)

évaluation (f) evaluation (n) *or* estimate (n)

évaluation (f) *[expertise]* valuation (n)

évaluation des dommages assessment (n) of damages

évaluation du rendement performance rating (n)

évaluer *[biens, coût]* evaluate (v) *or* estimate (v)

évaluer *[expertiser]* value (v)

évaluer les dommages assess (v) damages

évasion (f) fiscale tax avoidance

éventail (m) range (n)

éventualité (f) contingency (n)

éviter avoid (v)

ex-dividende ex dividend

exact(e) correct (adj)

exact(e) *[précis]* exact (adj) *or* accurate (adj)

examen (m) examination (n) *or* test (n)

examen (m) *[contrôle]* examination (n) *or* inspection (n)

examiner examine (v); consider (v)

excédent (m) excess (n) *or* surplus (n)

excédent de bagages excess baggage

excédentaire *[balance commerciale]* favourable (adj) (balance of trade)

excédents (mpl) de stock overstocks (n)

excédents (mpl) de personnel overmanning (n)

excéder exceed (v)

excellent(e) excellent (adj) *or* A1

excepté except (for)

exception: à l'exception de excluding

exceptionnel (-elle)
[inattendu]
exceptional (adj)
exceptionnel (-elle)
[très grand]
exceptional (adj) *or*
outstanding (adj)
exclure exclude (v)
exclusif (-ive)
exclusive (adj) *or* sole
(adj)
exclusion (f)
exclusion (n)
exclusivité (f)
exclusivity (n)
excuse (f) apology (n)
excuser: s'excuser
apologize (v)
exécuter
implement (v)
or fulfil(l) (v)
exécuter une com-
mande fulfil an order
exécutif (-ive)
executive (adj)
exécution (f)
implementation (n)
or fulfilment (n)
exécution de
commandes
order fulfilment

exemplaire (m)
copy (n)
exemplaire: en
deux exemplaires
in duplicate
exemplaire: en
trois exemplaires
in triplicate
exempt(e) exempt
(from)
exempt(e) de
droit *ou* de taxe
duty-free (adj)
exempt(e) d'impôt
tax-exempt (adj) *or*
tax-free (adj)
exempter exempt (v)
exemption (f)
exemption (n)
exemption (f) d'im-
pôt tax exemption
exercer exercise (v)
exercice (m)
exercise (n)
exercice (m) social
[financier] accounting
year *or* financial year
exonération (f)
d'impôt tax exemp-
tion *or* exemption
from tax

exonéré(e) d'impôt
exempt (adj) from tax
or tax-exempt (adj)
exonérer *[exempter]*
exempt (v) (from)
exorbitant(e)
[inabordable]
prohibitive (adj)
expédier *[des*
marchandises]
dispatch (v) *or* send
(v) *or* ship (v)
expédier par avion
airfreight (v) *[goods]*
expédier (un colis)
par avion *[poste]*
send (a package) by
airmail
expédier par
conteneurs
containerize (v) *or*
ship (v) in containers
expédier par courrier
ordinaire send (v) by
surface mail
expédier par exprès
express (v)
expédier par la
poste mail (v) *or*
post (v) *or* send (v)
by post

expédier par mer *ou*
par bateau send (v)
by sea
expéditeur (-trice)
[de lettre, colis]
sender (n)
expéditeur *[de*
marchandises]
shipper (n) *or*
consignor (n)
expédition (f)
[acheminement]
shipping (n) *or*
forwarding (n)
expédition (f)
[envoi] consignment
(n) *or* shipment (n)
expédition en vrac
bulk shipment
expéditionnaire (m)
shipping clerk (n)
expérience (f)
experience (n)
expérimenté(e)
experienced (adj)
expert (m) *[con-*
sultant] expert (n);
consultant (n)
expert (m) *[en*
bâtiments]
surveyor (n)

expert (m) *[en évaluation]* valuer (n)

expert-comptable (m) chartered accountant

expert en problèmes de gestion troubleshooter (n)

expertise (f) *[de bijoux, etc.]* valuation (n)

expertise (f) *[de dégâts, de bâtiment]* survey (n)

expertiser *[des bijoux, etc.]* value (v)

expertiser *[des dégâts, un bâtiment]* survey (v)

expiration (f) expiration (n); expiry (n) (date)

expirer *[n'être plus valable]* lapse (v)

expirer *[venir à expiration]* expire (v)

explication (f) explanation (n)

expliquer explain (v)

exploitation (f) *[entreprise]* enterprise (n)

exploitation agricole farm (n)

exploiter *[mettre en valeur]* exploit (v)

exploiter *[profiter de]* capitalize on (v)

export (m) *[exportation]* export (n)

exportateur (-trice) *[qui exporte]* exporting (adj)

exportateur (-trice) exporter (n)

exportation (f) export (n)

exportations (fpl) *[marchandisesexportées]* exports (n)

exporter export (v)

exposant(e) exhibitor (n)

exposer *[à un salon]* exhibit (v)

exposer *[des faits]* set out (v) *or* describe (v)

exposition (f) *[salon]* exhibition (n)

Ff

exprès (-esse)
[explicite] on
purpose (adj)
express (adj)
[rapide] express
(adj) (letter, delivery)
express: (envoyer)
par express (send)
by express delivery
exprimer express
(v) *[state]*
expropriation (f)
compulsory
purchase (n)
extérieur(e)
external (adj)
extérieur(e) à l'en-
treprise
out-house (adj)
externe
external (adj)
extra (adj) *[qual-*
ité] high (adj) *or*
top (adj) *or*
premium (adj)
extraordinaire
extraordinary (adj)

fabricant (m)
[constructeur]
manufacturer (n)
or maker (n)
fabrication (f)
production (n) *or*
manufacture (n)
fabrication
en série
mass production
fabrique (f) *[usine]*
factory (n)
fabriquer produce (v)
or manufacture (v)
fabriquer en série
mass-produce (v)
facile easy (adj)
facilité (f) facility (n)
facilités (fpl) de
crédit credit facilities
facilités (fpl) de
paiement easy terms
facteur (m) factor (n)
facteur de coût
cost factor
facteur décisif
deciding factor

facteur négatif
minus factor *or*
downside factor
facteurs cycliques
cyclical factors
facteurs de production
factors of production
**factor (m) [*société,
personne*]** factor (n)
**factoring (m) [*affac-
turage*]** factoring (n)
facturation (f)
invoicing (n) *or*
billing (n)
facture (f) invoice (n)
or bill (n)
facture avec TVA
VAT invoice
facture d'avoir
credit note
facture détaillée
itemized invoice *or*
detailed invoice
facture pro forma
pro forma (invoice)
facturer invoice (v) *or*
bill (v) *or* charge (v)
facultatif (-ive)
optional (adj)
failli(e) (n)
bankrupt (n)

failli(e) (adj)
bankrupt (adj)
failli concordataire
certificated bankrupt
failli non réhabilité
undischarged
bankrupt (n)
faillite (f) bankruptcy
(n) *or* failure (n)
**faillite: causer une
faillite** bankrupt (v)
faillite: faire faillite
fail (v) *or* go bust
(v) *or* crash (v)
**faire exécuter *ou*
faire observer**
enforce
**faire face aux
dépenses** meet
(expenses)
faisabilité (f)
feasibility
**fait(e) sur mesure
ou sur commande**
custom-built *or*
custom-made (adj)
falloir [*nécessiter*]
need (v) *or* take (v)
falsification (f) fake
(n) *or* forgery (n) *or*
falsification (n)

falsifier fake (v) *or*
forge (v) *or* falsify (v)
falsifier les comptes
falsify the accounts
faute (f) [blâme]
fault (n)
faute (f) [erreur]
fault *or* mistake (n)
or error (n)
faute de [manque
de] for lack of
faute de frappe
typing error
faute de quoi
failing which
faux (fausse) false
(adj) *or* wrong (adj)
or inaccurate (adj)
faux (fausse)
[falsifié]
counterfeit (adj) *or*
faked (adj)
faux (m) fake (n)
or forgery (n)
faux frais (mpl) incidental expenses (n)
faux poids (m) false
weight (n)
faveur: de faveur
complimentary (adj)
[ticket, etc.]

fax (m) [télécopie]
fax (n)
femme d'affaires
businesswoman (n)
ferme [définitif,
soutenu] firm (adj)
fermé(e) closed
(adj) *or* shut (adj)
fermer close (v) *or*
shut (v)
fermer [cacheter] seal
(v) (an envelope)
fermer à clé lock
(up) (v)
fermer un compte
close an account
fermer un compte
en banque close a
bank account
fermer un magasin,
un bureau [le soir]
lock up a shop, an
office
fermer un magasin,
une usine [pour tou-
jours] close down a
shop, a factory
fermeture (f)
closure (n);
closing (n) (down)
ferry (m) ferry (n)

fête (f) légale
statutory holiday (n)
feu (m) *[incendie]*
fire (n)
feuille (f) sheet (n)
(of paper)
feuille de paie pay
slip (n)
feuillet (m)
[publicitaire]
leaflet (n)
fiabilité (f)
reliability (n)
fiable reliable (adj)
fiche (f)
[bordereau] slip (n)
fiche (f) *[carte de*
fichier] index card
(n) *or* filing card
fiche (f) *[de contenu]*
docket (n)
fiche (f) *[électricité]*
plug (n)
fichier (m) card
index (n)
fichier d'adresses
address list (n) *or*
mailing list
fichier (m)
(informatique)
(computer) file (n)

fidélité (f) à la mar-
que brand loyalty (n)
fidélité de la clientèle
customer loyalty
fiducie (f) trust (n)
filiale (f) affiliated
company *or* associate
company
fin (f) end (n)
fin (f) *[clôture]*
close (n) *or* end (n)
fin d'exercice year end
fin de mois month end
final(e) final (adj)
or last (adj)
finance (f) finance (n)
financement (m)
financing (n) *or*
funding (n)
financement du
déficit budgétaire
deficit financing
financer finance (v)
or fund (v)
financer une
opération finance
an operation
finances (fpl)
finances (n)
financier (-ière)
financial (adj)

financièrement
financially (adv)
fini(e) ended (adj)
or finished (adj)
finir end (v) *or*
finish (v)
firme (f) *[entreprise]*
company (n) *or* firm
(n) *or* house (n)
fisc (m) Inland
Revenue (n)
fiscal(e) fiscal (adj)
fiscalisé(e) liable
to tax *or* taxed (adj)
fiscaliser put (v) a
tax on (something)
fixation (f) fixa-
tion (n) *or* fixing (n)
fixe *[prix]* fixed (adj)
or set (adj)
fixé(e) fixed (adj)
or set (adj)
fixer fix (v) *or* set
(v) *or* determine (v)
fixer des objectifs
set targets
fixer le prix du lingot
fix (v) the bullion
price (for gold)
fixer une date
fix a date

**fixer une réunion à
15h** fix a meeting
for 3 p.m.
**fixing (m) (du cours
de l'or)** gold fixing (n)
flamber *[augmenter]*
rocket (v) *or* go up (v)
rapidly
flexibilité (f)
flexibility (n)
florissant(e)
flourishing (adj) *or*
booming (adj)
flottant(e)
[devise]
floating (adj)
flotter *[devise]* float (v)
fluctuation (f)
fluctuation (n)
fluctuation (f)
[mouvement]
movement (n)
fluctuer fluctuate (v)
flux (m) flow (n);
outflow (n)
flux de trésorerie
cash flow
**flux: (production,
etc.) à flux tendus**
just-in-time (adj)
(production, etc.)

FMI (Fonds Monétaire International) IMF (International Monetary Fund)

foi: de bonne foi in good faith; bona fide

foire (f) commerciale trade fair (n)

fonction (f) function (n)

fonctionnaire (m) civil servant (n)

fonctionnement (m) [marche] working (n)

fonctionnement: en fonctionnement in operation or operative (adj)

fonctionner [appareil] work (v)

fonctionner [être en service] run (v) [buses, trains]

fonctionner: faire fonctionner operate (v)

fond (m) bottom (n)

fondé (m) de pouvoir person with power of attorney; proxy (n)

fonds (m) fund (n)

fonds (mpl) funds (n) or money (n)

fonds de commerce business (n); goodwill (n)

fonds de prévoyance contingency fund (n)

Fonds Monétaire International (FMI) International Monetary Fund (IMF)

fonds bloqués [actif gelé] frozen assets

fonds de roulement working capital (n)

fonds de secours emergency reserves

fonds publics public funds

force (f) de vente sales force (n)

force (f) majeure force majeure (n)

forcé(e) forced (adj)

forfait (m) flat rate (n) or fixed rate (n)

formalité (f) formality (n)

formalités douanières customs formalities

formation (f)
training (n)
formation dans l'en-
treprise in-house
training
formation dans un
centre spécialisé
off-the-job training
formation en gestion
d'entreprise
management training
formation sur le
tas *ou* sur le terrain
on-the-job training
former *[une société]*
form (v) *or* set up (v)
former (quelqu'un)
train (v) (someone)
formulaire (m) form
(n) **formulaire de**
candidature (à un
poste) application
form
formulaire de
déclaration de
sinistre insurance
claim form
formulaire de
déclaration en
douane customs
declaration form

formulaire
d'inscription
registration form
formulation (f)
wording (n)
fort(e) strong (adj)
fortune (f) fortune
(n) *or* wealth (n)
fortune: faire
fortune make a
fortune *or* make
a lot of money
foule (f) mass (n)
fourchette (f) de
prix price range (n)
fournir *[approvision-*
ner] supply (v) *or*
provide (v)
fournir: se fournir
(chez) buy at (v)
(someone's shop)
fournisseur (m)
supplier (n)
fournisseur du
gouvernement
government
contractor (n)
fournitures (fpl) de
bureau office sta-
tionery (n) *[paper]*
fragile fragile (adj)

frais (mpl) *[prix ou coût]* cost(s) (n) *or* charge(s) (n)

frais (mpl) *[dépense]* expenses (n)

frais administratifs *ou* frais de gestion administrative costs *or* charges

frais bancaires *[agios]* bank charges

frais de débarquement landing charges

frais de démarrage *ou* d'établissement start-up costs

frais de déplacement travel expenses

frais de distribution *ou* de diffusion distribution costs

frais de fabrication manufacturing overheads (n) *or* costs

frais de manutention handling charge

frais d'emballage packing charges

frais d'enlèvement collection charges *or* collection rates

frais d'entrepôt storage (n) (cost)

frais de port et d'emballage postage and packing (p & p)

frais de représentation *ou* frais professionnels expenses (n)

frais de transport shipping costs; carriage (n); freight (n)

frais de transport aérien air freight (charges)

frais de transports routiers haulage (n) (costs *or* charges)

frais financiers *[intérêts à payer]* interest charges

frais généraux *ou* frais d'administration générale overheads (n) *or* overhead costs *or* oncosts (n)

frais juridiques legal costs *or* legal charges

frais supplémentaires
additional charges
franc (m) *[unité*
monétaire: Suisse]
franc (n)
franc de port car-
riage free; post free
franchisage (m)
franchising
franchise (f)
franchise (n)
franchisé(e) (n)
franchisee (n)
franchiser
franchise (v)
franchiseur (m)
franchiser (n)
franco franco *or* free
franco à bord (FAB)
free on board (FOB
or f.o.b)
franco à quai price
ex quay
franco de port *ou*
franc de port carriage
free; post free
franco wagon free
on rail
fraude (f) fraud (n)
fraude fiscale tax
evasion (n)

frauder le fisc
evade (v) tax
frauduleusement
fraudulently (adv)
frauduleux (-euse)
fraudulent (adj)
free-lance (adj)
freelance (adj)
free-lance (mf)
freelance (n) *or*
freelancer (n)
fréquent(e)
frequent (adj)
fret (m) freight (n)
fret aérien air
freight
frontière (f)
border (n)
fuite (f) de capi-
taux flight (n) of
capital
fusion (f)
merger (n)
fusionner
merge (v)
futur(e) future
(adj)

Gg

gâcher spoil (v) *or* damage (v)

gagner earn (v)

gagner net net (v)

gain (m) gain (n) *or* profit (n)

gain net net profit

gain théorique paper profit

gain: faire un gain make (v) a profit *or* make money

galerie (f) marchande shopping arcade (n) *or* shopping mall (n)

gamme (f) [variété] range (n)

gamme de produits product line *or* product range

garant (m) [avaliste] guarantor (n) *or* guarantee (n)

garant: se porter garant de quelqu'un go (v) guarantee for someone

garant: se porter garant d'une dette guarantee (v) a debt

garantie (f) guarantee (n) *or* warranty (n)

garantie (f) [nantissement] collateral (n) *or* security (n) *or* cover (n)

garantir guarantee (v)

garantir [une émission d'actions] underwrite (v)

garde-meuble (m) furniture storage (n)

garder [détenir] hold (v) *or* keep (v)

gardien (m) de la sécurité security guard (n)

gare (f) (ferroviaire) (railway) station (n)

gaspillage (m) wastage (n)

gaspiller waste (v)

gauche [côté] left (adj)

gel (m) (des prix et des salaires) (price and wage) freeze (n)

gelé(e)
frozen (adj)
geler *[bloquer]*
freeze (v)
geler les crédits
freeze credits
général(e)
general (adj)
général(e) *ou*
généralisé(e)
across-the-board
général(e) *[global]*
overall (adj) *or*
comprehensive (adj)
gentleman's agree-
ment (m) gentleman's
agreement (n)
gérant(e) manager (n),
manageress (f)
gérer manage (v)
or run (v)
gérer une propriété
manage a property
gérer: mal gérer
mismanage (v)
gestion (f) *[admi-*
nistration]
administration (n)
or management (n)
gestion d'entreprise
business management

gestion de porte-
feuilles portfolio
management
gestion des stocks
stock control
gestion du personnel
personnel management
gestion: mauvaise
gestion misman-
agement (n)
gestionnaire (mf)
administrator (n) *or*
controller (n)
gestionnaire (m)
des stocks stock
controller
global(e) global *or*
comprehensive (adj)
gold-point (m)
gold point (n)
goodwill (m)
goodwill (n)
gonflé(e) *[prix]*
inflated (adj)
(prices)
goulet (m) *ou*
goulot (m)
d'étranglement
bottleneck (n)
gouvernement (m)
government (n)

gouvernemental [du gouvernement] government (adj)

gramme (m) (g) gram or gramme (n)

grand(-)livre (m) ledger (n)

grand(-)livre des achats bought ledger or purchase ledger

grand(-)livre des ventes sales ledger

grand(-)livre général general ledger or nominal ledger

grand magasin department store

grande surface (f) hypermarket (n) or superstore (n)

grande taille (f) [vêtements] outsize (n & adj) (OS)

grandissant(e) mounting (adj) or increasing (adj)

graphique (m) diagram (n) or graph (n) or chart (n)

graphique d'évolution flow chart or flow diagram

graphique des ventes sales chart

gratis [gratuitement] gratis (adv) or free (adv) (of charge)

gratuit(e) free (adj)

gratuitement free (adv) (of charge) or gratis (adv)

greffier (m) registrar (n)

grève (f) strike (n)

grève de protestation protest strike

grève de solidarité sympathy strike

grève du zèle ou grève perlée go-slow (n) or work-to-rule (n)

grève générale total strike or all-out strike

grève sauvage wildcat strike

grève sur le tas
sit-down strike (n)
or sit-down protest (n)
grève: se mettre en
grève *ou* faire (la)
grève strike (v) *or*
go on strike
gréviste (mf)
striker (n)
grille (f) grid (n)
grille (f) des salaires
wage scale (n) *or*
structure (n)
grimper climb (v)
gros (m) *ou* en gros
wholesale (m)
grosse (f) *[douze*
douzaines]
gross (n) (= 144
items)
grossiste (mf)
wholesale dealer (n)
or wholesaler (n)
groupage (m)
d'envois consolida-
tion (n)
groupe (m) group (n)
groupe de travail
working party (n)
groupe industriel
industrial group

groupes socio-
économiques
socio-economic
groups
grouper batch (v)
grouper [envoi]
consolidate (v)
[shipments]
grouper *[sur une*
liste] bracket (v)
together
guerre (f) des prix
price war *or*
price-cutting
war (n)
guilde (f) guild (n)

Hh

hall (m)
(d'exposition)
(exhibition) hall (n)
harmonisation (f)
harmonization (f)
harmoniser
harmonize (v)

hausse (f) *[augmen-tation]* increase (n)

haussier (m) *[spéculateur à la hausse]* bull (n)

haut(e) high (adj)

haut de gamme up-market (adj)

hautement qualifié highly qualified

hauteur (f) height (n)

hauteur: à hauteur de up to

hebdomadaire (adj) weekly (adj)

hectare (m) hectare (n)

heure (f) hour (n); time (n)

heure de fermeture closing time

heure d'enreg-istrement *[à l'aéroport]* check-in time (n)

heure d'ouverture opening time

heure/homme (f) *ou* heure travaillée man-hour (n)

heure: (de) l'heure per hour

heure: de bonne heure early (adv)

heures (fpl) de bureau office hours *or* business hours

heures de pointe peak period (n) *or* rush hour

heures d'ouverture business hours *or* opening hours

heures d'ouverture des banques banking hours

heures supplémen-taires *[de travail]* overtime (n)

holding (m) holding company

homme (m) *[ouvrier]* man (n)

homme d'affaires businessman (n)

homologuer *[authentifier]* authenticate (v)

honnête *[correct]* fair (adj)

honnête *[fiable ou sûr]* reliable (adj)

honoraire (adj)
honorary (adj)
honoraires (mpl)
[pour services] fee
(n); honorarium (n)
honorer sa signature
honour (v) one's
signature
honorer une traite
honour (v) a bill
horaire (m) *[indica-
teur]* timetable (n)
[train, etc.]
horaire (adj)
hourly (adv) *or* by
the hour; per hour
hors taxe *[taxe non
comprise]* exclusive
of tax
hors taxe *[exempt
de taxe]* duty-free
(adj); tax-free (adj)
hôtel (m) hotel (n)
hôtel classé graded
hotel
hôtel des ventes
(aux enchères)
saleroom (n) *or*
auction room
hôtelier (-ière)
hotelier (n)

hôtellerie (f)
hotel trade (n)
hyperinflation (f)
hyperinflation (n)
hypermarché (m)
hypermarket (n) *or*
superstore (n)
hypothèque (f)
ou prêt (m)
hypothécaire
mortgage (n)
hypothéquer
mortgage (v)

Ii

illégal(e) illegal
(adj) *or* unlawful
(adj); against
the law
illégalement
illegally (adv)

illégalité (f)
illegality (n)
illicite illicit (adj)
image (f) (d'une société) (corporate)
image (n)
image de marque
[réputation] public
image
imitation (f)
imitation (n)
immatriculer une société register (v)
a company
immédiat(e)
immediate (adj)
immédiatement
immediately (adv)
immobilier (-ière)
immovable (adj)
immobilisations (fpl) [actif immobilisé] fixed
assets (n)
immobilisations corporelles fixed
tangible assets
immobilisations incorporelles
fixed intangible
assets

immobiliser des capitaux lock up (v)
capitals
impair(e) odd (adj)
[not even]
impasse (f)
deadlock (n)
impayé(e) out-
standing (adj) *or*
unpaid (adj)
imparfait(e)
imperfect (adj)
imperfection (f)
imperfection (n)
implanter [une industrie] establish
(v) *or* set up (v)
implanter: s'im-
planter sur un marché penetrate (v)
a market
importance (f)
importance (n)
important(e)
important (adj)
or major (adj)
important(e) [massif ou lourd] important
or heavy (adj)
importateur (-trice)
(n) importer (n)

importateur (-trice) (adj) importing (adj)

importation (f) [action] importation (n) or importing (n)

importation: (article) d'importation imported (adj) (article)

importations (fpl) imports (n) or imported goods

importations visibles visible imports

importer import (v)

importer [avoir de l'importance] matter (v) or be important

import-export (mf) import-export (n & adj)

imposable [taxable] taxable (adj)

imposé(e) taxed (adj)

imposer [prescrire] impose (v)

imposer [taxer] tax (v)

imposition (f) taxation (n)

imposition directe direct taxation

imposition indirecte indirect taxation

impôt (m) tax (n); taxation (n)

impôt direct direct tax

impôt indirect indirect tax

impôt progressif graded tax or graduated income tax

impôt retenu à la source tax deducted at source

impôt sur le chiffre d'affaires turnover tax

impôt sur le revenu income tax

impôt sur les bénéfices des sociétés corporation tax

impôt sur les gains exceptionnels excess profits tax

impôt sur les grosses fortunes wealth tax

impôt sur les plus-values capital gains tax

imprévu (m) [éventualité] contingency (n)

**imprimante (f)
(d'ordinateur)**
(computer) printer (n)
**imprimante à
marguerite**
daisy-wheel printer
imprimante laser
laser printer
**imprimante ligne à
ligne** line printer
**imprimante
matricielle**
dot-matrix printer
imprimé (m) printed
matter (n)
**imprimé (m)
*[copie sur papier]***
hard copy (n)
imprimé(e) (adj)
printed (adj)
imprimer print
(out) (v)
imprimeur (m)
printer (n)
imputable
chargeable (adj)
imputation (f)
charging (n) *or*
charge (n)
imputer charge (v)
[to an account]

**inabordable *[exor-
bitant]*** prohibitive
(adj) *or* exorbitant
(adj) (price)
incendie (m) fire (n)
inchangé(e)
unchanged (adj)
incidence (f)
repercussion (n)
or effect (n)
incitation (f)
incentive (n)
inclure include (v)
or count (v)
inclus(e) *[compris]*
inclusive (adj)
inclusivement
inclusive (adv)
incompétent(e)
incompetent (adj)
**inconditionnel
(-elle) *[sans
réserve]***
unconditional (adj)
**incorporé(e) *[inté-
gré]*** built-in (adj)
incorporel (-elle)
intangible (adj)
incorporer *[intégrer]*
incorporate (v) *or*
build in (v)

incorrect(e)
incorrect (adj)
incorrectement
incorrectly (adv)
**inculpation (f) *[accu-*
*sation]*** charge (n)
inculper *[accuser]*
charge (v)
indemnisation (f)
[dédommagement]
compensation (n) *or*
indemnity (n)
indemniser
[dédommager]
indemnify (v) *or*
compensate (v)
indemniser
quelqu'un d'une
perte indemnify
someone for a loss
**indemnité (f) *[allo-*
*cation]*** benefit (n)
indemnité (f)
[dédommagement]
indemnity (n) *or*
compensation (n)
indemnité (de
déplacement, de
vie chère) (travel,
cost-of-living)
allowance (n)

indépendant(e)
independent (adj)
indépendant(e) *[qui
travaille à son compte]
self-employed (adj);
independent (adj)
index (m) index (n)
indexation (f)
indexation (n)
indexé(e) (sur l'indice
du coût de la vie)
index-linked (adj)
indexer index (v)
indicateur (m)
[horaire] timetable
(n) *[trains, etc.]*
indicateurs (mpl)
économiques eco-
nomic indicators (n)
indicatif (m)
(téléphonique)
(dialling) code (n)
indicatif de zone
[telephone] area code
indicatif du pays
[telephone]
country code
indicatif interna-
tional [telephone]
international
access code

indice (m) *[des prix, etc.]* index (n)
indice de crois-sance growth index
indice de la production industrielle manufacturing output index
indice des prix à la consommation retail price index (RPI)
indice des prix à la production producer price index (PPI)
indice du coût de la vie cost-of-living index
indice pondéré weighted index
indiquer *[spécifier]* specify (v)
indirect(e) indirect (adj)
indispensable necessary (adj) *or* essential (adj)
indisponibilité (f) unavailability (n)
industrialisation (f) industrialization (n)

industrialiser industrialize (v)
industrie (f) industry (n)
industrie à fort coefficient de capital capital-intensive industry
industrie clé key industry
industrie de base basic *or* primary industry
industrie de crois-sance growth industry
industrie de services service industry *or* tertiary industry
industrie de trans-formation manu-facturing industry *or* secondary industry
industrie légère light industry
industrie lourde heavy industry
industrie nationalisée nationalized industry

**industriel (-elle)
(adj)** industrial (adj)
industriel (m)
industrialist (n)
inefficacité (f)
inefficiency (n)
inexact(e) inaccurate
(adj) *or* wrong (adj)
inférieur(e) à
under; less than
inflation (f)
inflation (n)
**inflation par la
demande**
demand-led inflation
**inflation par les
coûts** cost-push
inflation
inflationniste
inflationary (adj)
influence (f)
influence (n)
influencer
influence (v)
**informaticien
(-ienne)[program-
meur]** computer
programmer (n)
**informaticien
(-ienne)-analyste**
systems analyst (n)

information (f)
information (n)
**information en
retour** feedback (n)
informatique (f)
information
technology (n)
**informatique (f)
[traitement de
données]** data
processing (n)
informatisé(e)
computerized (adj)
informatiser
computerize (v)
**informer [aviser,
renseigner]**
inform (v)
**informer [donner
des explications]**
brief (v)
infrastructure (f)
infrastructure (n)
ingénieur (m)
engineer (n)
ingénieur conseil
consulting
engineer
**ingénieur de
chantier** site
engineer

ingénieur de production *ou* **ingénieur-produit** product engineer
ingénieur de projet project engineer
initial(e) (adj) initial (adj) *or* opening (adj)
initiale (f) [lettre] initial (n)
initialer [signer de ses initiales] initial (v)
initiation (f) induction (n)
initiative (f) initiative (n)
injonction (f) writ (n)
injuste unfair (adj)
innovateur (-trice) (adj) innovative (adj)
innovateur (m) innovator (n)
innovation (f) innovation (n)
innover innovate (v)
inonder (le marché) flood (v) (the market)
inscrire [noter] enter (v)

inscrire [immatriculer ou enregistrer] register (v) *[in official list]*
inscrire à l'ordre du jour put (v) on the agenda
inscrire une propriété au cadastre register a property
inscrire: s'inscrire register (v)
inscrire: s'inscrire à l'arrivée (à l'hôtel) check in (v) (at the hotel)
insérer une annonce put (v) an ad (in the paper)
insolvabilité (f) insolvency (n)
insolvable insolvent (adj)
inspecter inspect (v)
inspecteur (-trice) inspector (n)
inspecteur de la TVA VAT inspector
inspecteur des impôts tax inspector

inspecteur du travail
factory inspector
inspection (f)
inspection (n)
**Inspection du
travail** factory
inspectorate (n)
**installations (fpl)
[bâtiments, etc.]**
facilities (n)
**installations portu-
aires** harbour facilities
instantané(e)
instant (adj) or
immediate (adj)]
**instituer [com-
mencer]** institute (v)
institut (m)
institute (n)
institution (f)
institution (n)
**institution (f)
financière** financial
institution
institutionnel (-elle)
institutional (adj)
instruction (f)
instruction (n)
**instructions pour la
livraison** delivery
instructions

**instructions relatives
à l'expédition** ship-
ping or forwarding
instructions
**instrument (m)
[document]**
instrument (n) or
document (n)
**instrument (m)
[outil]** implement (n)
or device (n)
**intégration (f)
horizontale** horizon-
tal integration (n)
**intégration (f)
verticale** vertical
integration
**intégré(e) [incor-
poré]** built-in (adj)
**intégrer [incor-
porer]** incorporate
(v) or build in (v)
**intenter un procès
à ou contre** take
(v) legal action
against or sue (v)
(someone)
interdiction (f)
ban (n)
**interdiction d'im-
porter** import ban

interdire ban (v) *or*
forbid (v)
intéressant(e)
interesting (adj)
intéressement (m)
[aux bénéfices]
profit-sharing
(scheme)
intéresser (quel-
qu'un) interest (v)
intérêt (m)
[considération]
interest (n)
intérêt (m) *[droit*
acquis] vested
interest
intérêt (m) *[d'un*
capital, d'une dette]
interest (n)
intérêt(s) com-
posé(s) compound
interest
intérêt couru
[d'un placement]
accrued interest
intérêt élevé
high interest
intérêt fixe
fixed interest
intérêt(s) simple(s)
simple interest

interface (f)
interface (n)
intérieur(e) inland
intérieur(e)
[national]
internal (adj) *or*
domestic (adj)
intérim (m)
[travail temporaire]
temporary work (n)
intérim: assurer
l'intérim de
quelqu'un deputize
(v) for someone
intérim: faire de
l'intérim temp (v)
intérim:
(président) par
intérim acting (adj)
(president)
intérimaire *[divi-*
dende, etc.]
interim (adj)
(dividend, etc.)
intérimaire
[remplaçant]
acting (adj)
(manager, etc)
intérimaire
[temporaire]
temporary (adj)

intermédiaire (mf)
middleman (n) *or*
intermediary (n)
international(e)
international (adj)
interne internal (adj)
Internet (m)
Internet (n)
interprète (mf)
interpreter (n)
interpréter *ou*
servir d'interprète
interpret (v)
interrompre *[sus-*
pendre] suspend (v)
interruption (f)
[arrêt] stop (n) *or*
suspension (n)
intervenir
intervene (v)
intervenir comme
médiateur
mediate (v)
intervention (f)
intervention (n)
interviewé(e)
interviewee (n)
interviewer (m)
interviewer (n)
interviewer
interview (v)

introduction (f)
introduction (n)
invalidation (f)
invalidation (n)
invalider
invalidate (v)
invalidité (f)
invalidity (n)
invendable
unsellable (adj)
invendus (mpl)
unsold items
inventaire (m)
inventory (n) *or*
stocklist (n)
inventaire (m) (des
stocks) *[action]*
stocktaking (n)
inventaire de posi-
tion picking list (n)
inventaire: faire
l'inventaire *[stocks]*
take (v) stock
inventaire: faire
l'inventaire *[mai-*
son] inventory (v)
the contents of a
house
inventaire: nous
faisons l'inventaire
we are stocktaking

inventorier *[faire l'inventaire]*
inventory (v)
inverse reverse (adj)
inverser reverse (v)
investi(e)
invested (adj)
investir invest (v)
investissement (m) *[placement]*
investment (n)
investissement à intérêt fixe
fixed-interest investment
investissement à l'étranger foreign investment
investissement: faire un investissement
invest (v)
investisseur (m)
investor (n)
investisseurs institutionnels
institutional investors
invitation (f)
invitation (n)

inviter (quelqu'un à) invite (v) (someone to)
irrégularité (f)
irregularity (n)
irrégulier (-ière)
irregular (adj)
irrévocable
irrevocable (adj)
isolé(e) [unique]
one-off (adj)
itinéraire (m)
itinerary (n)

Jj

jargon (m) administratif
officialese (n)
jauge (f) *[d'un navire]*
tonnage (n)
jauge brute
gross tonnage
jeter throw away (v) *or* discard (v)

**jeter: à jeter après
usage** disposable
(adj)
**jeu (m)
[ensemble]** set (n)
joindre [relier]
attach (v) or join (v)
joindre [contacter]
contact (v) or join (v)
joint-venture (f)
joint venture (n)
**jouissance (f) à vie
[usufruit]** life
interest (n)
jour (m) day (n)
[24 hours]
**jour (m) [journée
de travail]** day or
working day
jour de congé
day off
**jour de règlement
trimestriel**
quarter day
jour férié bank
holiday (n) or
public holiday (n)
jour: à jour
up to date
jour: par jour per
day or daily (adv)

jour: tous les jours
every day or daily
(adv)
journal (m)
newspaper (n)
**journal (m) [compt-
abilité]** journal (n)
**journal (m)
de l'entreprise**
house journal or
house magazine (n)
journal des ventes
sales book (n)
**journal professionnel
[revue]** trade journal
**journalier (-ière)
[quotidien]** daily
(adj)
journaliste (mf)
journalist (n) or
correspondent (n)
**journée (f) [de
travail]** day (n) or
working day (n)
juge (m) [arbitre]
adjudicator (n)
**juge (m) [magis-
trat]** judge (n)
**jugement (m) [de la
cour]** judg(e)ment
(n) or ruling (n)

jugement déclara-tif de faillite
adjudication (n) of bankruptcy
juger judge (v)
juridiction (f) jurisdiction (n)
juridique legal (adj) *or* referring to law
jusqu'à *ou* jusqu'à concurrence de up to
juste *[correct, exact]* right (adj); accurate (adj)
justificatif (m) *[preuve écrite]* documentary proof (n)
justificatif (m) comptable voucher (n) *[document from an auditor]*
justifier warrant (v) *or* justify (v); account for (v)

Kk Ll

kg (= kilogramme)
km (= kilomètre)
kilogramme (m) *ou* kilo (m) kilo (n) *or* kilogram (n)
kilomètre (m) kilometre (n)
label (m) *[éti-quette]* label (n)
label de qualité quality label
laisser entrer (quel-qu'un) *[admettre]* admit (v) *or* let in (v)
laisser flotter une devise float (v) a currency
laisser-passer *ou* laissez-passer (m) pass (n)
lancement (m) *[sur le marché]* launch (n) *or* launching (n)
lancement d'une société en Bourse floating (n) *or* flotation (n) of a company

lancer *[produit]*
bring out (v) *or*
launch (v)
**lancer à grand
renfort de publicité**
hype (v) *[product]*
**lancer une société
(en Bourse)** float
(v) a company
**lancer: se lancer
dans les affaires**
go (v) into business
**langage (m) (de
programmation)**
programming
language (n)
leasing (m) *[crédit-
bail]* lease (n) *[with
option to purchase]*
**lecteur (m) de
disques** *ou* **de
disquettes** disk
drive (n)
légal(e) *[juridique]*
legal (adj) *or*
referring to law
légal(e) *[légitime]*
rightful (adj)
légal(e) *[licite]*
legal *or* lawful (adj)
or according to law

législation (f)
legislation (n)
légitime
rightful (adj)
lettre (f) letter (n)
lettre commerciale
business letter
**lettre d'accompagne-
ment** covering note
or covering letter
lettre d'affaires
business letter
lettre d'embauche
letter of
appointment
lettre d'intention
letter of intent
**lettre de candida-
ture (à un poste)**
letter of application
lettre de change
[money] bill (n)
of exchange (n) *or*
draft (n)
lettre de crédit
letter of credit
lettre de rappel
reminder (n)
**lettre de réclama-
tion** letter of
complaint

lettre de recom-mendation letter of reference
lettre de relance follow-up letter
lettre de voiture waybill (n)
lettre personnelle private letter
lettre recom-mandée registered letter
lettre standard *ou* **lettre type** standard letter
levée (f) *[du cour-rier]* collection (n)
levée (f) d'une option exercise (n) of an option
lever *[supprimer]* lift (v) *or* remove (v)
lever *[percevoir]* levy (v)
lever la séance wind up (v) *or* close (v) a meeting
lever une option exercise (v) *or* take up (v) an option

liasse (f) pile (n) *or* batch (n) *[of orders, notes]*
libeller un chèque *[faire un chèque]* write out (v) a cheque
libérer free (v)
libérer decontrol (v)
libre free (adj) *[no restrictions]*
libre *[personne]* free (adj) *or* not busy
libre *[siège, table, etc.)* vacant (adj) *or* inoccupied (adj)
libre-échange (m) free trade (n)
libre-service (m) self-service (n) (store)
libre-service (m) de demi-gros cash and carry (n)
licence (f) licence (n) *or* permit (n); license (n) *[US]*
licence (f) d'exportation export licence *or* export permit

**licence (f)
d'importation**
import licence *or*
import permit
**licencié(e) pour
raisons
économiques** (be)
made redundant *or*
(be) laid off
**licencié(e): être
licencié [mis à la
porte]** get (v)
the sack
licenciement (m)
sacking (n) *or*
dismissal (n)
**licenciement (m)
[économique]**
redundancy (n) *or*
lay-off (n)
**licenciement
abusif ou injuste**
unfair dismissal
**licencier [con-
gédier]** sack (v)
or dismiss (v) *or*
fire (v)
**licencier [pour
raisons économiques]**
make (v) redundant
or lay off (v)

licite legal (adj) *or*
lawful (adj)
lié(e) par contrat
bound (adj) by contract
lien (m) [relation]
connection (n)
lier [relier]
connect (v)
lieu (m) place (n)
lieu (m) de réunion
meeting place *or*
venue (n)
lieu (m) de travail
place of work *or*
workplace (n)
ligne (f) line (n)
ligne de conduite
guideline (n)
**ligne de produits
[gamme]** product line
ligne téléphonique
telephone line
**ligne (téléphoni-
que) extérieure**
outside line
**ligne: en ligne
[informatique]**
on line *or* online
**ligne: en ligne
[au téléphone]**
on the phone

ligne: restez en ligne *[téléphone]* hold the line

limitation (f) limitation (n) *or* restriction (n)

limitation à la liberté du commerce restraint (n) of trade

limitation de temps time limitation; time limit (n)

limitations (fpl) des importations import restrictions

limite (f) limit (n)

limite d'âge age limit

limite de crédit *[plafond]* credit limit

limite de découvert overdraft limit

limité(e) limited (adj)

limiter limit (v) *or* restrict (v)

limiter le crédit restrict credit

lingot (m) *[d'or ou d'argent]* ingot (n)

lingot: (or *ou* argent) en lingots bullion (n)

liquidateur (m) liquidator (n)

liquidation (f) d'un société *[ordre]* liquidation (n) *or* winding up (n)

liquidation du stock *[avant fermeture]* closing-down sale

liquidation forcée *[d'une société]* compulsory liquidation *or* winding up order

liquidation (f) volontaire voluntary liquidation

liquider *[dette]* settle (v)

liquider *[écouler]* sell off (v)

liquider *[entreprise]* liquidate (v) *or* wind up (v) *[company]*

liquider du stock liquidate (v) *or* sell off (v) stock

liquidité (f) liquidity
liquidités (fpl)
[disponibilités]
liquid assets (n)
liste (f) list (n)
liste de colisage
packing list or
packing slip (n)
liste de sélection
(de candidats)
shortlist (n)
liste noire [mauvais
payeurs, etc.]
black list
liste rouge: être sur
la liste rouge be ex-
directory [telephone]
liste: faire une
liste list (v)
listing (m) [sortie
d'imprimante]
computer listing (n)
or printout (n)
litre (m) litre (n)
livraison (f) [envoi,
marchandises]
delivery (n)
livraison contre
remboursement
cash on delivery
(c.o.d.)

livraison de
marchandises
delivery of goods
livraison express
express delivery
livraison gratuite
free delivery
livre (m) [de
comptabilité]
account book or
ledger (n)
livre (f) [poids:
0.45 kg] pound (n)
livre (m) [publica-
tion] book (n)
livre (f) [unité
monétaire en
Irlande] (Irish)
punt (n)
livre de caisse
petty cash book
livre-journal (m)
[comptabilité]
daybook (n)
livre sterling [unité
monétaire au
Royaume Uni] pound
(n) (sterling)
livrer deliver (v)
livret (m) [de ban-
que] bank book (n)

livret (m) *[manuel]*
manual (n);
booklet (n)
livreur (m)
deliveryman (n)
**local (m) à usage
de bureau**
office space (n)
local(e) local (adj)
**locataire (mf) (à
bail)** tenant (n) *or*
lessee (n)
**locataire occupant
les lieux** sitting
tenant
**locataire principal
(e) *[sous-location]***
sublessor (n)
**location (f) *[immo-
bilière]*** letting (n)
**location (f) *[loge-
ment]*** rented
accommodation (n)
**location (f) *[de
voiture, machine]***
hire (n)
**logiciel (m) *[infor-
matique]*** (computer)
program (n) *or*
software (n)

logo (m) logo (n)
loi (f) law (n)
**loi de l'offre et de
la demande** law of
supply and demand
loi de prescription
statute (n) of
limitations
**loi des rendements
décroissants** law
of diminishing
returns
long (longue) long
(adj)
**long parcours (m)
*[vol]*** long-distance
(flight)
longue portée long
range
long: à long terme
long-term (adj)
**lot (m) (d'un
produit)** lot (n) *or*
batch (n) (of
product)
**louer *[donner en
location]*** lease (v)
or rent out (v) *or*
let (out) (v) *or* hire
out (v)

louer *[prendre en location]* lease (v) *or* rent (v) *or* hire (v)
louer du matériel en crédit-bail lease (v) equipment
louer un bureau *[donner à bail]* let an office (to someone)
louer une voiture hire a car
lourd(e) *[impor-tant]* heavy (adj) *or* important (adj)
lourd(e) *[poids]* heavy (adj)
loyer (m) rent (n) *or* rental (n)
loyer élevé high rent
loyer non rentable uneconomic rent
loyer symbolique nominal rent
loyer sans payer de loyer rent-free
lucratif(-ive) *[qui rapporte]* paying (adj) *or* profitable (adj)

lucratif: (organisation) sans but lucratif non profit-making (organization)
luxe: de luxe luxury (adj) (item)

Mm

machine (f) *[appareil]* machine (n)
machine à affranchir franking machine
machines (fpl) plant (n) *or* machinery (n)
macro-économie (f) macro-economics (n)
magasin (m) shop (n) *or* store (n)
magasin (m) *[entrepôt]* store (n); stockroom (n)

**magasin à succur-
sales multiples**
multiple store
or chain store
magasin d'usine
factory outlet (n)
**magasin de demi-
gros** cash and
carry (n)
magasin de détail
retail shop *or* retail
outlet (n)
magasin de discount
discount store *or*
discounter (n)
magasin du coin
corner shop
**magasin: grand
magasin** depart-
ment store (n)
**magasinier (m)
[entrepôt]** ware-
houseman (n)
**magazine (m)
[périodique]**
magazine (n)
magistrat (m)
judge (n)
mailing (m)
(direct) mailing (n)
main-d'oeuvre (f)

[personnel]
workforce (n) *or*
labour (force) (n)
**main-d'oeuvre (f)
[travail]** labour (n)
**main-d'oeuvre bon
marché** cheap
labour
**main-d'oeuvre
locale** local labour
**maintenance (f)
[entretien]**
maintenance (n)
**maintenance (f)
[vérification]**
service (n)
**maintenir [garder,
entretenir]** keep up
(v) *or* maintain (v)
**maintenir: se main-
tenir [prix, etc.]** be
firm *or* hold up (v)
maintien (m)
maintenance (n)
**maison (f) [fami-
liale]** house (n);
(family) home (n)
**maison (f) [firme,
entreprise]** house
or company (n) *or*
firm (n)

maison d'édition
publishing house
maison d'exporta-
tion export house
maison mère
parent company
maîtrise (f) [con-
trôle] control (n)
maîtriser [con-
trôler] control (v)
majeur(e) [impor-
tant] major (adj)
majoration (f) (de
prix) mark-up (n)
majorer (le prix
d'un article) mark
up (v) (an article)
majorité (f)
majority (n)
malentendu (m)
misunderstanding (n)
malgré in spite of
or regardless of
management (m)
[gestion]
management (n)
mandat (m)
[argent] money
order (n)
mandat (m) [pouvoir,
autorité] mandate (n)

mandat de paiement
bank mandate
mandat interna-
tional foreign
money order
mandat postal ou
mandat-poste (m)
money order or
postal order
manifeste (m)
manifest (n)
mannequin (m)
[personne]
model (n)
manoeuvre (m)
[travailleur manuel]
manual worker (n)
manque (m)
[pénurie]
shortage (n)
manque (m) [déficit]
shortfall (n)
manque de fonds
lack (n) of funds
manquer [un train
ou un avion] miss
(v) (a train, a plane)
manquer de [être à
court de] lack (v)
or be short of; run
out of (v)

manquer son but
miss one's target
manuel (m) [livret]
manual (n)
manuel d'entretien
service manual
manuel d'utilisa-
tion operating
manual
manuel (-elle)
manual (adj)
manufacturer
[fabriquer]
manufacture (v);
make (v)
manuscrit(e)
[écrit à la main]
handwritten (adj)
manutention (f)
handling (n)
manutention du
matériel
materials handling
maquette (f)
dummy (n) or
mock-up (n)
maquette (f) [mod-
èle réduit] model (n)
marasme (m) [crise
économique] slump
(n) or depression (n)

marchand(e) [négo-
ciant] merchant (n)
or dealer (n)
marchandage (m)
bargaining (n)
marchander haggle
(v) or bargain (v)
marchandisage (m)
merchandizing (n)
marchandise(s) (f)
merchandise (n) or
goods (n)
marchandises à
prix sacrifiés
cut-price goods
marchandises
dédouanées duty-
paid goods
marchandises de
première qualité
high-quality goods
marchandises en
transit goods in
transit
marchandises
exportées
exports (n)
marchandises
vendues en catas-
trophe distress
merchandise

marchandiseur (m)
merchandizer (n)
marche (f)
[fonctionnement]
running (n)
marche: en (bon)
état de marche
[machine] in
working order
marche: mettre en
marche *[machine]*
start (v) *or* put (v)
into operation
marché (m) market
(n) *or* marketplace (n)
marché (m) *[affaire*
ou accord] deal (n)
or bargain (n)
marché (m) *[Bourse]*
stock market
marché (m) *[place]*
market (n)
marché à la baisse
buyer's market
marché à la baisse
[Bourse] bear
market
marché à la hausse
seller's market
marché à la hausse
[Bourse] bull market

marché à terme
forward market;
futures market
marché captif
captive market
marché ciblé
target market
Marché Commun
Common Market
marché des changes
foreign exchange
market
marché des
matières premières
commodity market
marché d'exclusi-
vité closed market
marché étranger
overseas market
marché faible
weak market
marché gris grey
market
marché hors cote
[Bourse] over-the-
counter market
marché intérieur
domestic market *or*
home market
marché libre
open market

marché mondial
world market
marché monétaire
money market
marché noir
black market
marché potentiel
potential market
marché restreint
limited market
Marché unique *[UE]*
Single European
Market
marge (f) margin
(n) *or* mark-up (n)
marge bénéficiaire
profit margin
marge brute gross
margin
**marge brute
d'auto-financement
(MBA)** cash flow
marge d'erreur
margin of error
marge nette net
margin
marginal(e)
marginal (adj)
**marine (f) mar-
chande** merchant
navy (n)

maritime maritime
(adj) *or* marine (adj)
marketing (m)
marketing (n)
marque (f)
brand (n)
**marque *ou* nom
(m) de marque**
brand name
**marque de fabrique
ou de commerce**
trademark (n) *or*
trade name
marque déposée
registered
trademark
marquer mark (v)
**marqueur (m)
*[surligneur]***
marker pen (n)
**masse (f)
monétaire** money
supply (n)
**matériel (m)
*[équipement]***
equipment (n)
matériel de bureau
office equipment
matériel lourd
heavy equipment *or*
heavy machinery

**matériel publici-
taire** publicity
matter (n) *or*
display material
**matières (fpl)
premières** raw
materials (n)
**maturité (f)
économique**
mature economy (n)
mauvais(e)
bad (adj)
mauvais achat bad
buy (n)
mauvais payeur
slow payer (n)
mauvaise gestion
mismanagement (n)
**maximal(e)
[maximum]**
maximum (adj)
maximalisation (f)
maximization (n)
**maximaliser *ou*
maximiser**
maximize (v)
maximum (m)
maximum (n)
**maximum
ou maximal(e)**
maximum (adj)

**MBA (marge brute
d'auto-financement)**
cash flow (n)
médiane (f)
median (n)
médias (mpl)
mass media (n)
**médiateur (-trice)
(n)** mediator (n);
ombudsman (n)
**médiation (f) *[arbi-
trage]*** arbitration (n)
**médiation (f)
*[intervention]***
mediation (n)
**médiocre *[de
qualité inférieure]***
low-quality (adj)
**meilleur(e)
*[supérieur]***
better (adj) *or*
superior (adj)
**meilleur(e): le
meilleur, la
meilleure** the best
membre (m)
member (n)
**mémoire (f)
*[informatique]***
memory (n) *or*
storage (n)

mémorandum (m)
memorandum (n) *or*
memo (n)
mener *[diriger]*
direct (v) *or*
conduct (v)
mener des négocia-
tions conduct
negotiations
mensualité (f)
[paiement mensuel]
monthly payment
mensuel (-elle)
monthly (adj)
mensuellement
[chaque mois]
monthly (adv)
menues dépenses
(fpl) petty expenses
mérite (m) merit (n)
mériter merit (v)
or earn (v)
message (m)
message (n)
message éléctronique
email (n) *[message]*
messagerie (f)
vocale voicemail (n)
mesure (f) *[dimen-*
sion] measure (n)
or measurement (n)

mesure (f) *[dispo-*
sition] measure (n)
mesure de rende-
ment measurement
of profitability
mesure de sécurité
safety measure *or*
safety precaution
mesure de surface
square measure
mesure de volume
cubic measure
mesure fiscale
fiscal measure
mesure: fait(e) sur
mesure(s) made
(adj) to measure
méthode (f)
method (n) *or*
procedure (n)
méthode comptable
accounting procedure
méthode des coûts
marginaux mar-
ginal pricing (n)
mètre (n) (carré,
cube) (square,
cubic) metre (n)
mettre put (v)
mettre en caisse(s)
crate (v)

mettre en conteneurs
containerize (v) *or* put
into containers
mettre une annonce
advertise (v)
mettre à jour
[réviser] update (v)
mettre à la banque
bank (v)
mettre à la poste
post (v) *or* mail (v)
mettre à pied
[licencier] lay off
(v) (workers)
mettre au point
finalize (v)
mettre au point
[développer]
develop (v)
mettre en pratique
implement (v)
mettre en vente
sell (v) *or* offer (v)
(for sale)
mettre fin à
[terminer] end (v)
mettre fin graduelle-
ment phase out (v)
mettre les ressources
en commun pool (v)
resources

mettre par écrit
[rédiger] put in
writing
mettre son veto (à
une décision) veto
(v) (a decision)
mettre sous
séquestre
sequester (v) *or*
sequestrate (v)
mettre sur fiches
card-index (v)
mettre sur la liste
noire blacklist (v)
mettre sur palettes
palletize (v)
mettre sur pied
organize (v) *or*
set up (v)
meubles (mpl) de
bureaux office
furniture (n)
mi-temps: à
mi-temps part-
time (adj & adv)
micro-économie (f)
micro-economics (n)
micro-ordinateur (m)
microcomputer (n)
mieux (adv)
better (adv)

**mieux: le
mieux** best
milliard (m)
billion (bn) (n)
millier (m)
thousand (n)
million (m)
million (M) (n)
millionnaire (mf)
millionaire (n)
**minimal(e)
[minimum]**
minimum (adj)
minimum (m)
minimum (n)
minimum ou minimal
(e) minimum (adj)
ministère (m)
[du gouvernement]
ministry (n) or
department (n)
**Ministère de
l'Economie et du
Budget** Ministry of
Finance; the
Treasury [GB]
**Ministère des
affaires étrangères**
Foreign Office [GB]
ministre (mf) (gov-
ernment) minister (n)

**ministre (mf) [d'un
ministère impor-
tant]** secretary (n)
minorité (f)
minority (n)
minute (f) [temps]
minute (n)
mise (f) [offre]
bid (n) or offer (n)
(to buy)
mise à jour
update (n)
**mise à prix
[enchères]** opening
price (n); upset price
mise de fonds
outlay (n)
mise en chantier
house start (n);
housing start [US]
mise en conteneurs
containerization (n)
**mise en vigueur
[application]**
enforcement (n)
**mise initiale
[versement]** initial
investment (n)
**mise sous
sèquestre**
sequestration (n)

mise sur fiches
card-indexing (n)
mission (f)
commerciale trade
mission (n)
mixte mixed (adj)
mixte [conjoint]
joint (adj)
mobilier (-ière)
moveable (adj)
mobiliser
mobilize (v)
mobiliser des
capitaux mobilize
capital
mobilité (f)
mobility (n)
modalités (fpl) de
paiement modes
(n) of payment or
terms (n)
mode (m) mode (n)
mode (m) d'emploi
directions (n) for use
modèle (m) model
(n); design (n)
modèle de démon-
stration demonstra-
tion model
modèle déposé
registered design

modèle
économique
economic model
modèle réduit
[maquette] (scale)
model (n)
modem (m)
modem (n)
modéré(e)
moderate (adj)
modérer [limiter]
moderate (v)
moderne up to
date (adj) or
modern (adj)
modeste [peu
important]
small-scale
modification (f)
[amendement]
amendment (n) or
alteration (n) or
change (n)
modifier amend (v)
or alter (v) or
change (v)
moindre [inférieur]
lower (adj)
moins minus
or less
moins de less than

moins élevé(e)
lower than (adj)
moins-value (f)
depreciation (n) *or*
capital loss (n)
mois (m) month (n)
mois civil *ou* mois
complet calendar
month
mois: le mois
dernier last month
mois: par mois
per month *or*
monthly (adv)
moitié (f) half (n)
monde (m) world (n)
mondial(e)
worldwide (adj)
monétaire
monetary (adj)
monnaie (f) *[devise]*
currency (n)
monnaie (f) *[pièces]*
(small) change (n)
or cash (n)
monnaie conver-
tible convertible
currency
monnaie de
réserve reserve
currency

monnaie faible
soft currency
monnaie forte
hard currency
monnaie
inflationniste
inflated currency
monnaie légale *ou*
qui a cours légal
legal tender (n)
monopole (m)
monopoly (n)
monopole absolu
absolute monopoly
monopolisa-
tion (f) mono-
polization (n)
monopoliser
monopolize (v)
montage (m)
[assemblage]
assembly (n)
montant (m)
[somme] amount (n)
montant total
total amount
montant total de la
facture total
invoice value
montant versé
amount paid

monte-charge (m)
elevator (n)
monter [augmenter]
mount up (v)
monter en flèche
soar (v) or rocket
(v) or shoot up (v)
monter rapidement
escalate (v)
monter une affaire
[s'établir] set up
(v) in business
monter: faire
monter les prix
force (v) prices up
monter: se monter
[s'élever] amount
to (v) or run to (v)
or total (v)
moratoire (m)
moratorium (n)
mort(e)
dead (adj)
morte-saison (f)
off-season (n)
motivation (f)
motivation (n)
motivé(e)
motivated (adj)
mouvement (m)
movement (n)

mouvement (m)
[changement] shift
(n) or change (n)
mouvement (m)
[flux] flow (n)
mouvements de
capitaux move-
ments of capital
mouvements de
stocks stock
movements
moyen (m) [façon]
means (n) or ways (n)
moyen (légal)
d'échapper au fisc
tax loophole (n)
moyen de transport
transport facility (n)
moyen(s)
frauduleux false
pretences (n)
moyen (-enne)
average (adj) or
medium (adj)
moyen (-enne)
[taille]
medium-sized (adj)
moyen (-enne):
à moyen terme
medium-term
(adj)

moyenne (f) average (n) *or* mean (n)

moyenne pondérée weighted average

moyenne: en moyenne on an average

moyens (mpl) *[ressources]* means (n)

multilatéral(e) multilateral (adj)

multinationale (f) multinational (n)

multiple multiple (adj)

multiplication (f) multiplication

multiplier multiply

municipalité (f) local government (n)

muter *[transférer]* transfer (v) *or* move to new place

mutuel (-elle) mutual (adj)

mutuelle (f) (d'assurances) mutual (insurance) company

Nn

N° 1 du marché *[leader]* market leader (n)

nantissement (m) *[garantie]* guarantee (n) *or* collateral (n)

nation (f) nation (n)

nation endettée debtor nation

nation la plus favorisée most-favoured nation

national(e) national (adj); domestic (adj)

national(e) *[à l'échelon national]* nationwide (adj)

nationalisation (f) nationalization (n)

navire (m) ship (n)

navire-citerne *[pétrolier]* tanker (n)

navire marchand *[cargo]* merchant ship

néant (m)
[zéro] nil

nécessaire
necessary (adj)

nécessiter require
(v) *or* need (v)

négligeable
negligible (adj)

négligence (f)
negligence (n)

négligent(e)
negligent (adj)

négociable *[chèque]*
negotiable (adj)

négociant(e)
[marchand] dealer
(n) *or* merchant (n)

négociateur (-trice)
negotiator (n)

négociation (f)
negotiation (n)

négociation (f)
[marchandage]
bargaining (n)

négociations
salariales wage
negotiations

négocier
negotiate (v)

net (nette)
net (adj)

niveau (m)
level (n)

niveau de
réapprovision-
nement reorder
level

niveau des salaires
wage level

niveau des
stocks stock level

niveau élevé
high level

niveau très bas
low level *or* low (n)

nocturne (m) late-
night opening (n)

nolisage (m)
[affrètement]
charter (n);
chartering (n)

noliser *[affréter]*
charter (v)

nom (m) name (n)

nom de marque
brand name

nom: au nom de
on behalf of

nombre (m)
number (n)

nombre impair
odd number

nombre pair
even number
nomination (f)
[à un poste]
appointment (n)
nomination au
niveau du personnel
staff appointment
nommer *[à un*
poste] appoint (v)
non-livraison (f)
non-delivery (n)
non-paiement (m)
non-payment (n)
non-résident(e)
non-resident (n)
non-satisfaction:
en cas de
non-satisfaction
if not satisfied
normal(e) *[habituel]*
normal (adj) *or* usual
(adj)
normalisation (f)
[standardisation]
standardization (n)
normaliser *[standar-*
diser] standardize (v)
norme (f)
[standard] stan-
dard (n)

notaire (m)
notary public (n);
solicitor (n) *[GB]*
notation (f) finan-
cière credit rating (n)
note (f) *[d'hôtel,*
etc.] bill (n)
note (f) *[message]*
note (n) *or* memo (n)
note de crédit
credit note
note de débit
debit note
note de frais (de
représentation)
expense account
note financière
[d'une société]
credit rating (n)
noter *[prendre*
note] note (v)
noter *[consigner]*
record (v) *or*
register (v)
notification (f) *[avis]*
notification (n)
notifier notify (v)
nouveau (nouvelle)
new (adj)
nouveau: de
nouveau again

nouveau départ *ou*
nouvelle
orientation new
departure (n)
novateur (-trice)
pioneer (n)
nuit (f) night (n)
nul (nulle) null
(adj); void (adj)
nul et non avenu
null and avoid
numérique
numeric (adj) *or*
numerical (adj)
numéro (m)
[chiffre] number
(n) *or* figure (n)
numéro (m) *[d'une*
revue] issue (n)
numéro (m)
[exemplaire d'un
journal, etc.]
copy (n)
numéro de boîte
postale box
number
numéro de chèque
cheque number
numéro de
commande order
number

numéro de compte
account number
numéro de facture
invoice number
numéro de lot
batch number
numéro
d'enregistrement
registration
number
numéro de
référence
reference number
numéro de série
serial number
numéro de stock
stock code
numéro de
téléphone
telephone number
or phone number
numéro
d'immatriculation
registration
number
numéro vert *ou*
numéro
d'appel gratuit
freephone (n);
toll free
number *[US]*

numéro: **faire un
numéro (de télé-
phone)** dial (v) (a
number)
**numéroter
[pages, etc.]**
number (v)

Oo

objectif (-ive)
objective (adj)
**objectif (m) [but,
cible]** objective (n)
or aim (n) *or*
target (n)
objectif de vente
sales target
**objectifs à long
terme** long-term
objectives
obligataire (mf)
debenture holder (n)
**obligataire (mf)
[de bons du Trésor]**
bondholder (n)

**obligation (f)
[bon du Trésor,
titre]** bond (n)
**obligation (f)
[emprunt d'une
société]**
debenture (n)
**obligation (f)
[engagement]**
obligation (n)
**obligation au
porteur**
bearer bond
**obligation
convertible en
action(s)**
convertible bond
obligation d'Etat
government bond *or*
Treasury bond
**obligation non
remboursable**
irredeemable bond
**obligation
remboursable par
anticipation**
callable bond
obligatoire
compulsory (adj)
obsolescence (f)
obsolescence (n)

obsolescent(e)
obsolescent (adj)
obtenir *[se pro-*
curer] obtain (v)
or get (v)
occasion (f) *[bonne*
affaire] bargain (n)
occasion (f)
[opportunité]
opportunity (n)
occupant (m)
occupier (n) *or*
occupant (n)
occupation (f)
occupancy (n)
occupé(e) *[télé-*
phone] busy (adj)
or engaged (adj)
[line]
occupé(e)
[personne] busy
occuper occupy (v)
occuper: s'occuper
de attend to (v) *or*
deal with (v)
octroi (m)
grant (n)
octroyer *[accorder]*
grant (v)
officiel (-elle)
official (adj)

officiel (-elle)
[en bonne et due
forme]
formal (adj)
officiellement
officially (adv);
formally (adv)
officier (m) de
l'état civil
registrar (n)
officieusement
unofficially (adv);
off the record
officieux (-euse)
unofficial (adj)
offrant: le plus
offrant highest
bidder (n)
offre (f) offer (n)
offre (f) *[enchères]*
bid (n)
offre au comptant
cash offer
offre d'ouverture
opening bid
offre de lancement
[promotion]
introductory offer
offre exception-
nelle *[promotion]*
bargain offer

offre publique d'achat (OPA) takeover bid
offre publique de vente offer for sale
offre spéciale [promotion] special offer
offres (fpl) d'emploi appointments vacant *or* vacancies (n)
offrir [en cadeau] give (v)
offrir (de) [proposer] offer (v) (to)
offshore offshore (adj)
OIT (Organisation internationale du travail) ILO (International Labour Organization)
ombudsman (m) ombudsman (n)
omettre omit (v)
omettre de (faire quelque chose) fail (v) (to do something)
omission (f) omission (n)

onéreux (-euse) costly (adj) *or* expensive (adj) *or* highly-priced (adj)
OPEP (Organisation des pays exportateurs de pétrole) OPEC (Organization of Petroleum Exporting Countries)
opérateur (-trice) (n) [d'une machine] operator (n) *or* machinist (n)
opérateur (-trice) de saisie keyboarder (n)
opération (f) [affaire] operation (n)
opération [Bourse] operation *or* dealing *or* transaction (n)
opération à terme [Bourse] forward dealing; futures (n)
opération au comptant cash transaction
opération clés en main turnkey operation

**opération (f) de cou-
verture** hedging (n)
**opération multi-
devise** multicurrency
operation
opérationnel (-elle)
operational (adj)
**opinion (f)
publique** public
opinion (n)
opportunité (f)
opportunity (n)
**opposer une
demande recon-
ventionnelle**
counter-claim (v)
**opposer: s'opposer
à (une décision)**
veto (v) (a decision)
**opposition: faire
opposition à un
chèque** stop (v) a
cheque
option (f) d'achat
option (n) to purchase
option: en option
on option *or*
optional (adj)
ordinaire *[courant]*
ordinary (adj) *or*
usual (adj)

ordinaire *[standard]*
regular (adj) *or*
standard (adj)
ordinateur (m)
computer (n)
**ordinateur (m)
personnel** personal
computer (PC)
ordonnance (f)
order (n)
ordonner *[classer]*
order (v) *or* put (v)
in order
ordre (m) order (n)
or instruction (n)
**ordre (m)
*[classement]***
order (n)
ordre alphabétique
alphabetical order
**ordre
chronologique**
chronological
order
**ordre d'achat
*[commande]***
purchase order
**ordre de
prélèvement
automatique**
standing order (n)

ordre de virement bancaire *[pour un seul paiement]*
banker's order (n)
ordre du jour (m)
agenda (n)
ordre du jour: à l'ordre du jour
on the agenda
ordre: payez à l'ordre de *[sur un chèque]* pay to the order of
order: ou suivant ordre *[sur un chèque]* or order
organigramme (m)
organization chart (n)
organisation (f) *[entreprise]*
organization (n) *or* setup (n)
organization (f) *[disposition]*
organization (n) *or* arrangement (n)
organisation (f) *[institution]*
organization (n) *or* institution (n)

organisation hiérarchique *ou* verticale
line organization
Organisation internationale du travail (OIT)
International Labour Organization (ILO)
Organisation des pays exportateurs de pétrole (OPEP)
Organization of Petroleum Exporting Countries (OPEC)
organisation et mèthodes organization and methods
organiser
structure (v)
organiser *[mettre sur pied]* organize (v) *or* arrange (v)
organisme (m)
organization (n)
original (m)
original (n)
origine (f) origin (n)
osciller *[fluctuer]*
fluctuate (v)
outil (m) tool (n)
or implement (n)

outiller (une usine)
[équiper] tool up (v)
outre-mer abroad;
overseas
ouvert(e)
open (adj)
ouvert(e) à toute
proposition
open to offers
ouverture (f)
opening (n)
ouvrier (-ière)
worker (n)
ouvrier (-ière)
qualifié(e)
skilled worker
ouvrier (-ière)
spécialisé(e)
semi-skilled worker
ouvrier (-ière)
payé(e) à l'heure
hourly-paid worker
ouvriers (mpl)
qualifiés skilled
labour
ouvrir open (v)
ouvrir *[fonder,*
établir] establish
(v) *or* open (v)
ouvrir la séance
open a meeting

ouvrir un compte
open an account
ouvrir un compte
en banque open a
bank account
ouvrir une ligne
de crédit open a
line of credit

Pp

page (f) page (n)
pages jaunes (de
l'annuaire des télé-
phones) yellow pages
paie (f) *[salaire]*
pay (n) *or* wage
paiement (m)
[action] paying (n)
paiement (m)
[règlement]
payment (n) *or*
settlement (n)
paiement à la
commande cash
with order

paiement à la livraison cash on delivery (c.o.d.)

paiement annuel yearly payment

paiement au rendement *[salaire]* payment by results

paiement (au) comptant *ou* en espèces cash payment

paiement avec (une) carte de crédit payment by credit card

paiement d'avance payment in advance *or* prepayment (n); money up front (n)

paiement différé deferred payment

paiement en nature payment in kind

paiement intérimaire *[acompte]* interim payment

paiement libératoire final discharge

paiement mensuel monthly payment

paiement par chèque payment by cheque

paiement semestriel half-yearly payment

paiement symbolique token payment

paiements (mpl) échelonnés staged payments

pair: au pair at par

palette (f) pallet

palettiser palettize (v)

panel (m) de consommateurs consumer panel (n)

panne (f) *[défaillance]* failure (n) *or* breakdown (n)

panne: être en panne break down (v)

panneau (m) panel (n)

panneau d'affichage *ou* panneau publicitaire advertisement hoarding (n) *or* display board (n)

paperasserie (f)
paperwork (n)
paperasserie
administrative
red tape (n)
papier (m) paper (n)
papier à lettres
note paper (n)
papier cadeau
(gift) wrapping
paper
papier carbone
carbon paper
papier d'emballage
wrapping paper
papier en continu
ou **papier listing**
continuous
stationery (n)
papier kraft
brown paper
papier recyclé
recycled paper
paquet (m) *[bloc]*
block (n) *[of shares]*
paquet (m) *[colis]*
parcel (n)
paquet (m)
[emballage
commercial] pack
(n) *or* packet (n)

paquet (m) *[liasse]*
batch (n)
paquet d'en-
veloppes pack of
envelopes
paquet de ciga-
rettes packet of
cigarettes
paradis (m) fiscal
tax haven (n)
paraître *[sembler]*
appear (v) *or*
seem (v)
parapher *[signer*
de ses initiales]
initial (v)
parcours (m)
route (n)
parfait(e) perfect
(adj) *or* A1
parité (f) parity (n)
parrainage (m)
[sponsorisation]
sponsorship (n)
parrainer
[sponsoriser]
sponsor (v)
part (f) *[partie]*
share (n) *or* part (n)
part (f) *[valeur*
mobilière] share (n)

part du marché
market share
partage (m) de temps
time-sharing (n)
partage (m) d'un
poste (de travail)
job-sharing (n) *or*
work-sharing (n)
partager [diviser]
share (v) *or* divide
(v) among
partager [en com-
mun] share (v) *or*
use (v) with someone
partager un bureau
share an office
partenaire (m)
commercial trading
partner n
participation (f)
[contribution]
participation (n);
charge (n)
participation (f)
[intérêt financier]
(financial) interest (n)
or shareholding (n)
participation des
employés aux
résultats profit-
sharing (n)

participation (f)
symbolique
token charge (n)
partie (f) [part]
part (n)
partie (f) [juri-
dique] party (n)
partie contractante
contracting party
partie plaignante
plaintiff (n);
prosecution (n)
partir leave (v) *or*
go away (v)
partir à la retraite
retire (v) (from
one's job)
partout dans le
monde everywhere
(adv); worldwide
(adv)
passavant (m)
[douane] carnet (n)
passer à switch
over to (v)
passer par profits
et pertes write
off (v)
passer une
commande place
(v) an order

passer une écriture
post (v) an entry
passible de liable
to (adj) *or* subject
to (adj)
passif (m) *[dettes]*
liabilities (n)
passif exigible
current liabilities
patron (m) boss (n)
pause-café (f)
coffee break (n)
**pavé (m) numé-
rique** numeric
keypad (n)
**pavillon (m)
d'exposition *[hall]***
exhibition hall (n)
payable payable
(adj)
payable à l'avance
payable in advance
**payable à la livrai-
son** payable on
delivery
**payable à soixante
jours** payable at
sixty days
**payable à présenta-
tion *ou* à vue**
payable on demand

payé(e) *[réglé]*
paid (adj)
payé(e) *[travail]*
paid *[work]*
payé(e) d'avance
paid in advance *or*
prepaid (adj)
**payer *[une
facture, une note]***
pay (v) *or* settle (v)
(a bill)
**payer *[un
employé]*** pay (v)
(a worker)
**payer avec une
carte de crédit** pay
by credit card
payer comptant
pay cash
payer d'avance
prepay (v) *or* pay in
advance
**payer des
dommages-intérêts
*[indemniser]*** settle
(v) a claim
**payer les intérêts
d'une dette** service
(v) a debt
payer par chèque
pay by cheque

**payer par verse-
ments échelonnés**
pay in instalments
**payer: à payer
[impayé]**
outstanding (adj)
**payer: faire
payer** charge (v)
**payer: faire payer
trop cher**
overcharge (v)
payeur (m) payer (n)
**payeur: mauvais
payeur** bad payer
pays (m) country (n)
pays d'origine
country of origin
**pays en
développement
(PED)** developing
country
**pays exportateurs
de pétrole** oil-
exporting countries
pays industrialisés
industrialized
countries
**pays producteurs
de pétrole**
oil-producing
countries

**PDG (président-
directeur général)**
chairman and mana-
ging director or CEO
péage (m) toll (n)
pénaliser
penalize (v)
pénalité (f)
penalty (n)
**pénétration (f) du
marché** market
penetration (n)
pénétrer [entrer]
enter (v) or go in
(v) or go into (v)
**pénétrer un marché
[s'implanter]**
penetrate (v) a
market
**pension (f) de
retraite** (retire-
ment) pension (n)
pénurie (f)
shortage (n)
**pénurie (f) de
main-d'oeuvre**
manpower shortage
**PEPS (premier
entré, premier
sorti)** FIFO (first
in first out)

PER (coefficient de capitalisation des résultats) P/E ratio (price/earnings ratio)

percepteur (m) tax collector (n) *or* collector of tax

perception (f) des impôts tax collection

percevoir collect (v)

perdre lose (v)

perdre de l'argent lose money

perdre des arrhes forfeit (v) a deposit

perdre par confiscation forfeit (v)

perdre une commande lose an order

performance (f) performance (n)

performance (f) [efficacité] efficiency (n)

périmé(e) [passport, etc.] no longer valid *or* out of date

période (f) [durée] period (n)

période d'essai [employé] probationary period *or* probation (n)

période d'exercice d'une fonction tenure (n)

période d'expansion boom (n)

périodique (adj) periodic *or* periodical (adj)

périodique (m) [revue] periodical (n) *or* review (n) *or* magazine (n)

périphériques (mpl) (d'ordinateur) peripherals (n)

périssable perishable (adj)

permanence (f) téléphonique answering service (n)

permettre allow (v) *or* permit (v)

permis (m) [autorisation] permit (n) *or* licence (n); license (n) *[US]*

permis d'exporta-tion export licence *or* export permit
permis de séjour *[carte de séjour]* residence permit
permis de travail work permit
permission (f) *[autorisation]* permission (n) *or* authorization (n)
personnalisé(e) personalized (adj)
personne (f) person (n); individual (n)
personne désignée nominee (n)
personne: par personne per person *or* per capita *or* per head
personnel (m) staff (n) *or* personnel (n)
personnel (m) *[main-d'oeuvre]* workforce (n)
personnel clé key personnel *or* key staff

personnel de base *ou* **personnel réduit** skeleton staff
personnel de bureau office staff *or* clerical staff
personnel de direction managerial staff; management (n)
personnel d'en-cadrement managerial staff
personnel de vente *[commerciaux]* sales team *or* sales force *or* sales staff
personnel de vente très motivé highly motivated sales staff
personnel hôtelier hotel staff
personnel régulier regular staff
personnel temporaire temporary staff
personnel (-elle) *[privé]* personal (adj)

perspectives (fpl)
prospects (n)
perte (f) loss (n)
perte de valeur
[diminution]
decrease in value
perte d'exploita-
tion trading loss
perte d'une
commande loss
of an order
perte nette net loss
perte sèche dead
loss *or* write-off (n)
perte théorique
paper loss
pertes (fpl) *[gaspil-*
lage] wastage (n)
peser weigh (n)
petit(e) small (adj)
petit actionnaire
minor shareholder (n)
petite caisse (f)
petty (adj) cash
petite entreprise
small-scale enterprise
petite monnaie
small change
petites annonces
classified ads *or*
small ads

petites dépenses
petty expenses
petites et
moyennes enter-
prises (PME) small
(and medium-sized)
businesses
pétrole (m) oil (n)
pétrolier (m)
[navire-citerne]
tanker (n)
peu not (very)
much (adv)
peu actif (-ive)
[marché] slack
(adj)
peu à peu little by
little
peu important(e)
unimportant (adj)
peu important(e)
[de bas niveau]
low-level (adj)
peu important(e)
[de taille modeste]
small-scale (adj)
phase (f) stage (n)
photocopie (f)
photocopy (n)
photocopier
photocopy (v)

**photocopieur (m)
ou photocopieuse
(f)** photocopier (n)
or copier (n) or
copying machine (n)
**PIB (produit
intérieur brut)** GDP
(gross domestic
product)
pièce (f) [morceau]
piece (n)
pièce (f) [salle]
room (n)
pièce de monnaie
coin (n)
**pièce détachée ou
pièce de rechange**
spare part (n)
pièce jointe
attachment (n)
[to email]
**pièce jointe (p.j.)
[in letter]**
enclosure (n)
(encl. or enc.)
**pièces et main
d'oeuvre (PMO)**
labour and spare
parts
place (f) [espace]
room (n)

place (f) [rang]
place (n)
place du marché
marketplace (n)
**placement (m)
(financier)**
investment (n)
**placement de père
de famille** blue-
chip investment
placement sûr safe
or risk-free investment
placer place (v)
**plafond (m)
[limite]** ceiling (n)
or limit (n)
plafond de crédit
credit limit or
lending limit
plafond des prix
price ceiling
**plaindre: se
plaindre (de)** com-
plain (v) (about)
plainte (f)
complaint (n)
plan (m) [dessin]
plan (n) or draft (n)
plan (m) [projet]
plan (n) or project
(n) or scheme (n)

plan d'ensemble
[d'un immeuble]
floor plan
plan d'occupation
des sols (POS)
zoning regula-
tions (n)
plan d'urgence
contingency plan
plan (m) social *ou*
de développement
de la société
corporate plan
plancher (m)
floor (n)
planificateur (m)
planner (n)
planification (f)
planning (n)
planification à long
terme long-term
planning
planification dans
l'entreprise
corporate planning
planification de la
main-d'oeuvre
manpower planning
planification
économique
economic planning

planifier *[projeter]*
plan (v)
plateforme (f) de
chargement
loading ramp (n)
plein(e) full (adj)
pli (m) envelope (n)
pli: sous pli séparé
under separate
cover
plomb (m) de la
douane customs
seal (n)
plus more; plus
plus âgé; plus
important
senior (adj)
plus-value (f)
capital gains (n)
plus-value de
change exchange
premium (n)
PME (petites et
moyennes
entreprises) small
(and medium-sized)
businesses
PNB (produit
national brut) GNP
(gross national
product)

poche (f) pocket (n)
pochette (f) (en papier, en plastique) (paper, plastic) bag (n)
poids (m) weight (n)
poids brut gross weight
poids inexact [faux poids] false weight
poids lourd [camion] heavy goods vehicle (HGV)
poids maximum weight limit or maximum weight
poids net net weight
point (m) point (n)
point (m) [question] matter (n) or business (n) [to discuss]
point de départ starting point
point de vente outlet (n); point of sale (POS)
point de vente électronique electronic point of sale (EPOS)

point de référence benchmark (n)
pointe: de pointe up to date (adj); latest (adj)
police (f) d'assurance insurance policy (n)
police d'assurance-vie assurance policy (n)
politique (f) policy (n)
politique (de fixation) des prix pricing policy
politique budgétaire budgetary policy
politique en matière de crédit credit policy
politique générale (de l'entreprise) code of practice (n)
polycopier duplicate (v)
pondération (f) [indemnité de résidence] weighting (n)

pont (m) bridge (n)
pont (m) *[de navire]* deck (n)
pontée (f) deck cargo
populaire popular (adj)
port (m) *[de mer]* port (n) or harbour (n)
port (m) *[d'ordinateur]* port (n)
port (m) *[transport]* carriage (n)
port d'attache (d'un navire) port of registry
port d'embarquement port of embarkation
port d'escale port of call
port dû *ou* **en port dû** carriage forward or freight forward
port en lourd *[charge d'un navire]* deadweight cargo
port franc free port
port payé *[poste]* postage paid *or* postpaid (adj)

port payé *ou* **en port payé** *[transport]* carriage paid
port pour porte-conteneurs container terminal (n)
portable *ou* **portatif (-ive)** portable (adj)
porte (f) door (n)
porte-à-porte (m) *[démarchage]* canvassing (n) *or* door-to-door selling
porte-à-porte: faire du porte-à-porte canvass (v)
porte-conteneurs (m) container ship (n)
porte-documents (m) briefcase (n)
porte-documents personnalisé personalized briefcase
portefeuille (f) (d'actions) portfolio (n) (of shares)
porter intérêt bear (v) interest
porter plainte complain (v)

**porter une
signature** bear (v)
a signature
porteur (m)
bearer (n)
**poser sa candida-
ture à un poste**
apply (v) for a job
**poser sa candida-
ture une deuxième
fois** reapply (v)
positif (-ive)
positive (adj)
position (f)
position (n) *or* state
of affairs (n)
position (f) *[rang]*
rank (n)
position de force
[négociations] bar-
gaining power (n)
**position d'un
compte (bancaire)**
bank balance (n)
position financière
financial position
posséder possess
(v) *or* own (v) *or*
hold (v)
possibilité (f)
possibility (n)

possible possible
(adj)
possible *[potentiel]*
potential (adj)
**possible: aussitôt
que** *ou* **dès que
possible** as soon as
possible (asap)
postal(e)
postal (adj)
postdater
postdate (v)
poste (f) *[service
postal]* post (n) *or*
postal system (n)
poste (f) *ou* **bureau
(m) de poste** post
office (n)
poste aérienne
airmail (n)
poste centrale
general post office
poste restante
poste restante
**poste: mettre à la
poste** post (v) *or*
put (v) in the post
or mail (v)
poste (m) *[compt-
abilité]* item (n) *or*
entry (n)

poste (m) *[emploi]*
position (n) *or*
job (n)
poste (m)
[téléphonique]
extension (n)
poste clé key post
poste d'amarrage
[d'un navire]
berth (n)
poste de travail
[ordinateur]
workstation (n)
poste exceptionnel
[comptabilité]
extraordinary *or*
non-recurring item
poste frontière
customs entry
point (n)
poste vacant *ou*
poste à pourvoir
vacancy (n)
poster post (v) *or*
put (v) in the post
or mail (v)
pot-de-vin (m)
backhander (n) *or*
bribe (n)
potentiel (m)
potential (n)

potentiel (-elle)
(adj) potential (adj)
pourboire (m) tip
(n) *[money]*
pour cent (%) per
cent (%)
pourcentage (m)
percentage (n)
pourcentage de
remise percentage
discount
poursuite (f)
[continuation]
continuation (n)
poursuite(s)
(judiciaire(s))
prosecution (n) *or*
action (n)
poursuite en dom-
mages-intérêts
action for damages
poursuivre *[continuer]*
proceed (v) (with)
poursuivre en
justice take (v) to
court *or* prosecute
(v) *or* sue (v)
poursuivre: se pour-
suivre *[continuer]*
continue (v) *or* go on
(v) *or* proceed (v)

poussée (f)
boost (n)
pousser [relancer]
boost (v)
pouvoir (m)
d'achat purchasing
power (n); spending
power
pratique [utile]
handy (adj) or
convenient (adj)
**pratique (f) [acti-
vité]** practice (n)
**pratique malhon-
nête** sharp practice
**pratiques restric-
tives** restrictive
practices
préalable prior (adj)
or previous (adj)
préavis (m) notice
(n) or advance notice
**préavis (m) [aver-
tissement]** notice
(n) or warning (n)
précédent(e)
[antérieur] former
(adj) or previous
(adj)
précis(e) accurate
(adj)

précision (f)
precision (f) or
accuracy (n)
précision (f)
[detail] detail (n)
précision: avec
précision with
accuracy or
accurately (adv)
préemballer
prepack (v) or
prepackage (v)
préférence (f)
[priorité]
preference (n)
préférer prefer (v)
préfinancement (m)
pre-financing (n)
prélèvement (m)
[retenue]
deduction (n)
prélèvement
automatique
[banque] direct
debit (n)
prélèvement
fiscal tax
deductions [from
salary]
premier (-ière)
first (adj)

**premier entré,
premier sorti
(PEPS)** first in first
out (FIFO)
premier trimestre
first quarter (n)
**première offre
[enchères]**
opening bid
première qualité
premium quality *or*
first quality
prendre take (v)
**prendre des
dispositions** make
(v) provision for
**prendre des
mesures** take
action
prendre du retard
fall (v) behind *or*
be late
prendre fin end (v)
**prendre fin
[expirer]** expire (v)
**prendre la
succession de
quelqu'un** take
over from some-
one else

**prendre livraison
d'un envoi** accept
(v) delivery of a
shipment
prendre note
take note
**prendre sa retraite
ou partir à la
retraite** retire (v)
(from one's job)
**prendre un appel
[répondre au
téléphone]** take
a call
**prendre un
congé** take time
off work
prendre un risque
take a risk
**prendre une
décision** reach (v)
or come to (v) a
decision
préoccupation (f)
concern (n) *or*
worry (n)
**préposé(e) (n) à la
réception** recep-
tion clerk (n);
receptionist (n)

**préposé(e) à la
vente des billets**
booking clerk
**préposé(e)s au(x)
comptoir(s)**
counter staff
près de close to
or near
présent(e) present
(adj)
présentation (f)
presentation (n)
**présentation (f)
[exposition]**
display (n)
**présentation [d'une
personne]**
introduction (n)
présenter [donner]
present (v) *or*
give (v)
présenter [exposer]
display (v)
**présenter [une
personne à une
autre]** introduce (v)
**présenter une
traite à
l'acceptation**
present a bill for
acceptance

**présenter une traite
au recouvrement** pre-
sent a bill for payment
**présenter: se
présenter** report
(v) *or* go to (v)
**présenter: se
présenter à
l'enregistrement**
check in (v)
**présenter: se
présenter à un
entretien** report
(v) for an interview
présentoir (m)
display stand (n) *or*
display rack (n)
**présentoir de
produits en vrac**
dump bin (n)
**président(e) [d'une
assemblée]**
chairman (n)
**président(e) [d'une
société, d'un
comité]** chairman
(n); president (n)
**président-directeur
(m) géneral (PDG)**
Chairman and
Managing Director

presse (f) press (n)
prestation (f)
[Sécurité sociale]
benefit (n)
prestation de
service service
rendered
prestige (m)
prestige (n)
prêt(e) ready (adj)
prêt (m) loan (n)
prêt à court terme
short-term loan
prêt à long terme
long-term loan
prêt bancaire
bank loan
prêt bonifié *ou* de
faveur soft loan
prêt hypothécaire
mortgage (n)
prêt immobilier
mortgage (n) *[GB]*
prétendre claim (v)
or suggest (v)
prêter lend (v) *or*
loan (v)
prêter de l'argent
advance (v)
money *or* lend (v)
money

prêteur (m)
lender (n) *or*
moneylender (n)
prêteur (sur
hypothèque)
mortgagee (n)
preuve (f) proof (n)
preuve écrite
documentary
evidence
prévenir *[devancer]*
pre-empt (v)
préventif (-ive)
preventive (adj)
prévention (f)
prevention (n)
prévision (f)
[estimation]
forecasting (n)
prévisions (fpl)
forecast (n)
prévisions à long
terme long-term
forecast
prévisions de
trésorerie cash
flow forecast
prévisions des
besoins en main-
d'oeuvre man-
power forecasting

prévisions des ventes sales forecast

prévisions du marché market forecast

prévoir forecast (v)

prévoir *[prendre des dispositions]* make provision for *or* provide for

prévu(e) projected (adj) *[sales]*

prime (f) bonus (n)

prime (f) *[cadeau promotionnel]* free gift (n)

prime d'assurance (insurance) premium (n)

prime d'encouragement merit award *or* merit bonus

prime de fin de contrat terminal bonus

prime de rendement productivity bonus

prime de renouvellement *[assurance]* renewal premium

prime de risques risk premium

prime de vie chère cost-of-living bonus

prime d'incitation au travail incentive bonus

principal(e) principal (adj) *or* main (adj) *or* chief (adj)

principe (m) principle (n)

prioritaire *[lettre]* express (letter)

prioritaire *[privilégié]* preferential (adj)

priorité (f) *[préférence]* preference (n)

prise (f) de contrôle takeover (n)

prise de décision decision making (n)

prise de position dans les négociations bargaining position (n)

privatisation (f) privatization (n)

privatiser privatize (v)

privé(e) *ou* privatif
(-ive) private (adj)
privé(e) *[person-*
nel] personal (adj)
privé: en privé
privately (adv)
privé: en privé
[officieusement]
off the record
privilégié(e)
[prioritaire]
preferential (adj) *or*
preferred (adj)
prix (m) *[coût]*
price (n) *or* cost (n)
prix (m) *[tarif]*
price *or* rate (n)
prix à la portée de
tous popular price(s)
prix à quai landed
costs *or* price ex quay
prix au comptant
cash price
prix avec rabais
discount price
prix catalogue list
price *or* catalogue
price
prix compétitifs
keen prices *or*
competitive prices

prix convenu
agreed price
prix courant *ou*
actuel current
price
prix coûtant cost
price
prix de clôture
[Bourse] closing
price
prix de détail retail
price
prix de facture
invoice value
prix de gros trade
price
prix de location
rental (n)
prix d'émission
(d'une action)
offer price
prix départ usine
factory price *or*
price ex works
prix de revente
resale price
prix de revient
cost price
prix de revient *[coût*
de production]
production cost

prix de seuil
threshold price
prix de soutien
support price
prix de vente
selling price
prix de vente
conseillé manufac-
turer's recom-
mended price (MRP)
prix d'intervention
intervention price
prix d'origine *ou*
coût (m)
historique
historic(al) cost
prix d'ouverture
[Bourse] opening
price
prix du billet fare (n)
prix du marché
market price
prix du pétrole oil
price
prix du transport
freight (n) *or*
carriage (n) (cost)
prix entrepôt price
ex warehouse
prix exceptionnel
bargain price

prix ferme firm price
prix fixe set price
or fixed price
prix fort full price
prix gonflé(s)
inflated price(s)
prix imposé set
price
prix imposé:
politique des prix
imposés resale
price maintenance
prix le plus bas
lowest price; rock-
bottom price
prix livré supply
price
prix maximum
maximum price
prix minimum fixé
[aux enchères]
reserve price *or*
upset price
prix moyen
average price
prix net net price;
all-in price
prix plafond ceiling
price
prix raisonnable
fair price

prix réduit cut price

prix sacrifié
knockdown price *or*
bargain price

prix spot *[Bourse]*
spot price

prix stables stable
prices

prix tout compris
delivered price

prix unitaire *ou* prix
de l'unité unit price

prix: à prix réduit
cut-price (adj)

problème (m)
[difficulté]
problem (n) *or*
trouble (n)

problème (m)
[sujet] matter (n)
or problem (n)

problème (m) de
trésorerie liquidity
crisis *or* cash flow
problem

procédé (m)
process (n)

procédé industriel
industrial process

procédure (f)
procedure (n)

procédure de sélec-
tion selection
procedure

procédures
juridiques judicial
processes

procès (m) court
case (n) *or* lawsuit
(n) *or* trial (n)

procès-verbal (m)
minutes (n) (of
meeting)

processus (m)
process (n)

procuration (f) *[à
la place d'un autre]*
proxy (n)

procuration (f)
[mandat] power of
attorney (n)

procuration: par
procuration by proxy;
per procurationem
(per pro *or* pp)

procurer procure (v)

procurer: se
procurer obtain (v)

procurer: se pro-
curer des fonds
raise (v) money *or*
secure (v) funds

procurer: qu'on peut se procurer obtainable (adj) *or* available (adj)

producteur (-trice) producer (n)

productif (-ive) productive (adj)

production (f) production (n) *or* output (n)

production intérieure domestic production

production record peak output

production totale total output

productivité (f) productivity (n)

produire [fabriquer] produce (v) *or* make (v)

produire [présenter ou montrer] produce (v) (documents)

produire [rapporter un intérêt, etc.] carry (v) *or* produce (v) (an interest)

produire en excédent [surproduire] overproduce (v)

produire un bénéfice show (v) a profit

produit (m) product (n)

produit (m) [revenu] revenue (n)

produit d'appel [article-réclame] loss-leader (n)

produit dérivé [sous-produit] by-product (n) *or* spinoff (n)

produit des ventes sales revenue

produit fini end product *or* finished product *or* final product

produit grand public mass market product

produit intérieur brut (PIB) gross domestic product (GDP)

produit national brut (PNB) gross national product (GNP)

produit semi-fini semi-finished product

produits (mpl) products (n) *or* goods (n)

produits à marque du distributeur own brand goods *or* own label goods

produits concurrentiels competing *or* competitive products

produits de consommation consumable goods *or* consumables (n)

produits dérivés [Bourse] derivatives (n)

produits manufacturés manufactured goods

produits maraî-chers produce (n)

professionnel (-elle) professional (n & adj)

professionnel (-elle) [maladie] occupational (adj) (disease)

professionnel (-elle) [revue] trade magazine (n) *or* trade journal (n)

profil (m) profile (n)

profil de poste job description (n)

profit (m) profit (n) *or* earnings (n)

profit: à profit at a profit

profit: faire un profit make (v) a profit

profit: faire un profit brut gross (v)

profit: faire un profit net net (v)

profiter [se déve-lopper] thrive (v)

profiter de quelque chose [tirer avantage de] take (v) advantage of something

programmation (f)
(computer)
programming (n)
programme (m)
programme (n) *or*
scheme (n)
programme (m)
[logiciel] pro-
gramme (n) *or* pro-
gram *or* software (n)
programme de
recherche research
programme
programme pilote
pilot scheme
programmer (un
ordinateur) program
(v) (a computer)
programmeur
(-euse) (computer)
programmer (n)
progrès (m)
progress (n)
progresser
progress (v)
progressif (-ive)
[échelonné]
graduated (adj)
progressif (-ive)
[graduel]
gradual (adj)

projet (m) plan (n)
or project (n)
projet de loi bill
(n) *[in Parliament]*
projet pilote pilot
project
prolongation (f)
extension (n)
prolonger
extend (v)
prolonger une
traite renew (v) a
bill of exchange
promesse (f)
promise (n)
promettre
promise (v)
promotion (f)
[avancement]
promotion (n) (to a
better job)
promotion (f)
[publicité]
promotion *or*
publicity (n)
promotion (f)
[offre spéciale]
special offer (n)
promotion des
ventes sales
promotion

**promotion: en
promotion** on
special offer
**promotionnel
(-elle)**
promotional (adj)
promouvoir *[donner
de l'avancement]*
promote (v)
prompt(e) *[rapide]*
prompt (adj)
pronostic (m)
forecast (n)
pronostiquer
forecast (v)
**proportionnel
(-elle)**
proportional (adj)
**proportionnel
(-elle) (à la valeur)**
ad valorem
proportionnellement
in proportion to
**proposer (quelque
chose, quelqu'un)**
propose (v) *or*
suggest (v)
proposer *[motion]*
move (v) (that)
proposer *[offrir]*
offer (v)

**proposer de (faire
quelque chose)**
propose to (do
something)
proposition (f)
proposal (n) *or*
suggestion (n)
proposition (f)
[offre] offer (n)
propriétaire (mf)
proprietor (m),
proprietress (f);
owner (n)
propriétaire (mf)
*[d'un logement
locatif]* landlord
(m), landlady (f)
**propriétaire
légitime** rightful
owner (n)
propriété (f) *[droit]*
ownership (n)
propriété (f)
[maison, terrain]
property (n); house
(n); estate (n)
propriété collective
collective ownership
**propriété en com-
mun** *[copropriété]*
joint ownership

propriété privée
[droit] private
ownership
propriété privée
[maison, terrain]
private property
prorata: au prorata
pro rata
prospect (m)
[acheteur, client
potentiel]
prospective client *or*
buyer (n)
prospecter *[faire du*
démarchage]
canvass (v)
prospection (f)
[démarchage]
canvassing (n)
prospectus (m)
prospectus (n) *or*
leaflet (n)
prospère
flourishing (adj) *or*
booming (adj)
prospérer
flourish (v)
protection (f) du
consommateur
consumer
protection (n)

protectionniste
[tarif] protective
(adj) *[tariff]*
protéger protect
(v); safeguard (v)
protestation (f)
protest (n)
protestation: en
signe de protes-
tation in protest
protester contre
quelque chose
protest (v) (against
something)
protêt (m)
protest (n)
protocole (m)
d'accord heads of
agreement (n)
protocole financier
financial agreement
provenance (f)
[origine] origin (n)
province (f)
[campagne]
country (n) *[not*
town]
province (f)
[division de
certains pays]
province (n)

provision (f) *[avance,*
acompte] advance
(n) *or* deposit (n)
provision (f)
[comptabilité]
reserve (n)
provision (f)
[stock] supply (n)
or reserve (n)
provision pour
dépréciation
allowance (n) for
depreciation
provisions (fpl):
faire des provisions
stock up (v)
provisoire
provisional (adj)
pub (f) *[publicité]*
publicity (n); (TV)
commercial (n)
pub: faire de la pub
(pour un produit)
promote (v) or adver-
tise (v) or plug (v)
public (publique)
public (adj)
publication (f)
assistée par ordi-
nateur (PAO) desk-
top publishing (DTP)

publicitaire
advertising (adj)
publicitaire: les
publicitaires
(mfpl) publicity
people *or*
advertising staff
publicité (f)
publicity (n) *or*
advertising (n)
publicité (f)
[annonce]
advertisement (n)
or ad (n)
publicité à
l'échelon national
national advertising
publicité avec
coupon-réponse
coupon ad
publicité de produit
product advertising
publicité directe
direct-mail
advertising
publicité excessive
ou **grosse publicité**
hype (n)
publicité: faire
de la publicité
advertise (v)

publier publish (v)
publipostage (m)
direct mail *or*
direct-mail
advertising (n)

Qq

quai (m) *[gare]*
platform (n)
quai (m) *[port]*
quay (n) *or*
wharf (n)
qualifications (fpl)
professionnelles
professional
qualifications (n)
qualifié(e)
qualified (adj) *or*
skilled (adj)
qualifié: non
qualifié(e)
[ouvrier] unskilled
(adj)
qualité (f)
quality (n)

qualité courrier
[imprimante] near-
letter-quality (NLQ)
qualité inférieure
poor quality
qualité marchande
saleability (n)
qualité supérieure
top quality *or*
premium quality
quantité (f)
quantity (n)
quart (m) quarter
(n) *[25%]*
quartier (m) (d'une
ville) district (n) *or*
area (n) (of town)
quartier
commerçant
commercial district
quartier des
affaires business
centre
quatrième
trimestre fourth
quarter (n)
question (f)
question (n)
question (f) *[point]*
matter (n) *or* business
[to be discussed]

question (f) à l'ordre du jour item (n) on the agenda

quittance (f) [reçu] receipt (n)

quitter [partir] leave (v)

quitter [les lieux] vacate (v) (the premises)

quitter l'hôtel [régler la note au départ] check out (v) (of hotel)

quitter: ne quittez pas [téléphone] hold the line, please!

quorum (m) quorum (n)

quorum: atteindre le quorum have (v) a quorum

quota (m) quota (n)

quota (m) d'importation import quota

quotidien (-ienne) daily (adj)

Rr

rabais (m) [réduction de prix] price reduction or mark-down

rabais: au rabais at a discount or at cut price; reduced (adj)

rabais: faire un rabais reduce (v) or knock off (v) (price)

rachat (m) [prise de contrôle] takeover (n)

rachat contesté contested takeover

rachat de l'entreprise par ses salariés management buyout (MBO)

rachat avec capitaux garantis par l'actif de la société leveraged buyout (LBO)

racheter buy back (v)

racheter une police d'assurance *[résilier]* surrender (v) a policy

racket (m) racketeering (n)

racketteur (m) racketeer (n)

radier quelque chose d'une liste cross off (v)

raison (f) *[explication]* explanation (n)

raison sociale corporate name

raison: en raison de owing to

rajustement (m) *ou* **réajustement (m)** readjustment (n)

rajuster *ou* **réajuster** readjust (v)

ralentir slow down (v)

ralentissement (m) slowdown (n)

ralentissement (m) *[baisse]* decline (n)

rang (m) place (n) *[in a competition]*

rapide fast (adj) *or* quick (adj)

rapide *[express]* express (adj)

rapide *[prompt]* prompt (adj)

rapidement fast (adv) *or* quickly (adv)

rappel (m) *[avertissement]* reminder (n) *or* chaser (n)

rappel (m) de salaire back pay (n) *or* retroactive pay rise (n)

rappeler *[au telephone]* phone back (v)

rappeler (quelque chose à quelqu'un) remind (v) (someone of something)

rappeler une référence quote (v) a reference number

rapport (m) *[compte-rendu]* report (n)

rapport (m) *[taux ou ratio]* ratio (n)
rapport annuel annual report
rapport confidentiel confidential report
rapport d'avancement du travail progress report
rapport de faisabilité feasibility report
rapport intérimaire interim report
rapport qualité/ prix excellent good value (for money)
rapporter *[intérêt ou dividende]* yield (v) *or* earn (v) *or* produce (v) (interest)
rapporter *[produire un bénéfice]* bring in (v) *or* produce (v)
rapporter: qui rapporte money-making (adj)

rapporter brut *[faire un profit brut]* gross (v)
rapprochement (m) *[réconciliation]* reconciliation (n)
rapprochement de comptes reconciliation of accounts
ratage (m) *[échec]* failure (n) *or* flop (n)
rater *[échouer]* fail (v) *or* flop (v)
rater *[but, train]* miss (v) (target, train)
ratification (f) ratification (n)
ratifier ratify (v)
ratio (m) *[rapport, taux]* ratio (n)
ratio d'endette-ment *[effet de levier]* leverage (n) *or* gearing (n)
rationalisation (f) rationalization (n)
rationaliser rationalize (n)
rayer *[supprimer]* delete (v)

rayon (m)
department(n)
[in shop]
**rayon (m) *[comp-
toir]*** counter (n)
**rayon (m)
*[étagère]*** shelf (n)
rayonnage (m)
shelving (n) *or*
shelves (n)
réaction (f)
response (n) *or*
reaction (n)
**réaction (f) *[infor-
mation en retour]***
feedback (n)
**réajustement (m)
ou rajustement (m)**
readjustment (n)
réajuster *ou* rajuster
readjust (v)
**réalisation (f)
d'actif** realization
(n) of assets
**réalisation (f) d'un
projet** realization
of a plan
**réaliser un projet
ou un plan** realize
(v) a project *or*
a plan

**réaliser une
propriété *ou* des
biens [vendre]**
realize a property *or*
realize assets
**réaménagement
(m) (d'un magasin,
etc.)** refitting (n)
(of a shop, etc.)
**réaménagement
(m) (d'une zone)**
redevelopment (n)
**réaménager (un
magasin, etc.)** refit
(v) (a shop, etc.)
**réaménager (une
zone)** redevelop (v)
**réapprovision-
nement (m)**
restocking (n)
**réapprovisionner:
se réapprovisionner**
restock (v);
reorder (v)
réassurance (f)
reinsurance (n)
réassurer
reinsure (v)
**récépissé (m) de
douanes** customs
receipt (n)

réception (f)
reception (n)
réceptionner
[prendre livraison]
accept (v) delivery
(of a shipment)
réceptionniste (mf)
receptionist (n) *or*
reception clerk (n)
récession (f)
recession (n)
recettes (fpl)
receipts (n) *or*
revenue (n)
recettes (fpl) *[rentrées]* takings (n)
recettes nettes net
receipts
recettes publicitaires revenue from
advertising
receveur (m)
[percepteur]
collector (n)
receveur des
contributions
indirectes Excise
officer (n)
recevoir receive (v)
recherche (f)
[étude] research (n)

recherche des
besoins des
consommateurs
consumer research
recherche
documentaire *ou*
d'information data
retrieval (n)
Recherche et
développement (R
et D) Research and
Development (R & D)
recherche: faire des
recherches
research (v) *or* do
some research (on)
récipient (m) *[contenant]* container (n)
réciprocité (f)
reciprocity (n)
réciproque
reciprocal (adj)
réclamation (f)
[plainte]
complaint (n)
réclamation (f)
[demande ou revendication] claim (n);
demand (n)
réclame (f) *[publicité]* advertising (n)

réclamer *[demander]* ask for (something)

réclamer *[exiger]* demand (v)

réclamer (des dommages-intérêts) claim (v) (for damages)

réclamer un droit claim a right

recommandation (f) *[conseil]* recommendation (n)

recommandation (f) *[référence]* reference (n) *[report on person]*

recommander *[conseiller]* recommend (v) *or* suggest (v)

recommander (une lettre) register (v) (a letter)

recommander (un produit, etc.) recommend (v) (a product, etc.)

recommencer *[reprendre]* resume (v)

réconciliation (f) *[rapprochement]* reconciliation (n)

reconduire un crédit *ou* une dette roll over (v) credit *or* a debt

reconfiguration (f) (d'un emprunt) restructuring (n) (of a loan)

reconnaissance (f) recognition (n)

reconnaissance (f) de dette IOU (I owe you)

reconnaître *[avouer]* admit (v) *or* confess (v)

reconnaître officiellement un syndicat recognize (v) a union

record (m) *[meilleur]* record (n)

record (m) *[maximum]* peak (n)

record : qui bat tous les records record-breaking (adj)

recouvrable
[récupérable]
recoverable (adj)
recouvrement (m)
recovery (n) *[getting
something back]*
**recouvrement de
créances** debt
collection
recouvrer recover
(v) *[get something
back]*
**recouvrer une
créance** collect (v)
a debt
rectification (f)
rectification (n)
**rectifier [modifier
ou corriger]** rectify
(v) *or* amend (v)
**reçu (m) [quit-
tance]** receipt (n)
recul (m) [revers]
setback (n)
**récupérable
[recouvrable]**
recoverable (adj)
récupération (f)
recovery (n)
*[getting some-
thing back]*

récupéré(e) [sauvé]
salvaged (adj)
**récupérer
[recouvrer]** recover
(v); get back (v)
**récupérer son
argent** recoup (v)
one's losses
**recyclage (m)
[d'une personne]**
retraining (n)
**recyclage (m) [d'un
produit]** recycling (n)
**recycler [un pro-
duit]** recycle (v)
**recycler: se
recycler** retrain (v)
**R et D (Recherche
et developpement)**
R & D (Research and
Development)
**rédaction (f) d'un
acte de cession**
conveyancing (n)
**redevances (fpl)
[d'auteur, etc.]**
royalties (n)
**rédiger [chèque,
facture, etc.]** write
out (v) *or* draw up
(v) *or* make out (v)

rédiger [mettre par écrit] put in writing
rédiger un contrat draw up (v) a contract
rédiger une facture make out (v) or raise (v) an invoice
redistribuer redistribute (v)
redressement (m) [amélioration] turnround (n) [making profitable]
redressement (m) d'impôt tax adjustments
redresser: se redresser stage (v) a recovery or rally (v)
réduction (f) reduction (n) or cut (n)
réduction (f) [action] reducing (n) or cutting (n); lowering (n)
réduction (f) [remise ou escompte] discount (n)
réduction de prix [rabais] price reduction or price cut; mark-down (n)

réduction de salaire salary cut or cut in salary
réduction des frais cost-cutting (exercise)
réduction d'impôt tax abatement (n) or tax reduction (n)
réduire [diminuer] reduce (v) or cut (v)
réduire [éroder] erode (v)
réduire la valeur [amortir] write down (v)
réduire le prix d'un article mark down (v) an article
réduire les dépenses cut down (v) on expenses
réduire suivant un barème scale down (v)
réélection (f) re-election (n)
réélire re-elect (v)
réembaucher ou réemployer ou réengager re-employ (v)

réemploi (m)
re-employment (n)
réévaluation (f)
*[augmentation de
la valeur]* reva-
luation (n)
**réévaluation
(f) *[nouvelle
évaluation]***
reassessment (n)
**réévaluer
*[augmenter la
valeur]* revalue (v)
**réévaluer *[évaluer
de nouveau]***
reassess (v)
réexportation (f)
re-export (n)
réexporter
re-export (v)
**référence (f)
*[recommandation]***
reference (n)
**référer: se référer
à** refer (v) to
**refinancement
(m) d'un prêt**
refinancing of
a loan
refus (m) refusal
(n); rejection (n)

**refus de faire des
heures supplémen-
taires** overtime
ban (n)
refuser refuse (v)
or turn down (v) *or*
reject (v)
**refuser d'honorer
un accord** repudiate
(v) an agreement
**refuser tout
paiement** waive (v)
a payment
régime (m) plan
(n) *or* scheme (n)
régime de retraite
pension scheme
régime fiscal tax
system
région (f) *[zone]*
area (n) *or* region (n)
régional(e)
regional (adj)
registre (m)
register (n)
**registre (m) *[grand
livre comptable]***
ledger (n)
**registre des action-
naires** register of
shareholders

registre des administrateurs d'une société register of directors

registre du commerce et des sociétés (RCS) companies' register

règle (f) rule (n)

réglé(e) *[payé]* paid (adj)

règlement (m) *[d'un compte]* payment (n) *or* settlement (n)

règlement (m) *[montant]* payment (n) *or* remittance (n)

règlement avec (une) carte de crédit payment by credit card

règlement d'une dette discharge (n) *[of debt]*

règlement par chèque payment by cheque

réglementaire *[statutaire]* statutory (adj)

réglementation (f) regulation (n)

réglementé(e) par l'Etat government-regulated (adj)

réglementer regulate (v) *[by law]*

règlements (mpl) rules (n) *or* regulations (n)

régler *[un appareil]* tune (v)

régler *[un débit]* regulate (v)

régler *[payer]* pay (v) *or* settle (v) *or* remit (v)

régler avec (une) carte de crédit pay by credit card

régler la note *ou* **l'addition** pay the bill

régler par chèque pay by cheque *or* remit by cheque

régler un compte settle an account

régler une dette pay up (v) *or* discharge (v) a debt

régler une facture
pay *or* settle (v) an
invoice
régulier (-ière)
[habituel]
regular (adj)
réimportation (f)
reimportation (n)
réimportation (f)
[marchandise]
reimport (n)
réimporter
reimport (v)
réinvestir
reinvest (v)
réinvestissement
(m) reinvestment (n)
rejeter *[refuser]*
reject (v)
relance (f) *[de*
l'économie]
recovery (n)
relancer *[activer*
une commande]
chase (v) (an order)
relancer l'économie
boost (v) the economy
relatif à relating to
relatif à l'organisa-
tion *ou* **à la structure**
organizational (adj)

relation (f) *[lien]*
connection (n)
relation (f)
[personne] contact
(n) [person]
relations (fpl)
[rapports]
relations (n)
relations entre
employeurs et
employés
industrial relations
relations publiques
public relations (PR)
relevé (m) de
compte statement
(n) of account
relevé de compte
bancaire bank
statement
relevé mensuel
monthly statement
relevé semestriel
half-yearly statement
relever (directe-
ment) de quelqu'un
report to (v) *or* be
responsible to
someone
relier join (v) *or*
connect (v)

reliquat (m) [reste]
remainder (n)
**remboursable
[avance]**
refundable (adj)
**remboursable
[obligations]**
redeemable (adj)
remboursable [prêt]
repayable (adj)
**remboursement
(m) [d'emprunt, de
dette]** repayment
(n); redemption (n);
payback (n)
**remboursement de
frais** reimburse-
ment or refund (n)
of expenses
**remboursements
d'un prêt
hypothécaire
[versements]** mort-
gage (re)payments
rembourser pay
back (v) or repay
(v); refund (v)
**rembourser une
dette** pay off (v) or
clear (v) or redeem
(v) a debt

**remerciements
(mpl)** thanks (n)
**remettre [à plus
tard]** postpone (v)
or put back (v) or
defer (v)
remettre [donner]
hand in (v); hand
over (v)
**remettre un chèque
à l'encaissement**
cash (v) a cheque
**remettre en état
[réparer]** repair (v)
**remise (f)
[escompte]** dis-
count (n) or rebate
(n) or reduction (n)
remise à plus tard
postponement (n)
or deferment (n)
**remise
commerciale ou
professionnelle**
trade discount;
trade terms
**remise de base ou
remise habituelle**
basic discount
remise de gros
wholesale discount

remise sur quantité quantity discount *or* volume discount
remonter [se redresser] rally (v)
remplaçant(e) replacement (n) [person]
remplacement (m) replacement [item]
remplacer replace (v)
remporter un contrat win (v) a contract
rémunérateur (-trice) paid (adj) (work); well paid (adj)
rémunération (f) remuneration (n) *or* pay (n)
rémunération (f) [honoraires] fee (n) [for services]
rémunéré(e) [compte, etc.] interest-bearing (adj) (account, etc.)
rémunéré(e) [travail] paid (adj) (work)

rémunérer (un compte) pay (v) interest (on account)
rémunérer (quelqu'un) remunerate (v) *or* pay (v) (someone)
rémunérer (un travail) remunerate *or* pay for (v) (work)
rencontrer *ou* se rencontrer meet (v)
rendement (m) [capacité] capacity (n) [production]
rendement (m) [intérêt] yield (n) *or* return (n) [on investment]
rendement (m) [production] output (n); through-put (n)
rendement (m) [productivité] productivity (n)
rendement brut gross yield

rendement effectif
effective yield
rendement net
net yield
rendez-vous (m)
appointment (n);
meeting (n)
rendre compte de
[faire rapport]
report on (v)
rendre compte de
[justifier] account
for (v)
rendre compte: se
rendre compte de
realize (v) *or*
understand (v)
renoncement (m)
waiver (n) *[of right]*
renoncer à *[aban-*
donner] abandon (v)
renoncer à
[refuser] waive (v)
renoncer aux
poursuites *ou* à un
procès abandon (v)
an action
renouvelable *[crédit]*
revolving credit
renouveler
renew (v)

renouveler un
abonnement renew
a subscription
renouveler un bail
renew a lease
renouveler une
commande reorder
(v) *or* repeat (v)
an order
renouvellement
(m) renewal (n)
renouvellement
d'un bail *ou* **d'un**
abonnement
renewal of a lease
or of a subscription
renouvellement de
mandat
reappointment (n)
rénovation (f)
[magasin, etc.]
refitting (n) *or*
renovation (n)
rénover *[magasin,*
etc.] refit (v) *or*
renovate (v)
renseignement (m)
(piece of)
information (n)
renseigner *[informer]*
inform (v)

renseigner: se renseigner enquire (v) *or* inquire (v)

rentabilité (f) [*profitabilité*] cost-effectiveness (n) *or* profitability (n)

rentabilité (f) [*aspect économique*] economics (n)

rentabilité d'un investissement return on investment (ROI)

rentable cost-effective (adj) *or* economic (adj)

rentable [*productif*] profit-making (adj) *or* productive (adj)

rentrée (f) [*recette*] take (n)

rentrée (f) [*revenu*] revenue (n)

rentrer dans ses frais break even (v)

renvoi (m) [*à plus tard*] postponement (n) *or* deferment (n)

renvoi (m) [*d'un employé*] dismissal (n) *or* sacking (n)

renvoi injustifié wrongful dismissal

renvoyer [*licencier*] dismiss (v) *or* sack (v) (someone)

renvoyer [*retourner*] return (v) [send back]

renvoyer une lettre à l'expéditeur return a letter to sender

réorganisation (f) reorganization (n)

réorganiser reorganize (v)

réparation (f) repair (n)

réparer fix (v) *or* repair (v) *or* mend (v)

répartir un risque spread (v) a risk

répercussion (f) repercussion (n) *or* knock-on effect

repère (m) benchmark (n)

répertoire (m) d'adresses directory (n) *or* address list (n)

répertoire d'adresses par professions classified directory
répertoire d'entreprises commercial directory or trade directory
répertoire des noms de rues *[sur un plan]* street directory
répéter repeat (v)
repli (m) *[baisse ou recul]* downturn (n)
répondant (m) reference (n) *[person]*
répondeur (m) téléphonique answerphone (n) or answering machine
répondre (à une lettre, une question) reply (v) to or answer (v) (a letter or a question)
répondre à la demande *[satisfaire]* meet (v) or satisfy (v) a demand

répondre au téléphone answer (v) the phone *or* take (v) a call
réponse (f) answer (n) *or* reply (n)
réponse: en réponse à votre lettre in answer *or* in reply to your letter
reporté(e) *[différé]* deferred (adj) *or* postponed (adj)
reporté(e) *[montant]* carried (adj) forward
reporter *[montant]* carry (v) forward
reporter *[remettre à plus tard]* defer (v) *or* postpone (v) *or* put back (v)
reporter: se reporter à refer (v) to
reprendre *[recommencer]* resume (v)
reprendre les négociations resume negotiations
représentant(e) (sales) representative (n) *or* rep (n)

représentant(e) à
la commission
commission rep
représentatif (-ive)
representative (adj)
représenter [faire
de la représenta-
tion] represent (v)
reprise (f) [contre
un achat] part
exchange (n) or
trade-in (n)
reprise (f)
[économique]
upturn (n) or revival
(n) or recovery (n)
reprise (f) [à
l'achat d'une mai-
son] fixtures and
fittings [amount]
reprocher blame (v)
reproduction (f)
copy (n) or
duplicate (n)
reproduire [faire
une copie] copy (v)
or duplicate (v)
réputation (f)
[image de marque]
reputation (n) or
brand image (n)

requérant(e)
claimant (n)
requête (f)
[demande]
request (n)
réseau (m)
network (n)
réseau (m) de
distribution
distribution network
réservation (f)
reservation (n) or
booking (n)
réservation (f) à
l'avance advance
booking
réservation (f) en
bloc block booking
réserve (f) [argent]
reserve (n) or
provision (n)
réserve (f) [entre-
pôt] stockroom (n)
or store (n)
réserve (f) [mar-
chandises] store
(n) or stock (n)
réserve de
matières premières
stock of raw
materials

réserve: faire des
réserves stock up
(v) *or* stockpile (v)
réserve: sans
réserve
unconditional (adj)
réserve: sous
réserve conditional
(adj) *or* qualified
(adj)
réserve: sous
réserve de
subject to
réserves (fpl)
[fonds de secours]
emergency reserves
réserves (fpl)
[provisions]
reserves (n) *or*
supplies (n);
stockpile (n)
réserves bancaires
(bank) reserves
réserves de devises
currency reserves
réserves de
trésorerie cash
reserves
réserves occultes
[caisse noire]
hidden reserves

réserver *[retenir]*
reserve (v) *or*
book (v)
réserver une table
ou une place book
(v) a table *or* a seat
résidence (f)
[séjour]
residence (n)
résident(e) (n)
resident (n)
résident(e) (adj)
resident (adj)
résiliation (f)
cancellation (n) *or*
annulling (n)
résiliation (f)
[police d'assurance]
surrender (n)
résilier *[annuler]*
annul (v) *or* cancel
(v) *or* rescind (v)
résilier un contrat
terminate an
contract
résilier une police
d'assurance
surrender (v) a
policy
résolution (f)
resolution

résoudre un problème solve (v) a problem

respect: non respect breach (n) (of contract, of warranty)

respecter respect (v)

respecter un délai meet (v) a deadline

responsabilité (f) [charge] responsibility (n)

responsabilité (f) [légale] liability (n) or responsibility (n)

responsabilité contractuelle contractual liability

responsabilité limitée limited liability

responsable (adj) [légalement] liable (adj) or responsible (adj) (for)

responsable (mf) [chef] manager (n) or head (n) or director (n)

responsable de clientèle account executive (n)

responsable de la comptabilité analytique cost accountant (n)

responsable de la distribution distribution manager

responsable de la formation training officer (n)

responsable de la publicité advertising manager

responsable de l'information information officer (n)

responsable de relations publiques public relations man

responsable de suivi progress chaser (n)

responsable du contrôle de qualité quality controller (n)

**responsable d'un
entrepôt
[magasinier]**
warehouseman (n)
**responsable d'une
équipe de
représentants** field
sales manager
**resquiller dans
une queue** jump
(v) the queue
**resserrer (le
contrôle)** tighten
up (v) (on)
ressources (fpl)
resources (n)
**ressources finan-
cières** financial
resources
**ressources
humaines**
human resources
**ressources
naturelles**
natural resources
reste (m)
remainder (n)
rester remain (v)
restrictif (-ive)
restrictive (adj)

**restriction (f) [con-
trôle ou limitation]**
restriction (n)
restructuration (f)
restructuring (n)
**restructuration
d'une société**
restructuring of the
company
restructurer
restructure (v)
résultat (m)
result (n)
résultat (m) [effet]
effect (n)
**résultat net
[bénéfice net]**
final result or
bottom line
retard (m) delay
(n) or hold-up (n)
**retard: être en
retard** be late; be
overdue
retarder hold up
(v) or delay (v)
retenir keep back (v)
**retenir [de
l'argent]** deduct (v)
(money)

retenir [réserver]
reserve (v) or book (v)
retenir une
chambre reserve or
book a room
retenue (f) à la
source [impôt]
withholding tax (n)
retenues fiscales
tax deductions (n)
[from salary]
retirer withdraw
(v) [an offer]
retirer de l'argent
de la banque
withdraw (v) money
from the bank
retirer un gage
redeem (v) a pledge
retirer une OPA
withdraw (v) a
takeover bid
retour (m) [d'un
lieu] return (n)
[going back]
retour (m) [renvoi]
return (n) [sending
back]
retour à l'envoyeur
return to sender

retourner [ren-
voyer] return (v)
[send back]
retourner [revenir]
return (v) [go back]
retrait (m) with-
drawal [of money]
retraite (f)
retirement (n)
retrancher [déduire]
deduct (v)
rétribuer
[rémunérer]
remunerate (v)
rétroactif (-ive)
retroactive (adj)
réunion (f) [assem-
blée] meeting (n)
réunion (f) [con-
grès] conference (n)
réunion du conseil
d'administration
board meeting
réunion du person-
nel staff meeting
réunion du service
commercial sales
conference
réunir gather (v)
together

réunir [les éléments d'une liste] bracket (v) together

réunir: se réunir meet (v)

réussir succeed (v) *or* be successful *or* do well

réussir à manage to (do) *or* succeed in (doing)

révéler [divulguer] disclose (v)

révéler [faire apparaître] show (v)

revendeur (m) [détaillant] retail dealer (n) *or* retailer (n)

revendication (f) claim (n)

revendication (f) salariale wage claim

revente (f) resale (n)

revenu (m) [intérêt, etc.] income (n) *or* earnings (n) *or* revenue (n)

revenu du travail income (n)

revenu brut [du travail] gross income

revenu fixe fixed income

revenu imposable taxable income

revenu locatif rental income

revenu net [salaire net] net income *or* net salary; real income

revenu non imposable non-taxable income

revenu personnel personal income

revenus (mpl) [d'un pays] earnings (n) *or* revenue (n)

revenus invisibles invisible earnings

revers (m) setback (n)

réviser [mettre à jour] update (v)

réviser [revoir] reassess (v) *or* review (v)

réviser *[vérifier les comptes, etc.]* audit (v)
réviser une machine service (v) (a machine)
révision (f) comptable auditing (n)
révision de salaire salary review (n)
révision d'une machine service (n) (of a machine)
révoquer revoke (v)
revue (f) *[périodique]* magazine (n) *or* periodical (n)
revue commerciale trade magazine
revue professionnelle journal (n)
risque (m) risk (n)
risque d'incendie fire risk
risque financier financial risk
risquer risk (v) *or* venture (v)
ristourne (f) *[remise]* rebate (n) *or* discount (n)

rompre les négociations break off (v) negotiations
rompre un accord *ou* un contrat break (v) an agreement
rotation (f) des stocks stock turnround (n) *or* stock turn (n)
rotation du personnel turnover (n) of staff *or* staff turnover
royalties (fpl) royalties (n)
ruée (f) rush (n)
rupture (f) breakdown (n) *[talks]*
rupture de contrat breach (n) of contract
rupture: être en rupture de stock be out of stock

Ss

SA (société anonyme) *[cotée en Bourse]* Plc *or* plc (Public limited company)**S.A.R.L. (société à responsabilité limitée)** Ltd (limited liability company)
sac (m) *[pochette]* bag (n)
sac (m) en papier paper bag
saisie (f) *[confiscation]* seizure (n)
saisie de données au clavier keyboarding (n)
saisir (v) *[un article non payé]* repossess (v) *or* seize (v)
saisir *[des données]* input (v) information (into a computer)
saisir [des données au clavier] keyboard (v)

saison (f) season (n) *[time of year]*
saisonnier (-ière) seasonal (adj)
salaire (m) salary (n) *or* pay (n); wage (n)
salaire au rendement payment by results
salaire brut gross salary
salaire de départ ou de débutant starting salary
salaire horaire hourly wage
salaire minimum (SMIC) minimum wage
salaire net net salary *or* net income
salaire attrayant ou intéressant attractive salary
salaire payé pendant les vacances holiday pay
salaire régulier regular income
salarié(e) (adj) salaried (adj)

salarié(e) (n) *[employé]*
employee (n)
(receiving a salary)
salle (f) [pièce]
room (n)
**salle d'embarque-
ment *[aéroport]***
departure lounge (n)
salle d'exposition
showroom (n)
**salle de conférences
ou de réunion**
conference room
**salle de réunion
(du conseil d'ad-
ministration)**
boardroom
**salle de transit
*[aéroport]*** transit
lounge *or* transit
lounge (n)
**salle des ventes
*[enchères]*** auction
room
**salon (m) *[exposi-
tion]*** show (n) *or* fair
(n) *or* exhibition (n)
**salon réservé aux
personnages de mar-
que** VIP lounge (n)

**sanctionner *[péna-
liser]*** penalize (n)
sans without
sans *[moins]* minus
or less
**sans cesse
*[continuellement]***
continually
**sans emploi *[au
chômage]***
unemployed (adj)
**sans-emploi: les
sans-emploi** the
unemployed (n)
**sans-travail: les
sans-travail** the
unemployed (n)
santé (f) health (n)
satisfaction (f)
satisfaction (n)
**satisfaction dans le
travail *ou* au travail**
job satisfaction
satisfaction du client
customer satisfaction
**satisfaire *[un
client]*** satisfy (v)
**satisfaire *[la
demande]*** meet (v)
or satisfy (v) *or*
keep up with (v)

saturation (f)
saturation (n)
saturer saturate (v)
saturer le marché
saturate the market
sauf *[excepté]*
except; excepted
sauf erreur ou
omission errors
and omissions
excepted (e. & o.e.)
sauvegarder *[don-*
nées] back up (v);
save (v) *[computer*
file]
sauvegarder
[protéger]
safeguard (v)
sauver (une
société) salvage (v)
sauvetage (m)
salvage (n)
sceau (m) seal (n)
sceller *[fermer]*
seal (v)
sceller *[mettre un*
sceau] put (v)
a seal
schéma (m)
[diagramme]
diagram (n)

second(e) *[deux-*
ième] second (adj)
secondaire second-
ary (adj); subsidiary
(adj)
secret (m) secret (n)
secret (-ète)
secret (adj)
secrétaire (mf)
secretary (n)
secrétaire de
direction personal
assistant (PA)
secrétaire
général(e) *[d'une*
compagnie]
company secretary
secrétaire intéri-
maire temp (n)
secrétaire particulière
private secretary
secteur (m) sector
(n); division (n)
secteur (m)
[domaine] area (n)
secteur (m)
[d'une ville] area
(n) (of a town)
secteur (m) *[d'un*
représentant]
territory (n)

secteur difficile
problem area
secteur primaire
[industrie de base]
primary industry
secteur privé
private sector
secteur public
public sector
secteur secondaire
[industrie de
transformation]
secondary industry
or manufacturing
industry
secteur tertiaire
[industrie de
services] tertiary
industry *or* service
industry
sécurité (f) safety
(n) *or* security (n)
sécurité de l'em-
ploi security of
employment *or* job
security
sécurité sociale
social security
séduire *[attirer]*
appeal to (v) *or*
attract (v)

séjour (m) stay (n)
séjour (m) *[rési-*
dence] residence (n)
séjour: carte (f)
de séjour residence
permit (n)
séjourner stay (v)
sélection (f) *[choix]*
selection (n)
sélectionné(e)
[candidat]
shortlisted (adj)
sélectionner (des
candidats) short-
list (v) (candidates)
selon *[suivant]*
according to
selon échantillon
as per sample
semaine (f)
week (n)
sembler *[paraître]*
appear (v)
semestre (m)
(comptable)
half-year (n)
semi-remorque
(mf) articulated
lorry (n)
séparé(e) (adj)
separate (adj)

séquestration (f)
sequestration (n)
séquestre (m)
sequestrator (n)
séquestre:
administrateur
séquestre (m)
sequestrator (n)
séquestre: mettre
sous séquester
sequester (v) *or*
sequestrate (v)
séquestre: mise (f)
sous séquester
sequestration (n)
séquestrer
sequester (v) *or*
sequestrate (v)
série (f) series (n)
service (m)
[bureau]
department (n) *or*
division (n)
service (m)
[pourboire] service
(n) (charge)
service (m) *[tra-*
vail] service (n)
service après-vente
(SAV) after-sales
service

service clients
customer service
department (n)
service colis
(postaux) parcel
post (n)
service commercial
sales department
service d'entretien
service department
service de la
comptabilité acc-
ounts department
service de la
production *ou* de
la fabrication
production
department
service de la
publicité publicity
department
service de
reproduction
photocopying
bureau
service des achats
purchasing *or*
buying department
service des expédi-
tions dispatch
department

service des exportations *ou* **service export** export department
service des réclamations [assurances] claims department
service des réclamations [plaintes] complaints department
service des relations publiques public relations department
service du contentieux legal department
service (du) marketing marketing department
service du personnel personnel department
service informatique computer department
service postal [la Poste] Post (n) *or* postal system

service: être de service be on duty
service: être en service [train, bus] run (v)
serviette (f) [porte-documents] briefcase (n)
servir serve (v)
servir de [agir en tant que] act as (v)
servir les intérêts d'une dette service (v) a debt
servir d'interprète interpret (v) *or* act as interpreter
servir un client serve a customer
servir: se servir de [utiliser] use (v)
servitude (f) [on land] right (n) of way
seuil (m) threshold (n)
seuil (m) de rentabilité breakeven point
seul(e) only (adj)
seul(e) [exclusif] sole (adj)

**seul propriétaire
(m)** sole owner *or*
sole trader
**siège (m) social
[*d'une société*]**
registered office
or head office
**signaler [*faire
rapport*]** report (v)
signataire (mf)
signatory (n)
signature (f)
signature (n)
**signature (f) d'un
contrat** signing (n)
of a contract;
completion (n) of a
contract
**signer [*un chèque,
un contrat, etc.*]**
sign (v)
**signer de ses
initiales [*parapher*]**
initial (v)
**signer en qualité
de témoin** witness
(v) an agreement
simple [*unique*]
single (adj)
simple associé
junior partner (n)

sistership (m)
sister ship (n)
**site (m)
[*emplacement*]** site
(n) *or* situation (n)
site (web) (m)
website (n)
situation (f) [*état*]
situation (n)
situation (f) [*site*]
situation (n) *or*
site (n)
**situation
critique [*urgence*]**
emergency (n)
**situation de mono-
pole** monopoly (n)
situation financière
financial position
**situation légale
[*statut légal*]**
legal status
situé(e) situated
(adj)
**SME (système
monétaire
européen)** EMS
(European Monetary
System)
social(e) (adj)
social (adj)

société (f)
[association ou
club] society
or club (n) or
association (n)
société (f)
[immatriculée]
company (n);
corporation (n) [US]
société (f) [non
immatriculée]
partnership (n)
société à but
lucratif profit-
oriented company
société affiliée
associate company
société anonyme
(S.A.) [cotée en
Bourse] Public
Limited Company
(Plc)
société à
responsabilité
limitée (S.A.R.L.)
limited liability
company (Ltd)
société commerciale
trading company
société coopérative
cooperative society

société cotée en
Bourse listed
company
société d'affac-
turage ou de
factoring factor (n)
société de Bourse
firm of stockbrokers
société de crédit
finance company
société de crédit
immobilier building
society
société de location
de matériel
plant-hire firm
société de services
service company or
service bureau
société de services
et d'ingénierie
informatique (SSII)
computer bureau ;
software company
société d'investisse-
ment à capital
variable (SICAV)
unit trust (n)
société en comman-
dite simple (SCS)
limited partnership

société exporta-trice *ou* **d'exporta-tion** export house *or* export company

société familiale family company

société fiduciaire trust company

société indépen-dante independent company

société mère *[maison mère]* parent company

société prête-nom shell company

société qui a un fort coefficient d'endet-tement highly-geared company

sol (m) floor *[surface]*

solde (m) *[d'un compte]* balance (n)

solde (m) *[vente au rabais]* sale (n) *or* clearance sale

solde (m) à ce jour; solde à reporter balance carried down *or* carrried forward

solde à moitié prix half-price sale

solde à nouveau; ancien solde; solde reporté balance brought down *or* brought forward

solde à recevoir balance due to us

solde créditeur credit balance

solde débiteur debit balance

solde de dividende final dividende

solde de trésorerie cash balance

solde en banque *[position d'un compte bancaire]* bank balance

solde: en solde on sale; reduced to clear

soldes (mpl & fpl) sales (n)

solder un compte *[arrêter]* balance (v)

solder un compte *[régler]* settle (the balance of) an account

solliciter *[demander]* request (v) *or* ask (v) (for)

solliciter des com-mandes solicit (v) orders

solliciter un emploi apply (v) for a job

solution (f) *[réponse]* solution (n)

solution de problèmes *[action]* problem solving (n)

solvabilité (f) solvency (n)

solvable solvent (adj) *or* credit-worthy (adj)

sommaire *[approxi-matif]* rough (adj)

somme (f) *[addi-tion]* addition (n); calculation (n)

somme (f) (d'argent) *[montant]* sum (n) *or* amount (n) (of money)

somme due amount owing

somme totale (grand) total (n)

sondage (m) d'opinion opinion poll (n)

sondage: faire un sondage d'opinion poll (v) a sample of the population

sortant(e) outgoing (adj)

sortie (f) d'imprimante (computer) printout (n) *or* listing (n)

sorties (fpl) *[dépenses]* outgoings (n)

souche (f) *[d'un chéquier, etc.]* counterfoil (n) *or* stub (n)

soulever (une question) raise (v) (a question)

soumission (f) *[pour un contrat, un travail]* tender (n)

soumission cachetée sealed tender

soumissionnaire (mf) tenderer (n)

soumissionner un travail tender (v) for a contract

souple (adj) [horaire] flexible (adj) [hours]

source (f) source (n)

source de revenu(s) source of income

souscrire subscribe (v)

souscrire une assurance take out (v) a policy or an insurance policy

sous-équipé(e) underequipped (adj)

sous-locataire (mf) sublessee (n)

sous-location (f) sublease (n)

sous-louer sublet (v) or sublease (v)

sous-payé(e) underpaid (adj)

sous-produit (m) by-product (n)

soussigné(e) (n ou adj) undersigned

sous-total (m) subtotal (n)

sous-traitance (f) subcontracting (n)

sous-traitance : donner en sous-traitance subcontract (v) or farm out (v) (work)

sous-traitant (m) subcontractor (n)

sous-traiter (v) [donner en sous-traitance] subcontract (v) or farm out (v) (work)

spécial(e) special (adj)

spécialisation (f) specialization (n)

spécialiser: se spécialiser specialize (v) (in)

spécialiste (mf) [expert] specialist (n) or expert (n)

spécialiste des techniques marchandes merchandizer (n)

specifications (fpl) specifications (n)

spécifier specify (v)

spéculateur (-trice)
speculator (n)
**spéculateur à la
baisse** *[baissier]*
bear (n) *[Stock
Exchange]*
**spéculateur à la
hausse** *[haussier]*
bull (n) *[Stock
Exchange]*
sponsor (m) *[com-
manditaire]* spon-
sor (n) *or* backer (n)
sponsorisation (f)
[parrainage]
sponsorship (n)
sponsoriser *[par-
rainer]* sponsor (v)
stabilisation (f)
stabilization (n)
stabiliser stabilize (v)
**stabiliser: se stabi-
liser** stabilize; level
off (v) *or* level out (v)
stabilité (f)
stability (n)
stabilité d'emploi
security (n) of
tenure
stabilité des prix
price stability

stable stable (adj)
stage (m) *[étape]*
stage (n)
stage de formation
course (n) *or*
training (n);
traineeship (n)
**stage (m) de
recyclage** refresher
course (n)
stagiaire (mf)
trainee (n)
**stagiaire
diplômé(e)**
graduate trainee
stagnant(e)
stagnant (adj)
stagnation (f)
stagnation (n)
stand (m)
[d'exposition]
stand (n)
standard (m)
[norme] standard (n)
standard (adj)
[ordinaire] stan-
dard (adj)
**standard (m)
téléphonique**
(telephone)
switchboard (n)

standardisation (f) [normalisation] standardization (n)

standardiser [normaliser] standardize (v)

standardiste (mf) (switchboard or telephone) operator (n)

standing (m) [réputation] standing (n)

statisticien (-ienne) statistician (n)

statistique (adj) statistical (adj)

statistiques (fpl) statistics (n)

statuer [déclarer] rule (v)

statut (m) [position] status (n)

statut légal legal status

statuts (mpl) d'une société articles (n) of association

statutaire [réglementaire] statutory (adj)

stimuler (l'économie) stimulate (v) (the economy)

stipulation (f) stipulation (n) or provision (n)

stipuler stipulate (v) or state (v)

stock (m) [marchandises] stock (n); inventory (n) [US]

stock (m) [provision] supply (n) or stock

stock en fin d'exercise closing stock

stock initial ou stock d'ouverture opening stock

stocker [avoir en stock] stock (v)

stocker [faire des réserves] stockpile (v)

stockiste (mf) [dépositaire] stockist (n)

stop (m) [arrêt ou fin] stop (n)

stratégie (f) strategy (n) or strategic planning

stratégie commerciale marketing strategy
stratégie des affaires business strategy
stratégique (adj) strategic (adj)
structure (f) structure (n)
structure (f) en grille grid structure
structurel (-elle) structural (adj)
subalterne (adj) junior (adj)
subir des dégâts suffer (v) damage
subvention (f) subvention (n) *or* subsidy (n) *or* grant (n)
subventionné(e) par l'Etat government-sponsored (adj)
subventionner subsidize (v)
succéder à succeed (v) (someone)
succès (m) success (n)

succès: qui a du succès successful (adj)
succursale (f) branch office
suffisant(e) sufficient (adj) *or* adequate (adj)
suite à *[en réponse à]* further to
suivant *[conformément]* according to
suivant *[en fonction de]* depending on
suivant avis as per advice
suivre follow (v)
suivre une formation train (v)
suivre une ligne de produits carry (v) a line of goods
sujet (m) matter (n)
superdividende (m) surplus dividend
supérette (f) minimarket (n)
supérieur(e) (adj) *[meilleur]* superior (adj) *or* of better quality

supérieur(e) (n)
[personne]
superior (n)
supérieur(e) à
(adj) *[plus de]*
more than
supermarché (m)
supermarket (n)
superviser *[surveil-*
ler] supervise (v)
supplément (m)
[frais supplémen-
taires] surcharge (n)
or extra charge (n)
supplémentaire
(adj) additional
(adj) *or* supplemen-
tary (adj) *or* extra
(adj)
supporter *[des frais]*
bear (v) *or* pay for
(v) *[expenses]*
suppression (f) d'em-
plois job cuts (n)
supprimer cut out
(v) *or* remove (v)
supprimer *[rayer]*
cross out (v) *or*
delete (v)
sûr(e) (adj) safe
(adj)

surabondance (f)
[surplus] glut (n)
surbooking (m) *ou*
surréservation (f)
overbooking (n) *or*
double-booking (n)
surbooking: faire
du surbooking
overbook (v)
surcapacité (f)
excess capacity *or*
overcapacity (n)
surcharger
[encombrer le
marché] glut (v)
[the market]
surcoût (m)
surcharge (n)
surenchère (f)
counterbid (n)
surenchérir outbid (v)
surestarie (f)
demurrage (n)
surestimer
overestimate (v)
surévalué(e)
overvalued (adj) *or*
overrated (adj)
surévalué(e)
[marché]
overbought (adj)

surévaluer overvalue (v) *or* overrate (v)

surface (f) area (n)

surface (f) au sol floor space

surligneur (m) marker pen (n)

surpayer overpay (v)

surplus (m) *[excédent]* surplus (n) *or* excess (n)

surplus (m) *[surabondance]* glut (n)

surproduction (f) overproduction (n)

surproduire overproduce (v)

surréservation *[surbooking]* overbooking (n) *or* double-booking (n)

surréserver overbook (v) *or* double-book (v)

sursis (m) stay of execution (n)

surtaxe (f) à l'importation import surcharge (n)

surveillance (f) supervision (n)

surveillant(e) supervisor (n)

surveiller *[contrôler]* control (v)

surveiller *[superviser]* supervise (v)

survente (f) overcharging (n)

suspendre suspend (v) *or* stop (v)

suspendre les paiements stop payments

suspension (f) *[arrêt]* suspension (n) *or* stoppage (n)

suspension (f) des paiements suspension of payments

syndicaliste (mf) *[trade-unioniste]* trade unionist (n)

syndicat (m) *[financier]* syndicate (n)

syndicat (m) *[Trade-union]* trade union (n) *or* union (n)

syndicat de garantie underwriting syndicate

synergie (f) synergy (n)

système (m) system (n)

système comptable
accounting system
système d'exploita-
tion operating system
système en temps
réel *[ordinateur]*
real-time system
Système monétaire
européen (SME)
European Monetary
System (EMS)
système téléphonique
automatique interna-
tional international
direct dialling

Tt

table (f) table (n)
tables de mortalité
actuarial tables (n)
tableau (m) *[informa-*
tique] spreadsheet (n)
tableau (m) à
feuilles mobiles
flip chart (n)

tableur (m)
[programme
informatique]
spreadsheet (n)
(program)
tabulateur (m)
tabulator (n)
tâche (f) assign-
ment (n) *or* job (n)
tachygraphe (m)
tachograph (n)
taille (f) size (n)
taille courante
stock size
taille normale
regular size
talent (m) *[apti-*
tude] skill (n)
talon (m) *[d'un*
chèque, etc.] coun-
terfoil (n) *or* stub (n)
tampon (m) stamp
(n) *[device]*
tamponner stamp (v)
[mark]
tangible
tangible (adj)
tare (f) tare (n)
tarif (m) tariff (n)
or rate (n) *or*
price (n)

tarif (m) *[barème des prix]* scale (n) of charges *or* schedule (n) of charges
tarif (m) *[liste de prix, catalogue]* price list (n)
tarif (m) *[prix d'un billet de train, etc.]* fare (n)
tarif des heures supplémentaires overtime pay
tarif douanier customs tariff
tarif d'un aller simple *[voyage]* one-way fare
tarif en vigueur going rate
tarif horaire hourly rate
tarif postal postage (n); postal charge *or* postal rate
tarif privilégié preferential duty *or* preferential tariff
tarif protectionniste protective tariff

tarif réduit cheap rate *or* reduced rate
tarif tout compris inclusive charge *or* all-in price
tarifs d'expédition freight rates *or* charges
tarifs différentiels differential tariffs
tarifs publicitaires advertising rates
taux (m) rate (n); percentage (n)
taux d'amortissement depreciation rate
taux d'augmentation rate (n) of increase
taux de base bancaire (TBB) bank base rate *or* prime rate
taux de change rate of exchange *or* exchange rate
taux de change à terme forward rate
taux (de change) croisé cross rate

taux de change en vigueur current rate of exchange

taux de conversion conversion price *or* conversion rate

taux de croissance growth rate

taux de production rate of production *or* production rate

taux de rendement rate of return; yield (n)

taux de rende-ment d'une action earnings per share *or* dividend yield

taux d'erreur error rate

taux d'escompte discount rate

taux d'imposition tax rate

taux d'inflation rate of inflation

taux d'intérêt interest rate *or* rate of interest

taux directeurs leading rates

taux d'occupation occupancy rate

taux effectif global (TEG) annualized percentage rate (APR)

taux fixe [forfait] flat rate

taxable [imposable] taxable (adj)

taxe (f) [droit] tax (n) *or* duty (n)

taxe à l'achat purchase tax

taxe à l'exporta-tion export duty

taxe à l'importa-tion import duty

taxe comprise inclusive of tax *or* tax included

taxe d'aéroport airport tax

taxe d'apprentis-sage training levy

taxe différentielle sur les véhicules à moteur road tax

taxe propor-tionnelle *ou* ad valorem ad valorem tax

taxe sur la valeur ajoutée (TVA) value added tax (VAT)
taxe sur les ventes sales tax
taxe: hors taxe exclusive of taxe
taxe: toutes taxes comprises (TTC) inclusive of tax *or* tax included
technique (f) technique (n)
techniques de gestion management techniques
techniques de marketing marketing techniques
TEG (taux effectif global) APR (annualized percentage rate)
télécarte (f) phone card
télécommande (f) remote control
télécopie (f) *[fax]* fax (n)
télécopie: envoyer par télécopie fax (v) *or* send by fax

télécopieur (m) fax (machine)
téléphone (m) telephone (n) *or* phone (n)
téléphone à carte card phone
téléphone cellulaire cellular telephone
téléphone de conférence conference phone
téléphone interne internal telephone
téléphone mobile mobile phone
téléphone public pay phone
téléphoner telephone (v) *or* phone (v)
téléphoner à quelqu'un call (v) *or* phone someone
télétravail (m) teleworking (n)
télévision (f) television (n) *or* TV
télévision (f) en circuit fermé closed circuit TV

télex (m) telex (n)
télexer *[envoyer un télex]* telex (v)
témoin (m)
witness (n)
témoin: être
témoin witness (v)
temps (m) time (n)
temps complet *ou*
plein temps
full-time
temps d'ordinateur
computer time
temps libre spare
time *or* free time
temps partiel
part-time
temps de mise
en marche (d'une
machine) make-
ready time
temps improductif
ou **temps d'arrêt**
[machine]
down time
temps: à temps
on time
temps: en temps
voulu in good time
tendance (f)
trend (n)

tendance à la hausse
upward trend
tendances du
marché market
trends *or* market
forces
tendances économi-
ques *[conjoncture]*
economic trends
teneur (f) content
tenir une promesse
keep (v) a promise
tenir une réunion
ou **une discussion**
hold (v) a meeting
or hold a discussion
tenue (f) de livres
[comptabilité]
bookkeeping (n)
terme (m) *[péri-*
ode] term (n)
terme: à terme *[ache-*
ter, vendre] forward
termes (mpl) *[con-*
ditions] terms (n)
termes (mpl) *[formu-*
lation] wording (n)
terminaison (f)
[expiration] expiry
(n) (date) *or*
termination (n)

terminal (m)
d'aéroport airport
terminal (n)
terminal (m)
d'ordinateur
computer terminal
terminal (m)
maritime (pour
porte-conteneurs)
container terminal
terminal(e) (adj)
terminal (adj) [at
the end]
terminer [mettre
fin à] end (v) or
terminate (v)
terminer [exécuter]
complete (v)
terne (adj) flat
(adj) or dull (adj)
terrain (m) ou
terre (f) land (n)
test (m) [contrôle]
test (n)
test de faisabilité
feasibility test
test sur échanti-
llon acceptance
sampling (n)
tester [contrôler]
test (v)

ticket (m) [billet]
ticket (n)
ticket de caisse
sales receipt
ticket de prix
[étiquette de prix]
price ticket
tiers (m) [tierce
personne] third
party (n)
timbre (m) ou
timbre-poste (m)
(postage) stamp (n)
timbre (m)
[tampon] stamp (n)
[device]
timbre dateur date
stamp [device]
timbrer [coller un
timbre] stamp (v)
timbrer [tampon-
ner] stamp (v)
tirage (m)
[d'un journal]
circulation (n)
tiré (m) [banque]
drawee (n)
tirer à découvert
overdraw (v)
tirer un chèque
draw (v) a cheque

tireur (m) *[banque]*
drawer (n)
tiroir-caisse (m)
till (n)
titre (m) *[action,*
obligation] share
(n); bond (n)
titre (m) *[d'un*
livre] title (n)
titre (m) *[qualifica-*
tion] (job) title
titre au porteur
[obligation]
bearer bond
titre de premier
ordre *[valeur sûre]*
blue chip (n)
titres (mpl)
[valeurs] securities
(n) *or* stock (n)
titres d'Etat gilt-
edged securities
or gilts (n)
titulaire (mf)
holder (n)
Toile (f): la Toile
the web
Toile mondiale
World Wide Web
tomber *[avoir lieu]*
fall (v) *[on a date]*

tonalité (f) (du
téléphone) dialling
tone (n)
tonalité 'occupé'
engaged tone
tonnage (m) *[d'un*
navire] tonnage (n)
tonne (f) ton (n)
tonne (f) (métrique)
tonne (n)
tôt early (adv)
total (m) total (n)
total (m) *[montant*
total] total amount
total(e) (adj)
total (adj)
total général
grand total
total reporté
running total
touche (f) *[d'un*
clavier] key (n)
touche de contrôle
control key
touche de majus-
cules shift key
toucher un chèque
[encaisser] cash (v)
a cheque
toucher net
[gagner] net (v)

tous frais payés all expenses paid
tous les trois mois quarterly (adv)
tout compris all-in *or* inclusive (adj)
toutes taxes comprises (TTC) inclusive of tax *or* tax included
Trade-union (f) trade union (n)
trade-unioniste (mf) *[syndicaliste]* trade unionist (n)
trafiquer *[manipuler]* fiddle (v) (the accounts)
train (m) train (n)
train de marchandises freight train *or* goods train
train de marchandises en conteneurs freightliner (n)
traite (f) *[lettre de change]* draft (n) *or* bill (n)
traite à vue sight draft

traite bancaire bank draft *or* banker's draft *or* bank bill
traitement (m) de commandes order processing (n)
traitement de(s) données *[informatique]* data processing
traitement de texte word-processing
traitement par lots batch processing
traiter (une commande) process (v) (an order)
traiter avec quelqu'un *[faire affaire]* deal with (v) someone
traiter une affaire *[effectuer une transaction]* transact (v) business
tranche (f) [d'impôt] (tax) bracket (n)
transaction (f) (business) transaction (n)

**transaction bour-
sière** dealing (n) on
the Stock Exchange
transférer transfer (v)
transfert (m)
transfer (n)
**transfert (m)
(d'une traite)**
delivery (n) of (bill
of exchange)
**transformation (f)
[fabrication]**
manufacturing (n)
transit (m) transit (n)
transitaire (m) for-
warding agent (n)
**transmissible [cessi-
ble]** transferable (adj)
transport (m)
transport (n) *or*
carriage (n) *or*
shipping (n)
transport par avion
air transport
**transport par
chemin de fer** rail
transport
**transport par con-
teneurs** container-
ization (n) *or* shipping
(n) in containers

**transports (mpl)
en commun** public
transport
**Transports
Internationaux
Routiers (TIR)**
Transports
Internationaux
Routiers (TIR)
**transports (mpl)
routiers [camion-
nage]** road transport
or road haulage (n)
transporter
transport (v) *or*
carry (v) *or* ship (v)
**transporteur (m)
[entreprise de
transports]** carrier
(n) *or* shipper (n)
travail (m) labour (n)
travail (m) [emploi]
job (n) *or* work (n)
or employment (n)
**travail à la pièce *ou*
aux pièces**
piecework (n)
**travail à plein
temps** full-time
work *or* full-time
employment

travail à temps partiel ou à mi-temps part-time work or part-time employment
travail au noir moonlighting (n)
travail au noir [économie parallèle] black economy (n)
travail contractuel contract work
travail de bureau clerical work
travail en retard ou en attente backlog (n) (of work)
travail manuel manual work
travail posté [travail par équipe] shift work
travail temporaire casual work
travail urgent ou travail d'urgence rush job
travail en cours work in progress
travailler work (v)
travailler au noir moonlight (v)

travailleur (-euse) worker (n)
travailleur (-euse) à domicile homeworker
travailleur (-euse) au noir moonlighter (n)
travailleur (-euse) manuel (-elle) manual worker
travailleur (-euse) temporaire casual worker
treizième mois Christmas bonus (n)
trésorerie (f) cash flow (n)
tribunal (m) ou tribunaux (mpl) court (n) or law courts
trimestre (m) quarter (n)
trimestre (m) (juridique ou universitaire) term (n)
trimestriel (-elle) quarterly (adj)
trimestriellement [tous les trois mois] quarterly (adv)
triple triple (adj)

tripler triple (v) *or* treble (v)

troc (m) barter (n); bartering (n)

troisième âge (m) old age

troisième trimestre (m) third quarter (n)

trop-perçu (m) overpayment (n); overcharge (n)

troquer barter (v)

tuyau (m) tip (n) *or* advice (n)

TVA (taxe sur la valeur ajoutée) VAT (value added tax)

Uu

UE (Union européenne) EU (European Union)

UEM (Union économique et monétaire) EUM (Economic and Monetary Union)

un pour cent (1%) one percentage point

unilatéral(e) unilateral (adj) *or* one-sided (adj)

union (f) douanière customs union (n)

Union européenne (UE) European Union (EU)

unique *[isolé]* one-off (adj)

unique *[simple]* single (adj)

unité (f) unit (n)

unité (f) *[centre]* unit

unité de mémoire *[informatique]* storage unit

unité monétaire monetary unit

urgence (f) emergency (n)

urgent(e) urgent (adj)

usine (f) factory (n) *or* plant (n)

usufruit (m) life interest (n)

usure (f) wear and tear (n)

usure normale fair wear and tear
utile (adj) useful (adj)
utilisateur (-trice) user (n)
utilisateur (m) (final) end user
utilisation (f) utilization (n) *or* use (n)
utiliser [se servir de] use (v)
utiliser la capacité disponible use up (v) spare capacity

Vv

valable valid (adj)
valable: non valable not valid *or* invalid (adj)
valeur (f) value (n) *or* worth (n)

valeur actualisée discounted value
valeur à la cote [actions] market value
valeur au pair par value
valeur comptable book value
valeur de l'actif asset value
valeur de rachat [assurance] surrender value
valeur de rareté scarcity value
valeur de remplacement replacement value
valeur de reprise trade-in price
valeur déclarée declared value
valeur nette net value; net worth
valeur nominale face value *or* nominal value
valeur sûre blue chip
valeur: sans valeur worthless (adj)

valeurs (fpl) *[titres]*
shares (n) *or* stock
(n) *or* securities (n)
**valeurs convert-
ibles** convertible
loan stock
**valide (adj) *[val-
able]*** valid (adj)
valide: non valide
not valid *or* invalid
(adj)
validité (f)
validity (n)
valise (f) case (n)
or suitcase (n)
valoir be worth
valoir *[coûter]*
cost (v)
variable *[qui fluctue]*
fluctuating (adj)
variation (f)
variation (n)
variation (f) *[écart]*
variance (n)
**variations (fpl)
saisonnières** sea-
sonal variations
varié(e) *[divers]*
miscellaneous (adj)
varier *[diversifier]*
diversify (v)

véhicule (m)
vehicle (n)
vendable
saleable (adj)
vendeur (m) ven-
dor (n) *or* seller (n)
**vendeur *[dans un
magasin]*** shop
assistant (n) *or*
sales clerk
**vendeuse (f)
*[dans un magasin]***
saleslady (n);
salesgirl (n)
vendre sell (v)
**vendre *[commer-
cialiser]*** market (v)
vendre à terme
sell forward
vendre aux enchères
auction (v)
**vendre (des
marchandises) au
détail** retail (v)
(goods)
**vendre moins cher
(que)** undersell (v)
**vendre moins
cher qu'un con-
current** undercut
(v) a rival

vendre son entreprise sell (v) one's business *or* sell out (v)

vendre: à vendre for sale

vendre: se vendre sell (v)

vendre: se vendre à sell for (v); retail for

vendre: qui se vend le mieux best selling (item) *or* best seller (n)

vendu(e) sold (adj)

vendu(e): non vendu(e) unsold (adj)

venir à échéance mature (v) *or* fall (v) due

vente (f) sale (n)

vente (f) *[action]* selling (n)

vente à domicile house-to-house selling

vente agressive hard selling

vente au comptant cash sale *or* cash deal

vente au détail retail (n); retailing (n)

vente aux enchères auction (n) *or* sale by auction

vente avec possibilité de reprise des invendus sale or return *or* see-safe (n)

vente de fin de saison end of season sale

vente directe direct selling

vente en gros wholesale (selling)

vente forcée *[en catastrophe]* distress sale

vente forcée *[liquidation]* forced sale

vente non agressive soft sell

vente par correspondance (VPC) mail order

vente(s) (f) par téléphone telesales (n) *or* telephone sale(s)

vente réglée avec (une) carte de crédit credit card sale

vente: en vente on sale

ventes (fpl) sales

ventes à terme forward sales

ventes enregistrées book sales

ventes intérieures domestic sales *or* home sales

ventes nettes net sales

ventes prévues projected sales

ventes record record sales

ventilation (f) breakdown (n)

ventiler les frais break down (v) *or* itemize (v) expenses

vérificateur (m) [contrôleur] controller (n)

vérification (f) verification (n) *or* check (n)

vérification [contrôle] control (n) *or* monitoring (n)

vérification (f) [inspection] inspection (n)

vérification comptable [audit] audit (n)

vérification générale des comptes general audit

vérifié(e) [comptes] audited (adj)

vérifié(e): non vérifié(e) [comptes] unaudited

vérifier verify (v) *or* check (v)

vérifier [contrôler] control (v) *or* monitor (v)

vérifier [inspecter] inspect (v)

vérifier les comptes audit the accounts

véritable [authentique] genuine (adj) *or* real (adj)

véritable *[vrai]*
real (adj)
versement (m)
payment (n) *or*
instalment (n)
versement annuel
yearly payment
verser de l'argent
pay (out)
verser de l'argent
(sur un compte)
deposit (v) money
(in the bank)
verser un acompte
ou **une provision**
pay (v) money down
or on account
verser un dividende
pay (v) a dividend
verser un intérêt
pay (v) interest
veto (m) veto (n)
via *[par]* via
viable viable (adj)
vice (m) de fabrica-
tion defect (n)
vide empty (adj)
vidéoconférence (f)
videoconference (n)
vieux, vieil (vieille)
old (adj)

vigile (m) security
guard
vigueur: en vigueur
[prix] going (adj)
(price, rate)
virement (m)
bancaire bank
transfer (n)
virement (m) de
crédit transfer of
funds
virgule (f)
(décimale) decimal
point (n)
visa (m) visa (n)
visa d'entrée
entry visa
visa de transit
transit visa
visa permanent
(bon pour
plusieurs entrées)
multiple-entry visa
viser (à) *[avoir pour*
but] aim (at) (v)
visite (f) call (n)
visite d'affaires
business call
visite de routine *ou*
habituelle
routine call

visite impromptue (d'un représentant) cold call
visiter call on (v) *or* visit (v)
vitrine (f) *[devanture]* shop window (n)
vitrine (f) *[meuble, armoire vitrée]* display case (n) *or* showcase (n)
voiture (f) car (n)
voiture de location hire car
voix (f) prépondérante casting vote (n)
vol (m) *[de marchandises]* theft (n)
vol (m) *[avion]* flight (n)
vol à l'étalage *ou* **vol dans les rayons** shoplifting (n)
vol charter charter flight
vol régulier scheduled flight
voleur (-euse) thief (n)

voleur (-euse) à l'étalage shop-lifter (n)
volume (m) volume (n)
volume (m) *[capacité]* capacity (n) *or* space (n)
volume d'affaires volume of trade *or* volume of business
volume de ventes volume of sales *or* sales volume
volumineux (-euse) bulky (adj)
vote (m) vote (n)
vote par procuration proxy vote
voter vote (v)
voter *[adopter une motion]* carry (v) *[a motion]*
voyage (m) trip (n); journey (n)
voyage d'affaires business trip
voyage de retour homeward journey

vrai(e) *[véritable]*
real (adj); genuine
(adj)
vrac: en vrac loose
(adj); in bulk
**VRP (Voyageur-
Représentant-
Placier)** represen-
tative (n) *or* rep (n)

Ww Zz

**wagon (m) (de
marchandises)**
[train] goods
wagon (n) *or*
freight car (n)

warrant (m)
warrant (n)
web (m): le web
the web
zéro (m) zero
zéro: à taux zéro
zero-rated (adj)
zone (f) *[région]*
area (n) *or* region (n)
**zone de libre-
échange** free
trade area
zone dollar
dollar area
zone franc
franc area
zone franche
free zone
zone industrielle
industrial estate (n)
zone piétonnière
shopping precinct (n)

501

Business correspondence

La correspondance commerciale

Sample Curriculum Vitae

CURRICULUM VITAE pour Madame Joséphine Cotterel
5A rue de Brives, 75015 Paris
Téléphone: (01) 886 88 54 Portable: (07914) 248553
E-mail: jfcotterel@freenet.fr

Objectif:

Occuper un poste professionnel de directrice des ressources humaines, avec un rôle de chef d'équipe au sein d'une compagnie de premier ordre. Les postes futurs impliqueront la gestion des relations avec le personnel à l'échelle française ou internationale.

Expérience professionnelle:

2000 — présent Société internationale de commerce et navigation S.A., Paris

Conseillère en politique de ressources humaines
Je fournis des conseils professionnels sur toutes les questions relatives à la politique des ressources humaines, y compris la formation et les relations avec les salariés. J'ai développé la politique pour la France, et mis en œuvre les changements de politique au sein de l'entreprise.

1996 — 1999   Société internationale
de commerce et navigation
S.A., Paris

Conseillère en ressources humaines:
Maritime, Expédition/Navigation, et Aviation
Je fournissais des conseils sur le recrutement
à 3 services du groupe d'entreprises mondial:
Produits maritimes, Expédition/Navigation et
Aviation. J'ai coordonné plusieurs procédures
de recrutement interne et externe, participant
à toutes lesétapes, des annonces publicitaires
à la sélection des candidats.

1993 — 1995   Société GP France
Exploration et Production,
Le Havre

Expert-conseil en ressources humaines:
Ingénierie des puits de pétrole
Je fournissais des conseils sur toute une
gamme de questions, ayant également
"sur une grande échelle d'une compagnie.

Etudes/Qualifications:

1999 —2001	Titulaire d'une maîtrise en sciences de Relations avec le Personnel, *Université de Paris XII, Paris*
1996 —1998	Diplômée de l'Institut de Commerce supérieur
1990 —1993	Licence en psychologie expérimentale (mention bien), *Université du Havre*
1982 —1990	Baccalauréat série A2, *Lycée St Etienne, Le Havre, Seine Maritime*

Echantillon de Curriculum Vitae

CURRICULUM VITAE for Ms. Josephine Catterall
5A, Hanton Street, London, SE13 1DF
Tel: (020) 8868 9854 Mobile: (07914) 248553
E-mail: jfcatterall@hotmail.com

Objective:

To become a professional HR manager with a team-leader role within a blue-chip company. Future positions to involve managing employee relations on a UK or global basis.

Work History:

Dec 1999 — present GP International Trading and Shipping Company Ltd., London

Human Resources Policy Adviser
Provided professional advice on all HR policy matters including employee relations and training. Developed UK policy and implemented policy changes within the business.

May 1996 — Nov 1999 GP International Trading and Shipping Company Ltd., London

Human Resources Adviser: Marine, Shipping, and Aviation
Provided recruitment advice to 3 departments of the Global Businesses group: Marine Products, Shipping, and Aviation. Coordinated several internal and external recruitment processes through all stages from advertising to candidate selection.

Sept 1993 — April 1996 GP UK Exploration and Production, Southampton

Human Resources Consultant: Oil-well Engineering
Provided advice on a range of issues, including helping to manage a large-scale company relocation.

Education/Qualifications:

1999 — 2001   MSc in Employee Relations, University of Westminster, London

1996 — 1998	Graduate of the Chartered Institute of Personnel and Development
1990 — 1993	BA (Hons) Experimental Psychology (Class Iii), University of Bristol
1982 — 1990	'A' Levels: Biology (A), French (A), German (B), *St Stephen's School, Ely, Cambs*

Sample covering letter for job application

Adrienne Griffon
20 rue Racine
75012 Paris

Madame Jeanne Simonet
Chef du personnel
Data Technique S.A.
60300 Beauvais

Paris, le 25 mars 2003

Madame,

Je suis très intéressée par le poste de directrice commerciale chez Data Technique S.A., comme décrit dans votre annonce du 20 mars dans le journal Le Monde.

Dans le poste que j'occupe actuellement en tant que directrice commerciale adjointe chez Bureautique Sarl, j'ai contribué à une augmentation de 15% de notre part de marché, au cours de l'année passée. Je comprends d'après votre site Web et votre rapport annuel que Data Technique a également augmenté sa part de marché cette année, et compte faire de même pour l'exercice financier prochain. Je pense que ma compétence professionnelle et mes qualifications seraient tout à fait adéquates pour con-venir à votre plan de croissance.

Comme requis dans votre annonce, je joins à cette lettre une copie de mon C.V., dans lequel vous trouverez tous les détails sur mes qualifications et mon expérience professionnelle. Je serais enchantée si vous décidez de considérer ma candidature pour ce poste et j'ai hâte de recevoir une réponse de votre part.

Veuillez agréer l'expression de mes salutations distinguées.

Adrienne Griffon

Document ci-joint

Echantillon de lettre de motivation

Adrienne Griffiths
20 Shakespeare Road
London
SE18 2PB

Jane Stevenson
Senior Personnel Officer
DataTech Ltd
Botley Road
Oxford
OX2 1ZZ

25 March 2003

Dear Ms Stevenson

I am very interested in the position of sales manager at DataTech Ltd as described in your advertisement of 20 March in the Guardian newspaper.

In my current position of deputy sales manager for Parker Smith Plc I have helped to increase our market share by 15% in the past year. I see from your website and annual report that DataTech have also increased their market share this year and are aiming to do the same in the next financial year, and I feel my track record and qualifications would fit in well with these plans for growth.

As requested in the advertisement, I enclose a copy of my CV which gives full details of my qualifications and work history. I would be very pleased to be considered for this position and I look forward to hearing from you.

Yours sincerely

Adrianne Griffiths

Encl.

Sample letter making a job offer

Data Technique S.A.
Route de Chantilly
60300 Beauvais
Tél: 03 22 48 71 18

Madame Adrienne Griffon
20 rue Racine
75012 Paris

Beauvais, le 10 avril 2003

Madame,

Réf.: Poste de directrice commerciale

Suite à votre entretien la semaine dernière, j'ai le plaisir de vous offrir le poste de directrice commerciale, où vous serez directement sous les ordres de David Bartot, le directeur des ventes de notre compagnie.

Votre salaire d'embauche sera 44500 Euros, avec une révision de salaire annuelle, à la date où vous entrerez dans notre compagnie. Les autres modalités seront celles décrites au cours de votre entretien.

Si cette offre vous est acceptable, je vous serais reconnaissante de bien vouloir m'en envoyer confirmation par écrit. Nous pourrons alors mettre au point les détails de votre contrat et date d'embauche, et discuter des frais de mutation éventuels auxquels vous pourriez avoir droit.

Veuillez accepter mes meilleurs vœux de réussite et agréer l'expression de mes salutations distinguées.

Jeanne Simonet
Chef du personnel
Data Technique S.A.

Echantillon de lettre offrant un emploi

DataTech Ltd
Botley Road
Oxford
OX2 1ZZ

Ms Adrianne Griffiths
20 Shakespeare Road
London SE18 2PB

10 April 2003

Dear Ms Griffiths

Re: Post of Sales Manager

Further to your interview last week I am pleased to be able to offer you the post of Sales Manager, reporting directly to David Wardlock, our Company Sales Director.

Your starting salary will be £29,635, with an annual salary review on the date of your joining the company. Other terms and conditions will be as outlined in the interview.

If this offer is acceptable to you I would be grateful if you could send me confirmation in writing. We can then finalize details of your contract and starting date and discuss any relocation expenses you may have to claim.

Best wishes

Yours sincerely

Jane Stevenson
Senior Personnel Officer
DataTech Ltd

Sample letter requesting product information

TOP MAISON
156 av. de la République
86000 Poitiers
Téléphone: 05 29 42 07 91

M. F. Durand
12 rue Clémenceau
69000 Lyon
France

Lyon, le 10 avril 2003

Monsieur,

Je vous remercie de votre demande de renseignements à propos de notre nouvelle gamme de produits de bricolage etaménagement de maison.

Suite à notre conversation ce matin, j'ai le plaisir de joindre à cette lettre notre catalogue, qui contient une liste complète de nos produits, avec leur prix et disponibilité.

Si vous avez des questions, n'hésitez pas à me contacter au numéro de téléphone

ci-dessus ou par e-mail à l'adresse:
info@nouvellesidées.fr

Je vous prie d'agréer l'expression de mes salutations distinguées.

Emilie Lebret
Directrice commerciale du service clients.

Echantillon de lettre d'envoi de renseignements

12 Smith Street
Manchester
M90 1AA

Customer Sales
New DIY Ideas Ltd
Butler Industrial Estate
Manor Park
Manchester SE12 8NU

24 June 2003

Dear Sir or Madam

I recently saw an advert for your new range of DIY products in my local paper and would be very interested to have more information on prices.

Could you send a copy of your catalogue to my home address above?

Thanking you in advance.

Yours faithfully

James Fox

Sample letter of complaint

47 rue des Bois
83200 Nice

Madame H. Lemante
La Boutique Informatique
123 rue Picasso
83200 Nice

Nice, le 20 mars 2003

Madame,

**Imprimante à jet d'encre défectueuse
(modèle numéro A1234)**

J'ai acheté une imprimante à jet d'encre
(modèle numéro A1234) dans votre
magasin le jeudi 13 mars (ci-joint une
copie du reçu). Malheureusement, l'imprimante semble être défectueuse et deux
techniciens de votre magasin n'ont pas
réussi à déterminer la cause du problème. Par conséquent, j'apprécierais un
remboursement in tégral de votre part
pour cette imprimante, ce dans les
meilleurs délais.

Veuillez me contacter à l'adresse ci-dessus, afin que je puisse organiser une heure à laquelle l'imprimante pourra être collectée et vous être renvoyée.

J'ai hâte d'avoir de vos nouvelles très bientôt et vous prie d'agréer l'expression de mes salutations distinguées.

Elizabeth Martin

Echantillon de lettre de réclamation

47 Highfield Road
York
YO2 3BP

Ms H Naughton
The Computer Shop Ltd
123 High Street
York
YO1 7HL

20 March 2003

Dear Ms Naughton

Faulty inkjet printer (model number A1234)

I purchased an inkjet printer (model number A1234) from your shop on Thursday 13 March (copy of receipt enclosed). Unfortunately, the printer appears to be faulty, and two engineers from your shop have not been able to isolate the cause of the problem. I would, therefore, appreciate a full refund on the faulty printer at your earliest convenience.

Please contact me at the above address so that we may arrange a time when the printer can be picked up and returned.

I look forward to hearing from you.

Yours sincerely

Elizabeth Kendall

www.ingramcontent.com/pod-product-compliance
Ingram Content Group UK Ltd.
Pitfield, Milton Keynes, MK11 3LW, UK
UKHW021009050325
455865UK00002B/14